THE

THE
HEADACHE
SOURCEBOOK

THE
HEADACHE
SOURCEBOOK

THE COMPLETE GUIDE
TO
MANAGING TENSION, MIGRAINE, CLUSTER, AND OTHER RECURRENT HEADACHES IN ADULTS, ADOLESCENTS, AND CHILDREN

JOEL PAULINO, M.D.
CEABERT J. GRIFFITH, M.P.A.S., P.A.

Contemporary Books

Chicago   New York   San Francisco   Lisbon   London   Madrid   Mexico City
Milan   New Delhi   San Juan   Seoul   Singapore   Sydney   Toronto

Library of Congress Cataloging-in-Publication Data

Paulino, Joel
    The Headache sourcebook : the complete guide to managing tension, migraine,
cluster, and other recurrent headaches in adults, adolescents, and children / Joel Paulino,
Ceabert J. Griffith
      p. cm.
    Includes bibliographical references and index.
    ISBN 0-7373-0545-2
      1. Headache—Popular works.   I Griffith, Ceabert J.   II. Title

RB128 .P38 2001
616.8'491—dc21

2001028223

Contemporary Books

A Division of The McGraw·Hill Companies

01 02 03 04 DOH/DOH 18 17 16 15 14 13 12 11 10 9 8 7 6 5 4 3 2 1

International Standard Book Number: 0-7373-0545-2

This book was set in Adobe Minion.
Interior design by Robert S. Tinnon
Printed and bound by R. R. Donnelley & Sons Co.

McGraw-Hill books are available at special quantity discounts to use as premiums
and sales promotions, or for use in corporate training programs. For more information,
please write to the Director of Special Sales, Professional Publishing, McGraw-Hill,
Two Penn Plaza, New York, NY 10121-2298. Or contact your local bookstore.

To our patients, who taught us the lion's share of what we know about headaches

Contents

Foreword

When pondering the power of modern technological breakthroughs that shape my practice of medicine, I marvel at our ability to continue to unravel the mysteries of the human machine. However, medical technology, even when infinitely precise, cannot on its own perform the basic task of medicine, that is to alleviate human suffering. As time constraints continue to shorten patient/provider interactions, patients have become dissatisfied with the conventional system of medicine and have begun to seek answers elsewhere.

In *The Headache Sourcebook*, Paulino and Griffith open the doors of the halls of medicine to their patients. In the process, they clearly and simply reveal what is understood and what mysteries remain to be solved regarding headache pain. However, they do not limit their scope to merely conventional medicine. Treating the whole patient, they delve into mind and body interactions, nonpharmacological interventions, herbal and alternative therapies, and coping methods for chronic conditions.

Great healers are great teachers. They bring a body of knowledge to suffering patients, and offer relief by helping them to understand their disorder. I anticipate that headache sufferers will find Paulino and Griffith's comprehensive analysis invaluable in their trek to manage this poorly understood but extremely common ailment.

ANTHONY A. DONATO, JR., M.D.
Associate Professor, Department of Medicine
Uniformed Services University of the Health Sciences
Bethesda, Maryland

Preface

Between clients, all Emily can think of is rushing home, crawling into bed in her darkened bedroom, and promptly falling asleep. During the past four days, sleep has been her only respite from the grip of a severe, throbbing headache over her left temple that has been almost completely unresponsive to a variety of high-dose painkillers, including extra-strength acetaminophen, naproxen, and ibuprofen. The accompanying nausea is unaffected by a diet of crackers, dry toast, flavored gelatin, and other favorite home remedies. Emily's clients are none the wiser. As a seasoned mental health professional with a long history of unconquered chronic headaches, she has grown adept at concealing any physical expressions that would betray her suffering.

You'd think that Emily would be used to the monthly visitations of vicious headaches by now. After all, this popular psychotherapist has been plagued by menstrual migraines since the summer following her fifteenth birthday. Nineteen years have come and gone and Emily is still helpless when faced with these dreaded head pains that adversely affect her personal, social, and professional life. She misses about twenty days of work each year (over $4,500 in lost wages), was spurned by her high school sweetheart, and regularly turns down invitations to parties—all because of repeated, disabling headaches. She has put off going to see a physician for an evaluation in hopes that she'd eventually "get used to it." Nearly two decades later, she hasn't. The passage of time has only served to further isolate her in a world of recurrent headache—a world of despair, anger, anxiety, depression, and loneliness.

But Emily is not alone in her suffering. As a matter of fact, she has plenty of company. The best estimates indicate that between forty and fifty million Americans are affected by tension-type, migraine, cluster, or other forms of chronic or repeated headaches.[1] By contrast, sixteen million Americans suffer from diabetes, thirty-seven million have arthritis, and forty-three million have high blood pressure—leaving headache the hands-down winner in the contest for most chronic medical conditions afflicting Americans. At any one time, an estimated twenty million people in the United States are experiencing headaches. Worldwide, upward of 93 percent of all men and 99 percent of all women will experience one or more headache episodes during their lifetimes, making headache the most prevalent of all human diseases.

The National Headache Foundation (NHF) estimates that ten million health care visits are made in the United States each year because of head pain. Approximately 2.5 percent of all visits made to emergency rooms annually are for headache complaints. It is the seventh leading "presenting complaint" (primary reason a patient seeks medical care) in ambulatory medical care settings.

Unfortunately, surveys show that for every person who seeks medical care for headaches, about two more don't, due in part to the false assumption that nothing can be done to relieve recurrent headaches. If that's not troubling enough, experts tell us that, of those headache sufferers who seek treatment, nearly 50 percent receive ineffective treatment.

Recurrent headache—the number one reason for lost productivity in the United States and the biggest reason for disability payments made to American workers—also costs lots of money to evaluate and treat. According to the NHF, businesses lose a staggering fifty billion dollars annually to absenteeism and payment of medical benefits to headache sufferers.[2] Migraine headaches alone affect twenty-five to thirty million adults and about one million children and cost a whopping eleven billion dollars per year to treat, and incur 157 million lost workdays.[3] Moreover, one out of seven U.S. workers curtails his work activities because of distracting head pain each day. Canadian public health authorities estimate that twenty-seven of one hundred lost workdays are due to migraine headaches, at an annual cost of $500 million. In a 1993 survey of American children with migraines, 10 percent of respondents missed one day of school over a two-week period, and 1 percent missed four days because of headache.[4]

Americans spend an additional four billion dollars annually on over-the-counter headache remedies such as aspirin, acetaminophen, naproxen, ibuprofen, and ketoprofen. Most sufferers have an incomplete understanding of their disease and lack an integrated approach to the management of their head pain. Many take narcotics and other prescription medications with little or no physician oversight. Sadly, in their desperate quest for pain relief, countless chronic headache sufferers become addicted to prescription painkillers—in effect, trading one distressing problem for another.

These statistics tell the chilling story of a single but far-reaching medical condition with enormous health, social, and economic effects. Is headache "a modern day pestilence," a contemporary disease that came into its own during the twentieth century? As it turns out, it's not. Headache has been around about as long as mankind has. The first-century physician Arateus of Cappadocia in Asia Minor accurately described the migraine headaches that afflicted many of his patients. The modern name *migraine* is not at all modern; in fact, it's derived from the term *hemikrania,* meaning "half a head," used by the second-century Greek physician and writer Galen to describe the characteristic one-sided head pain of migraine sufferers (also known as *migraineurs*). Written accounts from ancient civilizations stretching from Egypt to Sumeria and India tell stories of headache sufferers devastated by their disease. Although our premodern ancestors suffered from the scourge of headaches, however, we don't have to do so.

Recent advances in headache research have uncovered tantalizing clues to the causes of migraine, cluster, and other enigmatic types of headaches. Many novel treatments—acupuncture, progressive relaxation, elimination diets, aerobic exercise, and drug therapy, among others—are now available to manage even the most recalcitrant headache. Cutting-edge therapies notwithstanding, the cornerstone of headache management remains self-care with physician guidance.

Headache self-care begins with a thorough education about your headache: what it is, what it isn't, what causes it, how to manage it, and how to conquer it. Reading this book will provide you with the requisite headache education; it contains a comprehensive delineation of migraine, tension-type, cluster, and other forms of chronic headaches that affect adults, adolescents, and children. We'd like to emphasize caution, however. No health care information book, no matter how well written, can take the place of a physician or other health care professional. Your health care provider is the person best qualified to diagnose and guide you in the management of your recurrent headache.

On the other hand, no clinician can be an effective practitioner without a well-informed patient. As Plutarch put it,

> Each person ought neither to be unacquainted with the peculiarities of his own pulse (for there are many individual diversities), nor ignorant of any idiosyncrasy which his body has in regard to temperature and dryness, and what things in actual practice have proved to be beneficial or detrimental to it. For a man who has no perception regarding himself is but a blind and deaf tenant in his own body, who gets his knowledge of these matters from another, and must inquire of his physician whether his health is better in summer or winter, whether he can more easily tolerate liquid or solid foods, and whether his pulse is naturally fast or slow. For it is useful and easy for us to know things of this sort, since we have daily experience and association with them.

Good medicine is virtually useless if the patient has an incomplete understanding of her illness. This is especially true when it comes to chronic illnesses such as high blood pressure, diabetes, and recurrent headaches. Author and migraine sufferer Susan L. Burks, drawing on considerable personal experience, writes in her book *Managing Your Migraine,* "Just as it will benefit you as a headache sufferer to locate a doctor with a special attitude, you'll likewise find it to your advantage to acquire an in-depth knowledge of your own condition."[5]

Our first objective in writing *The Headache Sourcebook* is to help you become a better-informed patient, which will ultimately allow your health care team to better help you manage your chronic headaches. Another of our main objectives is to help you overcome the communication barrier between health care provider and patient. Recent surveys of patients with chronic illnesses, such as ulcers, arthritis, and asthma, show a widening gap between what a health care team has time to tell patients and what patients need to know about their conditions. This growing "disconnection" stems from time constraints imposed by the new way Americans get their health care. The proliferation of health maintenance organizations (HMOs), preferred provider organizations (PPOs), and other forms of managed-care networks places greater emphasis on seeing larger numbers of patients in less provider hours. What suffers in this new paradigm of health care delivery is the time it takes to fully educate patients. Consequently, persons who want to fully understand the nature of their diseases will have to take the initiative to tap into alternative resources to obtain complete health information. Information dissemination—via books like this one—is the only feasible way to close the doctor/patient information gap that seriously threatens to separate patients from their doctors.

Many well-meaning headache books on the market today are filled with the latest headache information, but fail to address this "disconnection" between chronic headache sufferers and their health care teams. Having lots of information is great, but you are still powerless if you don't know how to use it. This headache primer is unique because it will help bridge the widening communication gap between you as patient and your health care provider. We hope that this book, based on the very latest headache information discussed in easy-to-understand terms, will give you a detailed account of the information your health care professional does not have the time to teach you. Additionally, we hope that *The Headache Sourcebook* will help you formulate the right questions to ask your doctor and other members of your health care team. In this way, you can get the most "bang for your buck" during your visit to your doctor, even if he practices in a managed-care setting. It is our hope that you, your family and friends, your employer, and your health care providers will read this book, use it, and recommend it as a comprehensive guide to eliminate—or at least reduce—the frequency and intensity of recurrent headache pain.

HOW TO USE THIS BOOK

The Headache Sourcebook is organized into eighteen chapters, each detailing a specific aspect of recurrent headache pain. We recommend that you read the entire book, even if, for instance, you suffer only migraine headaches and spend most of your time digesting the information in chapter 5. The foreword and introduction set the tone for the book and will help you fully understand the "big picture" regarding chronic headache before you learn about the details. We suggest that before delving into the heart of the book you browse through the glossary to familiarize yourself with the terminology used throughout the book and that you refer to it thereafter as needed.

Chapter 1 discusses the biological basis of head pain and the major classifications of headaches and offers some historical perspective on chronic headache suffering. Chapter 2 lists some common myths about headaches held by both the general public and some medical professionals and, by pointing out headache facts, aims to dispel these misconceptions. In chapter 3, we examine the environmental, dietary, and psychological factors and the social habits and common drugs that can trigger recurrent head pain.

In chapter 4, we talk about the most prevalent of all headaches, tension-type headache—its causes, treatment, and prevention. We discuss migraine headache, the second most common type of chronic headache, in chapter 5, and detail migraine facts, migraine causes, who gets it, and how doctors diagnose and treat it. Chapter 6 will give you clear insight into cluster headache suffering, what causes it, and who gets it, and will delineate the state-of-the-art treatments for this enigmatic headache.

In chapter 7, we provide a full review of the features of mixed headaches and the ways clinicians diagnose and treat them. In chapters 8 and 9, we discuss the unique features of headache pain among women and children, respectively. We'll show you why headache in women is different from that in men, and why head pain in children is different from that in adults. Chapter 10 delineates the common medical conditions, such as sinus infections and high blood pressure, that can cause headache. Chapter 11 will inform you about the signs and symptoms that can signal the presence of brain tumors, brain infections, and other life-threatening forms of headaches.

Chapter 12 delineates the "Medical Evaluation of the Headache Patient." We'll talk about the most common laboratory tests and X-rays doctors order when evaluating a headache patient. Chapter 13 gives you some time-honored tips on working with your health care team and getting the most out of each health care visit. After reading chapter 14, "Which Practitioners Should Evaluate and Treat Your Headache?" you'll understand the roles of the various medical specialists and alternative medicine practitioners who evaluate patients with recurrent headache. Chapter 15 lists the nondrug strategies (such as yoga and biofeedback) you can employ to manage your headache, while chapter 16, "Headache Drugs," details the myriad drugs used to prevent and to abort chronic head pain.

Chapter 17, "How to Be a Savvy Consumer," will help you avoid becoming the victim of health care fraud. We'll also discuss ways to reduce the cost of your headache medications. Your friends and relatives play crucial roles in helping you rid yourself of your chronic headache, and in chapter 18 we teach them how to support you as you embark on your journey to freedom from headache. We also teach you how to get health care in today's managed-care market. The Epilogue summarizes all the information outlined in *The Headache Sourcebook*.

At the back of this book, you'll find helpful information such as a list of suggested readings, a comprehensive glossary of headache terms, and a complete list of resources for obtaining further information on chronic headache.

A note on the terminology used throughout this book: The terms *clinician, provider, health care practitioner,* and *health care provider* refer to health care professionals who practice medicine in the United States and Canada. These professionals include physicians, physician assistants, and nurse practitioners. Other health professionals who evaluate and treat individuals with headache pain include chiropractors, optometrists, dietitians, pharmacists, psychologists, acupuncturists, and occupational therapists. A physician is the final authority on matters related to chronic headache. Nonphysician providers, such as physician assistants, work in concert with a licensed physician when caring for patients with chronic headache. Therefore, a licensed physician ultimately makes the decisions about your health care.

Acknowledgments

We're deeply indebted to numerous persons who lent unconditional support to this project. We would like to especially thank our editors at Contemporary Books who provided us with the poking and prodding necessary to complete this book. Their passionate support of this project, wise counsel, and firm deadline mandates provided the framework for our motivation and productivity. It is nearly impossible to thank each and every person who in some small way gave life to this work.

JOEL PAULINO, M.D.

CEABERT J. GRIFFITH, M.P.A.S., P.A.

I would like to dedicate this book to my family and friends for all their support while I pursued this dream of writing a book. To Andy Donato and Rick Ricardo, thanks for being there through the years. To Bert Griffith, who did most of the hard work and research, thanks for giving me the opportunity to write this book with you. To my parents, Jaime and Asuncion Paulino, thanks for instilling in me the ethics of hard work and perseverance. Finally, to my wonderful wife, Connie,and my beautiful boys Nicholas and Nathaniel, for you have brought so much happiness into my life.

JP

No book is ever written without the unwavering support of family, friends, mentors, and colleagues, and this book is no exception. I owe my highest gratitude to my dear wife, Yuko Kinjo Griffith, who has been my steadfast emotional pillar and lifeblood. My four wonderful children—Michael, Vanessa, Kevin, and Meg—provided the daily inspiration needed to help me stay focused on my work. My parents, Ceabert and Dora Griffith, and my late grandmother, Beryl DaCosta, were my inspirations from the beginning. With esteemed friends like Joel Paulino, M.D., and John Harris, P.A.-C., and perennial mentors like Rod Hooker, P.A., Ph.D., and Steve Tiger, P.A.-C., providing invaluable counsel, I was bound to succeed in this endeavor.

CJG

THE
HEADACHE
SOURCEBOOK

Introduction

Are you a chronic headache sufferer with many unanswered questions about your condition? Do you even know what questions to ask? Are you wondering why you suffer repeated headaches, as well as what you can do to get protracted or permanent relief?

If you've answered "yes" to any of the preceding questions, we have wonderful news for you: If you follow the advice of your health care practitioner and the suggestions outlined in this book, you have an excellent chance of reducing the frequency and severity of your headaches and may even manage to stop them completely. We'll detail for you the lifestyle measures, self-care techniques, and drug treatments available to treat your headaches and prevent them from recurring, no matter how severe and disabling they are, and no matter how long you've suffered from them.

You'll understand why humans experience headaches and why many people get them over and over again. You'll learn that many individuals with chronic headaches tolerate their pain and suffer in silence—needlessly. Throughout the book we'll emphasize that recurrent headache can be effectively conquered, if only you'd practice a few time-honored strategies and, if indicated, take your medications as prescribed by your doctor.

HOW THIS BOOK CAN HELP YOU

You're probably reading this book because you want to learn more about the various forms of chronic headaches: what they are, who gets them, how they develop, why one gets them, how to treat them, and how to obtain long-lasting relief from them. You may not completely understand every-thing your doctor told you about your headache due to the time con-straints of a typical visit to a doctor's office. It is also likely that one of the following statements may apply to you:

- You experience repeated headaches; they're well controlled, but you want to learn more about your condition.
- Your health care provider previously diagnosed you with one of the many types of chronic headaches but you failed to follow the recommended treatments and continue to suffer recurrent head pain.
- You are the parent of a child who experiences repeated headaches and you want to learn more about his condition for your peace of mind and to feel confident in your ability to lend your support to him.
- You have a family history of chronic headaches and you want to educate yourself in case you develop headaches later on in life.
- You experience chronic headaches, but you haven't yet sought medical care and wonder how to go about getting a medical evaluation and treatment.
- You have recurrent headaches and, despite your clinician's reas-surances, you worry that your recurrent head pain is related to a serious, life-threatening problem, such as a brain tumor.
- As a health care provider, nurse, health insurance executive, employer, or health device manufacturer, you want to update your fund of knowledge regarding headaches and find a com-prehensive headache self-help book to recommend to others.

If you are a patient, it's your physician or other health care provider who will ultimately design a treatment plan based on the type of headaches you have and your age, gender, and other applicable sociodemographic and psychological factors. For example, if you are a woman whose headache is well controlled with ibuprofen, naproxen, or ketoprofen, your choice of headache medications greatly narrows if you become pregnant. You can no longer take these medications as they may have an adverse effect on your developing fetus; you may have to settle for acetaminophen (for example, Tylenol) during your pregnancy.

How well you follow your doctor's treatment plan will determine its success. If your provider is too busy to answer all your questions regarding your headaches, this book will help you better understand your disease and will provide answers to your unanswered questions. *The Headache Sourcebook* will therefore help make you a better-informed patient by supplementing the information provided by your doctor. For example, if your health care provider prescribes an *abortive* drug (a drug to stop a condition or symptom) and a *prophylactic* drug (a drug to prevent a condition or symptom) for your migraine headaches, this book will detail her rationale and show you why both drugs are equally important in helping you get rid of your pain.

If it's your child, spouse, parent, or other family member or friend who suffers chronic headaches, this book will provide you a complete education on the disease and motivate you to help your loved one live a headache-free life. If you or your loved one has never been diagnosed with chronic headaches, this book will show you how simple the evaluation can be and encourage you to seek medical attention. You'll also learn how easy it is to manage even the most severe headache pain with your physician's guidance.

WHAT CAN YOU DO TO HELP YOURSELF?

You may have gotten some insight into your headaches while watching your favorite morning TV newsmagazine or by reading a newspaper article on the subject. Now that you suspect what type of chronic headache you have, you—in collaboration with your physician—should take steps to treat it. In the chapters ahead, we'll walk you through the vast, often intimidating world of information about chronic headache. We'll show you how much power you have to ensure a life free of debilitating headaches.

Exercising this power begins with taking the responsibility for monitoring your overall health and maintaining a solid relationship with your health care team.[1] Only you can keep a headache diary to help your health practitioner determine what type of headache you have. Only you can avoid the foods or drugs that may trigger your headache, and only you can make sure you get enough exercise to thwart your tension-type headaches. Only you can remember to take your medications as your doctor prescribed or to regularly practice biofeedback measures. Your level of commitment can literally be the difference between having a daily headache and living a headache-free life.

Please be sure to apprise your physician of information you glean from this book, and check with him before implementing any of our recommendations. We're confident your provider will be happy that you've taken the initiative to become a well-informed consumer and that you aspire to be an equal partner in the management of your health. The ball is in your court; it's your turn!

IN SUMMARY

The Headache Sourcebook will help you to:

- become a better-informed patient by supplementing information provided by your health practitioner.
- demystify sometimes confusing headache information.
- effectively communicate with your health care team, and to accurately articulate your concern, fears, and expectations about your headaches.
- empower you to assume an active role in your health care.
- become headache-free!

CHAPTER ONE

What Is a Headache?

Very few people in the world can claim to have never suffered from a headache, yet so little is known about this common problem. Why does one's head ache? What causes the pain? We've all felt some type of pain, and many of us have felt headache pain, but few truly understand our bodies' complex physical structures and biochemical reactions involved in pain. Before learning what headache pain is, let's first try to understand the biology of pain in general.

WHAT IS PAIN?

What would life be without pain? For starters, it would mean no more headaches! It would also mean that you would not flinch if you broke your leg in a fall, and that surgeons could remove diseased gallbladders and cancerous prostates without subjecting their patients to the risk of general anesthesia. You could walk through a jungle filled with thorns without worrying about the painful sticks. There would be absolutely no pain to go along with the incessant bleeding. But would this be good for you? Would the lack of ability to feel pain help you live a carefree life or cause your early demise?

As good as the inability to feel pain sounds, it would be detrimental to your existence. Pain has only one important function: to warn that something has gone wrong in the body. Pain warns you of dangers that, if ignored, can lead to irreparable bodily harm. For example, unknowingly touching a hot stove without the ability to sense that your hand is burning will result in destruction of your skin, muscles, tendons, ligaments, bones—indeed, your

IF YOU COME TO THINK ABOUT IT, PHYSICAL PAIN HAS MANY SINGULARITIES. OF ALL HUMAN EXPERIENCES IT IS, AS LONG AS IT LASTS, THE MOST ABSORBING; AND IT IS THE ONLY HUMAN EXPERIENCE WHICH, WHEN IT COMES TO AN END, AUTOMATICALLY CONFERS A REAL IF NOT PERHAPS A VERY HIGH KIND OF HAPPINESS.

PETER FLEMING

entire hand. The wounds created by thorns can produce life-threatening hemorrhage or infections. As you can see, pain serves a protective function. It helps you guard against the many dangers lurking in your environment. Ultimately, pain helps our species survive.

According to renowned headache specialists and authors Drs. Alan Rapoport and Fred Sheftell, pain complements the interaction between your nerves that monitor your environment and your brain.[1] Your ability to sense pain is made possible by two bodily systems: the nervous system, which includes the brain and the 45 miles of spinal and peripheral nerves; and the endocrine system, which contains the glands and the hormones that help the glands communicate with each other. How pain develops is quite complicated, but we'll look at some examples to illustrate the intricacies.

When you're in a racquetball game and you're hit in the arm by the ball, the nerve endings under your skin at the point of impact are stimulated (irritated) and fire off a message to the brain. The transmission of the message is aided by a series of chemicals called *neurotransmitters.* The brain receives the message, interprets it as pain, and sends a response message to withdraw your arm, rub it, or otherwise protect it.

How you respond to such an injury—ignore it and keep playing, or stop to ice it and seek the help of your playing partner—is individualized and may have implications for how you perceive and respond to other forms of pain. Perhaps based on life experiences and expectations, each of us develops an individualized *pain threshold,* or the weakest stimulus that a person perceives and interprets as pain. *Pain tolerance* refers to the degree of severity each person assigns a pain stimulus. Thus, the severity of pain is partly subjective and largely relative. This is why some of us writhe in pain in response to a splinter in a finger, while others easily shake off the contusion of a heavy log falling on a foot.

An individual's pain threshold can be lowered by factors such as stress and depression, which affect the secretion of neurotransmitters like serotonin (discussed on page 9). Some pain researchers feel that some forms of headache pain have to do with the ways an individual perceives and responds to external stimuli such as a hectic Monday at the office. The anxiety of enduring a busy Monday may cause some persons to clench their teeth ("I hate Mondays with a passion"), which leads to tight muscles in both temples and, eventually, a muscle tension headache. Others respond with characteristic calm ("I can't do anything about Mondays; besides, I need this job") and never develop headaches.

WHY DOES YOUR HEAD ACHE?

The highly regarded fifth century B.C. Greek physician Hippocrates was the first to look at headache pain as a symptom of a disease. His contemporaries were skeptical; instead of a biological model for headache, they ascribed head pain to the work of demons. After the Dark Ages, scientists began to suspect that spiritual phenomena was a poor explanation for headaches and began to formulate various biologically based theories. It wasn't until 1940 that Harold Wolff and John Graham found that the drug ergotamine, used today to treat migraine and cluster headaches, constricted blood vessels and brought relief to headache sufferers. Further biological bases of some forms of headaches have since been uncovered. Headache researchers now better understand the intricate mechanisms involved in the development of headache.

A most important finding of headache research in the past three decades is that, for the most part, headache results from disordered biological mechanisms. One notable finding is that most primary headache sufferers (those whose headaches have no known cause) may be born with a propensity for their headaches. However, not everyone biologically predisposed to recurrent headaches gets them. The inherited tendency must be triggered by factors such as loud noise, changes in the levels of the body's hormones, emotional stress, or other external and internal factors. As headache researcher Dr. Michel Ferrari of Leiden University in the Netherlands said, "Certain patients will have a genetic predisposition but will develop migraine only when other, presumably environmental, factors are involved."[2] In chapter 3, we'll detail the myriad factors that can trigger headaches, such as chocolate, weather changes, stress, changes in sleep pattern, and birth control pills.

In addition to a hereditary tendency for head pain, there may be an environmental aspect to chronic headaches. Some clinicians and headache researchers believe that headache behavior can be a learned behavior, in which biologically predisposed children observe parents, siblings, or relatives during recurrent headache episodes.[3]

Let's now review the physiological basis of headache pain. As much as it sounds like science fiction, the human brain itself can't feel pain. Thus, if a neurosurgeon cuts into the brain matter of an awake patient during surgery, the patient will not feel pain! This is because the brain itself lacks the nerves that transmit pain messages. The arteries, veins, and some of the specialized nerves in the brain also lack the ability to sense pain. So, why is it that it hurts to touch a hot stove? Why do persons with tension-type headaches say they feel like there is "a tight band around my head"?

As far as the perception of pain goes, nerves outside the brain sense the prick of a pin or the thump of a car door to the head, and send the sensory input (message) to the brain, which interprets the sensation as pain. The pain a patient undergoing brain surgery would feel without an anesthetic occurs in the many nerves that serve the blood vessels and muscles on the scalp, face, and neck. Stimulation of these pain-sensitive structures outside the brain—usually by pressure from surrounding tissues—is what actually accounts for the pain of headaches. Stimulation of these sensors results in release of pain-provoking chemicals in the brain that affect the blood vessels in and around the skull and the muscles of the head, face, and neck.

Therefore, headache pain is a symptom that points to a disturbance in a system of the body, much like a runny nose is a symptom that a cold virus has invaded the upper respiratory system. Headache can be traced to problems with the neurological, endocrine, muscular, or vascular systems. One of the premier scientific findings of the 1960s and 1970s is the role of the brain chemical serotonin (sometimes referred to by its chemical name 5-HT) in the development of headache. Headache researchers have shown that, for reasons still unclear, serotonin floods the blood vessels of the brain, causing them to narrow.[4] This event leads to a drop in serotonin levels in the blood, dilation (widening) of the blood vessels, and the throbbing pain of a migraine headache. Other brain chemicals implicated in the development of headache include substance P, bradykinin, dopamine, and norepinephrine.

Headaches are also linked to hormonal factors. Researchers at the University of Mississippi Medical Center showed that women with changes in their gynecological health, such as the development of ovarian cysts and irregular menstrual cycles, are twice as likely to develop chronic headaches as are women without such changes.[5] The precise mechanism of this is unclear, as we'll discuss in chapter 8.

MAJOR CLASSIFICATIONS OF HEADACHES

Lay persons often think that it's unnecessary to name each type of headache—a headache by any name hurts the same!—but the numerous and distinct types of headaches demand accurate identification. In fact, the International Headache Society (IHS), the organization of headache specialists that sets the definitions and diagnostic criteria of all headache disorders, has identified 129 types of head and neck pain affecting humans.[6] For purposes of effective clinical treatment and follow-up, it's important to identify the type of headache you have. For example, migraine headache is managed differently than a headache caused by arthritis of the joint in the jaw. The former is treated with pain medication, while the latter is managed with pain medication as well as facial exercises and a mouth guard.

Most headaches fit into one of four categories:[7]

1. tension-type headaches;
2. vascular headaches;
3. those caused by environmental, hormonal, or lifestyle factors, and
4. those caused by diseases or other medical conditions.

The IHS divides all headaches into two large categories: 1) primary headaches and 2) secondary headaches.[8] Primary headaches, which include tension-type, cluster, and migraine headaches—and which make up 95 percent of all headaches—are not caused by any identifiable medical condition.[9] Although frustrating and demoralizing, rarely are primary headaches a cause for concern.

On the other hand, secondary headaches—which include headaches caused by allergies and severely high blood pressure—are those headaches that result from an identifiable medical problem. These headaches can be either benign (e.g., due to a sinus or ear infection) or life threatening (e.g., due to an infection of the brain or a stroke). Together, secondary headaches account for less than 5 percent of all headaches.

Headache can also be classified as either acute or chronic. An acute headache is a single event of short duration and is not related to previous, recurrent episodes. With or without painkillers, the acute headache sufferer will have a full and complete recovery without long-term effects. Most humans have had temporary head pain, such as headaches caused by exposure to paint fumes, unrelated to a pattern of recurrent headache.

On the other hand, chronic headaches, such as cluster and migraine headaches, represent a distinct pattern of head pains that recur for many years with varying frequency and duration. Unlike acute headaches, chronic headaches have multiple causes that may include heredity, lifestyle factors, biological factors, and exposure to environmental factors. Additionally, chronic headaches are not amenable to quick fixes, and the sufferer often has to team up with a health care professional to develop an effective treatment plan that may take some time. Because of the duration of the condition, the chronic headache sufferer may develop physical deconditioning and psychological and emotional illness. Physical deconditioning may be defined as a reduction in the body's ability to engage in normal activities of daily living such as walking upstairs and carrying a bag of groceries without undue effort.

The two most common types of primary headaches are tension-type and migraine. Many types of migraine have been identified, including menstrual migraine (occurs in women around the time of their periods), ophthalmoplegic migraine (primarily involves the eyes), vertebrobasilar migraine (centered in the brain), and hemiplegia migraine (causes symptoms on one side of the body). Mixed headaches—those with features reminiscent of both migraines and tension-type headaches—is the next most common form of headache. (See chapter 7.) Although less common, cluster headaches are severe and disabling enough (in fact, they're probably the most painful of all headaches) to have far-reaching effects. (See chapter 6.) We'll discuss the features of the various types of headaches and the ways their symptoms manifest. (Clinicians speak of how a disease "presents.") We'll also list ominous headache features that require immediate medical attention to rule out life-threatening conditions. (See chapter 11.)

WHO GETS RECURRENT HEADACHES?

Chronic headache is an equal opportunity offender. It knows no racial, ethnic, cultural, gender, or geographic boundaries. Accordingly, African Americans, Asian Americans, Native Americans, and Caucasians can suffer chronic headaches. Both men and women can get them. Adolescents as well as middle-aged and older individuals can be afflicted. Residents of the New England states, California, and the beautiful tropical islands of Hawaii and Guam can get chronic headaches.

Even the meekest among us can suffer from chronic headaches. In a June 1999 interview on CNN, Dr. Irving Fish, director of pediatric neurology at New York University Medical Center in New York, said "about 85 percent of children by the time they're seventeen have had headaches severe enough to mention them to their physicians."

An estimated 59 percent of adult Canadians report some form of headache. The Migraine Association of Canada estimates that 3.2 million Canadians suffer from migraine headaches. New Zealand health authorities estimate that 49 percent of New Zealanders suffer chronic headaches, while in Zimbabwe, the number stands at 20 percent of the population. In Canada and the United States, more women than men suffer from headache.

THE SOCIAL AND ECONOMIC EFFECTS OF CHRONIC HEADACHES

As the statistics we mentioned in the preface indicate, chronic headache is an incapacitating disorder that interferes with the quality of life for adults, children, and adolescents; reduces workplace productivity; and negatively affects interpersonal relationships. According to the National Headache Foundation, billions of dollars are spent annually in the United States on the care of head pain (including eleven billion dollars to treat migraines alone, and four billion dollars on over-the-counter painkillers).[10] Some chronic headache sufferers can cost their employers well over five thousand dollars a year in health premiums.

HISTORICAL PERSPECTIVES

As we said in the preface, the incidence of headache dates back to prehistoric times. Ancient, medieval, and modern history is replete with accounts of headache suffering. Many movers and shakers of the religious, political, entertainment, academic, and military worlds of time past were famous, not only for their individual contributions to civilization, but for having suffered chronic headaches.

In the New Testament, Saul of Tarsus was plagued by recurrent visual disturbances, piercing head pain, and stomach upset—symptoms un- doubtedly caused by migraine headache. The Atharvaveda of India, a book about magic formulas written between 1500 and 800 B.C., contains essays about headaches. The early Greeks also recorded many accounts of re- peated headaches. One tablet at Epidaurus (circa 1250 B.C.) listed Ages- tratos as a chronic headache sufferer.[11] Hippocrates (circa 460–370 B.C.) aptly described a male patient suffering from what is now known as mi- graine headache:

> Most of the time he seemed to see something shining before him like a light, usually in part of the right eye; at the end of a moment, a violent pain supervened in the right temple, then in all the head and neck, where the head is attached to the spine . . . vomiting, when it became possible, was able to divert the pain and render it more moderate.

In more recent times, known chronic headache sufferers include nat- uralist Charles Darwin, dramatist George Bernard Shaw, psychoanalyst Sigmund Freud, and political economist Karl Marx. In our own country, the eighteenth U.S. president and Civil War general Ulysses S. Grant was known to suffer chronic bouts of head pain. So did our third president, Thomas Jefferson, and famed football player Terrell Davis.

Skulls bearing evidence of holes cut into them to relieve head pain have been recovered in Europe and South America.[12] Trepanning, as this practice was called, dates back to the Stone and Bronze Ages, circa 3500–1000 B.C. The Incas of ancient Peru used it to treat chronic head pain. South Pacific Islanders practiced trepanning for epilepsy, insanity, and recurrent headaches as recently as the seventeenth century.[13] Fortunately, these radi- cal headache treatments have given way to less life-threatening measures. When it comes to headache management, we've come a long way, baby!

AN ATTACH [SIC] OF THE
PERIODICAL HEAD-ACH, WHICH
CAME ON ME ABOUT A WEEK
AGO RENDERING ME UNABLE
AS YET EITHER TO WRITE OR
READ WITHOUT GREAT PAIN.

THOMAS JEFFERSON

MORE RECENTLY

Despite the lack of an outright headache cure, there has never been a better time to be a headache sufferer. Doctors can now prescribe headache treatments that are effective and provide prompt relief. A perfect example occurred during Super Bowl XXXII in January 1998. Star running back Terrell Davis of the Denver Broncos forgot to take his headache medication until right before game time and had to sit out part of the first quarter with a severe migraine attack. Remarkably, his medication quickly took effect, allowing him to be a major influence on the outcome of the most popular one-hour event in American sports.

IN SUMMARY

- The human brain lacks the ability to feel pain. However, the muscles, skin, blood vessels, and other structures that surround the brain possess sensory receptors that relay information (such as the prick of a pin) to the brain, which interprets it as pain.
- The pain caused by headache has its origins in biochemical aberrations within the brain and associated structures, and in blood flow. Serotonin appears to be a major chemical in the development of headache pain.
- Some headache sufferers may have a genetic tendency to develop headaches. However, an inherited propensity must be coupled with factors that trigger the head pain.
- Headaches can be broadly classified as either primary (i.e., have no known causes, as in migraines) or secondary (i.e., have some known cause, as in brain infection).

- Headache is an equal opportunity offender, not partial to any particular racial, ethnic, age, or geographic group.
- Many historical personalities, such as Charles Darwin, Sigmund Freud, Ulysses S. Grant, and Thomas Jefferson, were chronic headache sufferers. More recent sufferers include talented football player Terrell Davis.

CHAPTER TWO

Common Myths and Facts About Chronic Headaches

With so many people having headaches, you'd think almost everyone would have her headache facts straight. However, that's not the case. Despite headache pain's ancient lineage and widespread prevalence, individuals—including some health care professionals—harbor deep misinformation about the disease.[1] The general feeling among the public is that headaches result from personality flaws, and that only uptight control freaks get them. This erroneous information serves no useful purpose and it creates confusion in people's minds, trivializing a particularly disabling disease. At worse, misinformation can lead to needless suffering and even death. Even headache sufferers themselves have come to accept the generally held view of their condition, and many are frustrated by a "trivial" illness that nonetheless seems to have a major effect on their lives.[2]

In this chapter, we aim to debunk some of the common myths about headache and show you that it is more than "just an ache in the head." Speaking of myths, this is also a good time to expose the cottage industry of quackery, a business that thrives on the desperation of people feverishly seeking cures for their chronic medical conditions. Capitalizing on widespread fallacies about headaches, charlatans know that many chronic headache sufferers are willing to try anything that promises to restore good health. We encourage you to read chapter 16, in which we'll tell you which unconventional devices and substances are worth trying and which you should avoid.

MYTH OR FACT?

"Not tonight, honey, I have a headache." How many times have you heard this line—by now an American cliché—in popular sitcoms and movies in the past few decades? As offhand as it might seem, this trite line leaves viewers with a negative image of headaches and headache sufferers. The sufferer is not really sick, she just isn't capable of intimacy and tells a lie to avoid close emotional and physical contact.

> DO NOT UNDERVALUE THE HEADACHE. WHILE IT IS AT ITS SHARPEST IT SEEMS A BAD INVESTMENT; BUT WHEN RELIEF BEGINS, THE UNEXPIRED REMAINDER IS WORTH $4 A MINUTE.
>
> MARK TWAIN

This and other negative stereotypical portrayals of headache sufferers have spawned myriad myths about the nature of the condition and the psychological makeup and motivation of those who have it. After a while, people who don't suffer headaches come to regard headache sufferers as fakes, out to exact sympathy and to deceive family, friends, coworkers, and employers. Small wonder that a common myth about headache is that all sufferers have underlying personality disorders.

JUST THE FACTS, PLEASE!

Let's look at some of the common myths and facts regarding chronic headache and headache sufferers:

MYTH: Headache is not a real medical problem like diabetes or thyroid disease.
FACT: According to the National Headache Foundation, society has not always viewed headache as a serious disability.[3] Many prominent headache researchers like Dr. Richard Lipton of Albert Einstein College of Medicine in the Bronx and headache specialists like Drs. Seymour Solomon and Ninan T. Mathew of the American Council on Headache Education have shown that headaches are a genuine biological disorder. The proliferation

of headache clinics and their large-scale success are further testimony to the legitimacy of chronic headache pain.

MYTH: Chronic headaches result from hypersensitivity to pain: "You must be one of those people who are overly aware of every little sensation in your body."

FACT: Anyone who says "it's just a headache" obviously has never experienced the throbbing, debilitating head pain of a migraine that makes it difficult to work, attend school, or enjoy a close family relationship.

It is true that the degree of pain sensitivity varies from person to person, but there is no scientific proof that chronic headache sufferers are overly sensitive to pain. In the book *Migraine: The Complete Guide,* the American Council on Headache Education states that "considering the intensity of their pain, many migraineurs have learned to be exceptionally stoic, carrying on many of the functions of everyday life despite a level of pain that would demolish someone experiencing it for the first time."[4]

MYTH: Headaches result from poor coping skills: "If you'd learn how to properly deal with stress and other emotions, you wouldn't be getting these god-awful headaches in the first place."

FACT: Years of careful scientific research have shown that most headaches have biological origins characterized by many biochemical changes in the brain. True, psychological factors such as stress, anger, and other emotions can trigger some headaches, but in many cases the biological predisposition must be present beforehand. In other words, many persons who get over-stressed and angry do not experience migraine headache; many headache sufferers get head pain without getting angry or stressed out. We'll offer a detailed discussion on the issue of headache triggers in chapter 3.

MYTH: Headache results from a personality disorder: "Those Type-A personalities always manage to keep getting migraine headaches; they have a migraine personality that they can't shake."

FACT: The scientific literature does not support the theory of a "migraine personality" (stereotyped as being an intensely ambitious, driven perfectionist) that supposedly predisposes one to migraine headaches.[5] In fact, many people who fit the profile of a "migraine personality" don't suffer from migraines or any other type of headache; many people with migraine headache don't fit the stereotype.

MYTH: Chronic headache is a woman's disease; that's why many more women than men get them.
FACT: The majority of women do not get repeated headaches, while many men suffer from chronic headaches. That hardly makes headache a gender-specific condition. Women who suffer from chronic headaches, such as female migraineurs, have unquestionable hormonal factors that influence their head pain. (See chapters 5 and 8.) Men, too, experience hormonally based chronic headaches. In fact, cluster headache, which affects six times more men than women, is believed to be related to the male hormone testosterone. (See chapter 6.)

MYTH: Smart and rich people don't get headaches; only poor, unaccomplished folks get them.
FACT : Headache is an equal opportunity offender, affecting persons from all walks of life and those with all levels of socioeconomic and intellectual endowments. As we pointed out in chapter 1, Charles Darwin and Thomas Jefferson, arguably two of the most intellectually gifted men in the past two hundred years, suffered from recurrent headaches.

MYTH: "It's all in your head; ignore your headache and it will eventually go away."
FACT: To be sure, headaches do affect the head. Headache pain, however, is as real as the pain of stomach ulcers and arthritis. Headaches can be a symptom of a litany of medical disorders, such as undiagnosed high blood pressure, glaucoma, or thyroid imbalance, or a migraine disorder that involves a series of physiologic changes in the brain, blood vessels, nerves,

and other structures in the head and neck. For example, a 1999 study conducted by Dr. Massimo Cirillo and associates at the Second University of Naples, Italy, found that a large number of individuals with severe headaches suffered from high blood pressure. Only a physician or another qualified health care provider is competent to diagnose the source of a headache.

MYTH: Once you develop headaches, there isn't much you can do; you just have to accept your fate and "live with it."

FACT: The last few decades have seen great advances in the treatment of the most severe headaches. Indeed, researchers are closing in on the specific causes of most types of headaches and have already developed effective treatments for migraines, clusters, and other enigmatic headache syndromes. For example, scientists have discovered the drug sumatriptan succinate (Imitrex), which specifically binds to areas in the brain normally occupied by the brain chemical serotonin and serotonin-like substances, major chemicals that contribute to the development of migraine, cluster, and other forms of headaches. (See chapter 16.)

IN SUMMARY

- Headache myths abound among both laypersons and health care professionals.
- Headache is a legitimate disorder that deserves the same recognition given to conditions like diabetes and thyroid disease.
- The majority of headache pain has a biological origin, with stress and other factors acting as triggers that set off the pain.
- Chronic headache is no trivial matter and has nothing to do with a personality disorder. True, some persons with certain stereotypical personality traits get headaches, but many well-adjusted persons also get recurrent headaches.

- Recurrent head pain affects both men and women. Although more women than men get migraine, more men than women get cluster headache. This has led to the belief that both of these types of headaches are largely influenced by hormonal factors.
- Chronic headache has nothing to do with intellectual capacity or socioeconomic status.
- Headache pain is not "all in the head." In many cases, these pains can be traced to physical conditions such as high blood pressure and glaucoma.
- Advances in the understanding of chronic headaches in the past few decades have led to the development of effective medications to manage all forms of headaches.

CHAPTER THREE

Headache Triggers

Now that you understand what pain is, and specifically what headache pain is, let's turn our attention to the many factors that can trigger headache in some individuals. Headache research and anecdotal evidence have shown that some external and internal substances and factors cause headache flares in some susceptible headache sufferers (see table 3.1). Some forms of migraine headaches are provoked by environmental factors (e.g., change in weather), foods and food additives (e.g., chocolate and monosodium glutamate), drugs (e.g., birth control pills), and social habits (e.g., drinking alcohol).[1] Dietary triggers play a larger role in headache activation than any other factor.

Headache-triggering factors are not the biological causes of headaches; instead, they activate or trigger headaches when the predisposed individual is exposed to them. The exact mechanisms by which headache triggers precipitate headache pain continues to puzzle scientists. However, headache experts believe that the initiating substance or event triggers an irregular pattern of electrical activity in the outer layer of the brain called the *cortex*.[2]

No two people—indeed, not even two members of the same family— have the same headache triggers. Some people find that a combination of triggers activates their headache attacks. For example, drinking red wine or eating cheese may not trigger a migraine headache, but eating cheese while drinking red wine may. Remember also that headache triggers can change during the course of a life, so be wary of new ones. Some people even "outgrow" some of their headache triggers.

About 10 percent of headache sufferers are fortunate enough to discover their headache triggers; for others, their triggers are subtle and difficult to

TABLE 3.1: COMMON FACTORS THAT TRIGGER HEADACHE

Environmental Factors

Bright or flickering lights	Air pollution
High altitude	Weather changes
Strong odors	Loud noise

Foods and Food Additives

Chocolate	Ice cream
Caffeine	Monosodium glutamate
Amines	Nitrites and nitrates
Sulfites	Gamma-aminobutyric acid
Salt	Artificial sweeteners
Onions	Beans
Nuts	

Nutritional Deficiencies

Vitamin/mineral deficiencies	Low blood sugar (hypoglycemia)

Lifestyle Factors

Anxiety	Stress
Depression	

Social Habits

Smoking	Secondhand smoke
Alcohol	

Drugs

Painkillers	Diet pills
Hormones	Decongestants
Cardiovascular drugs	Recreational drugs

identify. Obviously, the advantage of knowing what sets your head pain in motion is being able to avoid or minimize the inciting factors. Identifying your triggers makes it easier to manage your condition or reduce your disability. Think back to a previous headache—was it triggered by a sudden change in barometric pressure, eating chocolate, not sleeping well, or by your menstrual period? The best way to determine if you are a victim of headache triggers, and to determine what those triggers are, is to keep a headache diary. (See chapter 13 and Appendix A.) Use the list in exhibit 3.1 to help you fill out your headache diary.

> SWEET THINGS AND SPICES AND STRONG DRINK, ONE AFTER THE OTHER HE CONSUMES WITH EAGER SPEED AND THEN COMPLAINS ABOUT HIS TURBID MIND.
>
> JOHANN WOLFGANG VON GOETHE

In this chapter, we'll detail the many known and suspected factors that can precipitate headaches. The complete list of possible triggers is too numerous to catalog, but we'll discuss the most common ones. For practical purposes, we've placed these triggers into six categories:

1. Environmental factors
2. Dietary factors (food and food additives)
3. Nutritional deficiencies
4. Lifestyle factors
5. Social habits
6. Drugs

ENVIRONMENTAL HEADACHE TRIGGERS

Many environmental conditions—such as bright lights, changes in barometric pressure, a reduction in the amount of sunlight during winter, and allergic reactions—can trigger recurrent headache in predisposed individuals. In fact,

---

EXHIBIT 3.1: TRACKING YOUR HEADACHE TRIGGERS

Identify the factors that trigger your headaches and use the information to help complete your headache diary.

Environmental Factors

Bright or flickering lights	☐	Air pollution	☐
High altitude	☐	Strong odors	☐
Weather changes	☐	Loud noise	☐

Foods and Food Additives

Chocolate	☐	Citrus fruits	☐
Ice cream	☐	Gamma-aminobutyric acid	☐
Caffeine	☐	Amines	☐
Monosodium glutamate (MSG)	☐	Nitrites and nitrates	☐
		Nuts	☐
Tyramine	☐	Sulfites	☐
Salt	☐	Onions	☐
Artificial sweeteners	☐	Beans	☐

Nutritional Deficiencies

Vitamin/deficiencies	☐	Low blood sugar (hypoglycemia)	☐

Lifestyle Factors

Anxiety	☐	Depression	☐
Stress	☐		

Social Habits/Drugs

Smoking	☐	Diet pills	☐
Secondhand smoke	☐	Hormones	☐
Alcohol	☐	Decongestants	☐
Drugs	☐	Cardiovascular drugs	☐
Painkillers	☐	Recreational drugs	☐

any change in the environment that involves physiological adjustment and adaptation can provoke headache.

BRIGHT OR FLICKERING LIGHTS OR GLARE

Exposure to bright or flickering lights or glare is a common trigger of migraine and cluster headaches in predisposed sufferers. A survey of migraineurs conducted by Australian headache specialists Drs. George Selby and J. W. Lance revealed that the glare of bright light was a common headache trigger in 47 percent of the respondents.[3]

Bright or flickering lights can excite the brain, activating a chain of events that can lead to vascular headaches in some people. Staring into the glare of sunlight reflected from snow, water, sand, or a metallic surface can cause one to squint, tensing the muscles around the eyes. Prolonged exposure to bright and fast-moving images on a computer, TV, or movie screen can produce the same effects. These exposures may also cause the blood vessels in the head and neck to swell and dilate, further inducing vascular headache.

Migraineurs should wear both sunglasses and wide-brimmed hats when outdoors on bright sunny days. Promptly fix faulty fluorescent lights and place antiglare covers on computer monitors. Additionally, curtail your driving at sunset, sunrise, or night.

HIGH ALTITUDE

Sudden changes in oxygen pressure cause the blood vessels in the scalp—which are extremely sensitive to changes in the pressure of oxygen—to swell, precipitating headaches.[4] A drop in oxygen pressure due to high altitudes also makes less oxygen available to the brain. This explains why some migraineurs report headache flares during airplane travel, when climbing mountains and large hills, or during deep-sea diving. Living at elevations over 6,000 feet or driving up or down steep inclines or declines can trigger similar headaches.

Symptoms of altitude-associated sickness include headache, vomiting, confusion, fatigue, and weakness. Additionally, shortness of breath, dizziness, feeling faint, and insomnia may be present.

Headache sufferers sensitive to high altitudes may consider having extra oxygen available. If you decide to climb a mountain, do so only if you are physically fit. When possible, ascend gradually in stages, allowing time for acclimatization. Doctors often prescribe the drug Diamox or steroids for altitude sickness. Vitamin C, which helps the circulation of oxygen throughout the body, may also help to treat this condition.

WEATHER CHANGES

Weather changes induce modifications in the body's biological milieu, triggering migraine and other headaches in susceptible individuals.[5] Sufferers experience headaches when there's a change in ambient temperature, humidity level, and barometric pressure. Some migraine sufferers can foretell when a low-pressure weather front is about to roll in. Others are affected by the so-called "ill winds," such as the southern Californian Santa Ana, the hot, dry winds of the Arizona desert, the Israeli sharav, the Balkan bora, and the Argentine zonda.

Along with their typical headaches, sufferers sensitive to changes in weather can experience fatigue, difficulty concentrating, anxiety, and depression. These symptoms can occur prior to falling barometric pressure or with the arrival of inclement weather.

If you experience weather-sensitive headaches, talk to your health care provider about starting you on headache medicines prior to the foreseeable arrival of inclement weather or environmental pressure changes.

AIR POLLUTION

Many vascular headache sufferers can trace their head pain to the level of smog, automobile exhaust fumes, and other air pollutants. These individuals report an improvement in their symptoms upon leaving the offending environment. The problem is believed to be caused chiefly by high levels of carbon monoxide, which competes with oxygen for space in the oxygen-carrying pigments in the blood. Even slightly low levels of oxygen lead to headaches in susceptible individuals. Ozone is another airborne culprit that triggers headaches in some sufferers.

Short of moving to another location, the only way to combat air pollutants is to limit outside activities on days when air pollution is high. (Fortunately, many TV and radio stations routinely alert listeners when pollution reaches unhealthy levels.) Another strategy for dealing with this problem is to plan your annual vacation during peak pollution days to escape the offending environment.

ALLERGIC REACTIONS

Allergic reactions to food, beverages, and drugs can trigger migraine headaches in susceptible people.[6] Don't confuse an allergic reaction with environmental allergies that cause headaches (see chapter 10). During an allergic reaction, the body secretes histamines and other vasoactive substances that are involved in the immune response. (Vasoactive substances cause the blood vessels to narrow, then expand, thus resulting in a headache.) These vasoactive substances protect the body but cause the blood vessels in the head, neck, and elsewhere to swell, triggering the vascular changes that occur with migraines. The best antidote for allergic reactions to foods, beverages, and drugs is avoidance.

OTHER ENVIRONMENTAL FACTORS

Chronic exposure to loud noise in the form of music, machinery, and airplanes, as well as from other sources, can cause chronic headaches. Avoidance is the best preventive strategy, but when this is not possible, you should use earplugs. Some chronic headache sufferers—most notably migraine sufferers—are prone to headache flares upon exposure to strong odors such as perfume, tobacco smoke (discussed on page 41), petroleum products, and room deodorizers.[7]

Others report head pain, sore throat, sneezing, runny nose, and fatigue on exposure to the chemicals emitted by photocopiers and carbonless paper. These chemicals can be inhaled into the lungs or absorbed into the skin. Again, avoidance is the best way to prevent these products from triggering your headache pain. If you spend lots of time using a photocopying machine, walk away from the machine while it's copying. Washing your hands after handling irritating chemicals can also help.

DIETARY
HEADACHE TRIGGERS

There are no accurate estimates of the number of headache sufferers whose headaches are diet related. However, headache researchers over the past three decades have uncovered a number of food products that can trigger headaches in some people, as well as deficiencies of some substances that can have the same result. In their book *Guide to Headache Relief,* Dr. Paula Maas and coauthor Deborah Mitchell wrote that 10 percent of all migraine headache sufferers blame certain foods, beverages, nutritional supplements, and food additives for their chronic headaches.[8]

The exact mechanisms by which foodstuffs trigger headaches aren't entirely clear. The most commonly implicated foods in triggering migraine, cluster, and other forms of headaches include chocolate, monosodium glutamate (MSG), amines, nitrates, sulfites, artificial sweeteners, and nuts. In addition, gamma-aminobutyric acid (GABA), salt, ice cream, onions, beans, and caffeine are often implicated.

CHOCOLATE

Headache researchers have found that eating chocolate can trigger headaches in some sufferers. Chocolate contains a number of substances, including caffeine (discussed on page 36), the amine phenylethylamine (discussed on page 32), and ground cacao, that are responsible for triggering migraine headaches. Phenylethylamine can affect blood vessel tone, causing migraine and migrainelike headaches.

People with chocolate-induced headaches may have significantly lower levels of a platelet enzyme that is responsible for breaking down phenylethylamine than do nonsufferers.[9] Some migraine sufferers experience a strong craving for chocolate just before a migraine attack. Plain and bitter chocolate contain higher levels of phenylethylamine than do milk chocolate and white chocolate.

MONOSODIUM GLUTAMATE

Monosodium glutamate (MSG), derived from the amino acid glutamic acid, is a food flavor enhancer commonly found in a number of food additives and in most packaged, canned, and frozen entrees sold in supermarkets. It's also used to enhance the flavor of commercial soups, gravies, hot dogs, and many other foods.

The U.S. Department of Agriculture requires that all labels of processed meat and poultry products list MSG and all other additives by name to alert people who know they are sensitive to these enhancers. MSG is often listed as "hydrolyzed vegetable protein," "textured vegetable protein," "flavoring," "hydrolyzed plant protein," or "natural flavor" instead of a separate ingredient.[10] MSG is also commonly found in foods prepared in Chinese restaurants. A 7-ounce bowl of wonton soup, for example, contains about 3 grams of MSG, enough to trigger a migraine attack in susceptible people.[11]

MSG-induced headaches typically begin less than thirty minutes after foods containing it have been eaten. In most people, the head pain feels like a bandlike pressure around the forehead and pressure or throbbing over the temples. Some sufferers also experience dizziness, pressure in the chest, and abdominal cramps. Patients prescribed a low-sodium diet, such as those diagnosed with high blood pressure and congestive heart failure, should be aware that MSG is high in sodium.

AMINES

A group of vasoactive, nitrogen-based protein components called *amines* have been implicated as triggers of vascular headaches in predisposed individuals.[12] People with sensitivity to amines may have a biochemical defect (i.e., they lack a platelet enzyme) that impairs amine metabolism. Following are the amines thus far implicated and their sources:

- Dopamine, present in legumes such as peanuts, peas, broad beans, and soy.
- Tyramine, found in aged foods such as cheese, yogurt, buttermilk, sourdough, and overripe bananas; red wine, beer, dried or pickled meat, salami, nuts, figs, raisins, avocadoes, and fish also contain high levels of tyramine.
- Histamine, contained in cold-water fish such as salmon and tuna.
- Phenylethylamine, present in chocolate.
- Octopamine and synephrine, found in citrus fruits.
- Tryptamine, contained in tomatoes and pineapples.

NITRITES AND NITRATES

Nitrites and nitrates are a group of chemicals used since ancient times to preserve meat and prevent food from spoiling and as preservatives in many canned foods. These substances, listed as sodium nitrites, potassium nitrite, and nitric acid on ingredients labels, are added to foods to prevent botulism, an often fatal form of food poisoning. Foods that commonly contain nitrites and nitrates include bacon, salami, hot dogs, bologna, and sausage.

These substances have been linked to various cancers and vascular headaches. Nitrites and nitrates apparently trigger vascular headaches by widening (dilating) blood vessels that carry blood to the head and neck. The ability of nitrites and nitrates to dilate blood vessels is demonstrated when nitroglycerin (e.g., isosorbide dinitrite) is used in patients with angina, a condition in which blood vessels to the heart are narrowed by plaque and spasm. A common side effect of nitroglycerin is a throbbing, migrainelike headache (discussed on page 46).

SULFITES

Sulfites are a family of chemicals used as preservatives in foods, alcohol, and drugs. These chemicals are listed as potassium bisulfite, sodium sulfite, and sulfur dioxide in ingredients lists. Sulfites give fruits and vegetables a "fresh" appearance and are still used by some restaurants to enhance the appearance of salads. Wine makers also use sulfites to inhibit bacterial growth in wine. These chemicals, long implicated as asthma triggers, are believed to cause or worsen headache symptoms.

Foods that contain sulfites include frozen potato products, dried fruits, avocado dip, and soup, sauce, and gravy mixes. Beer and wine also contain "sulfiting" agents. Drugs that contain sulfites include intravenous and spray preparations.

Sulfite-induced sensitivity ranges from mild to severe. Symptoms include flushing, hives, difficulty breathing, nausea, vomiting, and headache. In extreme cases, ingesting these chemicals can lead to loss of consciousness and death.

ARTIFICIAL SWEETENERS

Aspartame, the low-calorie artificial sweetener sold as Nutrasweet, Spoonful, and Equal, has been implicated as a headache trigger in some patients with migraines.[13] It is an almost odorless crystalline powder with an intensely sweet taste and is derived from aspartic acid and the metyl ester of phenylalanine. Some scientists believe that aspartame may lower brain serotonin levels, a mechanism implicated in the development of migraine headache.

Aspartame is found in everyday products such as soft drinks, puddings, yogurt, chewing gum, and various desserts. Individuals susceptible to its effects should avoid products containing aspartame.

NUTS

Peanut and tree nut sensitivity affects three million Americans. Both have been implicated in headache flares. Peanuts, which contain large amounts of dopamine, have been associated with migraine flares in susceptible sufferers. Peanut butter is also a culprit. Walnuts, pecans, almonds, coconut, cashews, and pistachios can also trigger headaches.

GAMMA-AMINOBUTYRIC ACID

Gamma-aminobutyric acid (GABA) is a brain chemical, an inhibitory neurotransmitter that helps transmit messages between nerve cells. Chemically, GABA resembles MSG, and excess amounts can trigger head pain in some headache patients. Medically, GABA has been used to treat epilepsy and high blood pressure. The substance is found in the brain, kidneys, heart, and lungs, as well as in some plants.

SALT

Salt, or sodium, may play a role in setting off migraines and other vascular headaches in some individuals. Sodium is believed to cause platelets to clump, a condition thought to be present in the development of some vascular headaches. Excessive sodium also can lead to fluid retention and a rise in blood pressure in some people.

High concentrations of sodium are found in many canned foods and food additives. One tablespoon of soy sauce, for example, contains about 1,030 milligrams of sodium. Even lean ham contains about 1,025 milligrams of sodium per 3-ounce serving. Your daily intake of salt should not exceed 2,400 milligrams.

ICE CREAM

Some migraine sufferers, as well as persons not predisposed to headaches, develop pain behind the eyes, deep behind the bridge of the nose, or in the temples when they eat ice cream or very cold foods. Ice cream–triggered headache pain typically lasts about twenty to thirty seconds. The exact mechanism by which ice cream induces headaches in these individuals is not known, but some plausible explanations have been offered. Headache specialists Drs. Alan Rapoport and Fred Sheftell believe that the sudden cold of the ice cream shocks the warm tissues of the roof of the mouth and throat, causing nerve and blood vessel changes that lead to headaches.

If you suffer from ice cream headaches, you can avoid them by eating smaller, warmer bites.[14] Between bites, hold the ice cream in front of your mouth for a few seconds until the roof of your mouth cools down.

CAFFEINE

Caffeine is an ingredient in some migraine medications. How, then, can caffeinated beverages, including coffee, tea, and colas, and other sources of caffeine be implicated as triggers in some forms of chronic headaches? Research shows that excessive use, as well as a sudden cessation of caffeine, can trigger headaches. Like nicotine and alcohol, too much caffeine narrows blood vessels excessively, reducing blood flow to the brain and other vital organs. If your headaches are affected by caffeine, you should not consume more than 300 to 400 milligrams of caffeine—the amount in four cups of brewed coffee—per day. (Table 3.2 lists the caffeine content of common caffeinated drinks, foods, and drugs.)

TABLE 3.2: CAFFEINE IN FOOD AND MEDICINE

Source	Estimated caffeine (in milligrams)
Brewed coffee, one cup (5 ounces)	100–150
Instant coffee, one cup	85–100
Decaffeinated coffee, one cup	2–4
Cocoa, one cup	40–55
Chocolate bar	25
Cola	40–60
Anacin	32
Bromo Seltzer	32
Cope	32
Darvon Compound	32
Excedrin	65
Midol	32
Pre-mens	30
Vanquish	33

Adapted from A. M. Rapoport and F. D. Sheftell, *Headache Relief* (New York: Fireside, 1991).

Conversely, reducing caffeine intake can lead to the rebound dilation of blood vessels, and this too can touch off withdrawal headaches. The typical caffeine-withdrawal headache sufferer drinks lots of coffee at work and little or none on his days off, and therefore develops throbbing headaches while away from work. If this describes you and you are trying to stop using caffeine, you should gradually reduce your intake over a three- to seven-day period.

FRUITS

Citrus fruits, which contain octopamine and synephrine, have been fingered as precipitants of migraine headaches—especially oranges, grapefruits, lemons, and limes. Overripe bananas, which contain high amounts of tyramine, can trigger headaches in some people (see page 32). Dried fruit, which contains high levels of sulfites, can also activate migraines (see page 33).

NUTRITIONAL DEFICIENCIES THAT CAN TRIGGER HEADACHES

In addition to food triggers, vitamin/mineral deficiency and hypoglycemia (low blood sugar) can lead to headache flares.

VITAMIN/MINERAL DEFICIENCY

A few studies have shown a connection between the deficiency of vitamins or minerals and the development of headaches. Additionally, anecdotal evidence points to a possible relationship. In a 1991 study, adults suffering from both migraine and tension-type headaches were found to have significantly lower levels of magnesium compared to age-matched controls.[15] Other studies have shown that low levels of vitamins may be related to recurrent headaches. Headaches have also been reported in people with chromium, copper, and iron deficiencies.[16]

Renowned headache specialists Alan Rapoport and Fred Sheftell recommend multivitamins for persons not careful to eat a diet containing all the crucial vitamins.[17] Caution is in order, however. Too much of some vitamins—especially the fat-soluble vitamins A, D, E, and K—may be bad for you. Fat-soluble vitamins can build up to toxic levels in fat cells, causing potentially life-threatening problems. Excess vitamin A, for example, can lead to pseudotumor cerebri, a condition characterized by increased pressure in the brain. Check with your doctor before starting megadoses of any vitamins.

HYPOGLYCEMIA

Abnormally low blood sugar or hypoglycemia, caused by excessive dieting, fasting, or having too much insulin in the body, can trigger headaches.[18] Diabetics who take more insulin than they need are at risk of developing hypoglycemia, as are individuals who fast for extended periods due to dieting or other reasons.

People prone to chronic headaches and those without a history of headaches can be equally affected by hypoglycemia. Low blood sugar causes the secretion of adrenaline which, like the amines discussed on page 32, is vasoactive. In a complicated way, adrenaline can also stimulate insulin secretion, further lowering your blood sugar.

Besides a throbbing headache, other symptoms of hypoglycemia include dizziness, mental confusion, sweating, and clumsiness. To avoid hypoglycemia, eat frequently, don't skip meals, and eat complex carbohydrates (whole grains and whole beans) instead of food made from refined sugars (sugar donuts). Hypoglycemia can be potentially fatal if you are diabetic; report any hypoglycemic episode immediately to your doctor, or call an ambulance to take you to the nearest emergency room.

LIFESTYLE FACTORS THAT CAN TRIGGER HEADACHES

Lifestyle factors have been blamed for triggering headaches in susceptible individuals. Anxiety, stress, depression, and changes in sleep patterns are associated with changes in the body's biochemistry. These changes can affect brain function, blood vessel size, and blood flow. This is why, for example, an intensely stressful event can cause a heart attack in a person with coronary arteries narrowed by plaque buildup. Similarly, the biochemical changes caused by emotional factors can affect the blood vessels in some people susceptible to vascular headaches.

STRESS AND OTHER EMOTIONAL FACTORS

What do traffic jams, deadlines, financial troubles, sexual harassment, and failed marriages have in common? These factors are all stressors—events and issues that induce emotional stress that can trigger myriad physical ailments, including headache. Although emotional stress can't be measured like blood pressure, its effects are well known. Many headache sufferers trace the flare-ups of their head pain to events that cause emotional stress. In fact, stress is one of the most common precipitating factors of migraine, tension-type, and cluster headaches.[19] Factors associated with stress include mental fatigue, anxiety, boredom, frustration, excessive worry, poorly balanced diet, and depression.

Stress can lead to physical and biochemical reactions in the body—the so-called "fight or flight" response that prepares and energizes the body to confront or flee from danger. During the fight or flight response, the body releases a number of chemicals, including adrenaline and cortisol, that lead to the blood vessel changes that set off headache symptoms. As we said in chapter 1, stress lowers the pain threshold. Typically, stress-related head pain starts after the stressful event, during the letdown or relaxation period.

Some headache patients report having weekend-only headaches; letdown head pain brought on by a hectic preceding workweek.

Like stress, anxiety, frustration, and anger can cause the body to secrete adrenaline that can narrow blood vessels and precipitate a headache.

Depression has been shown to increase the frequency of migraine attacks in many sufferers. This is not surprising since the chemical changes that occur with depression negatively affect the body's ability to utilize the neurotransmitter serotonin. When we discuss the antidepressant drugs such as fluoxetine (Prozac) in chapter 16, it will become clear why depression can trigger headaches, and also why antidepressant drugs work well to prevent vascular headaches in people with frequent headache attacks.

DISRUPTED SLEEP PATTERN

Human brain function is regulated by a biological clock that is inextricably tied in with food intake, stress levels, and the sleep/wake cycle.[20] Any change in sleep patterns—either too much or too little—can affect brain wave patterns and trigger headaches in some people. Sleep disturbances can be caused by factors such as changes in time zone and activity level, medication usage, and caffeine intake. In addition, anatomical structures such as large tonsils, a small throat, and excess fat around the neck can affect sleep quality by causing sleep apnea (periods of stoppage of breathing during sleep).

The best solution for sleep disturbances is to maintain a regular sleep/wake schedule: Go to sleep and arise at the same time every day, even on weekends. If your migraines flare up despite a consistent sleep/wake schedule, talk to your health care practitioner about the possibility of undergoing a sleep study. Other strategies include eating a balanced diet and following a regular regimen of aerobic exercise. Sleep apnea requires professional medical evaluation.

SOCIAL HABITS THAT CAN
TRIGGER HEADACHES

If you are prone to headaches and you smoke, are subjected to second-hand smoke, or consume excess amounts of alcohol, beware! Nicotine and the by-products of cigarette smoke can cause chronic recurrent headaches in some susceptible people, as can alcohol. Nicotine damages your health regardless of whether you have chronic headaches and, as we'll discuss in chapter 10, it can predispose you to a stroke. Some individuals with chronic headaches can get away with using moderate amounts of alcohol; others have to abstain completely.

SMOKING AND SECONDHAND SMOKE EXPOSURE

Tobacco and tobacco by-products apparently trigger headaches through two mechanisms. First, the nicotine in tobacco narrows blood vessels throughout the body, including those in the neck that feed the brain. When this happens, the brain is denied the free flow of vital oxygen, as well as glucose and other nutrients that nourish it. The oxygen-starved brain undergoes abnormal brain wave patterns, and the individual can experience impaired vision and a number of cognitive changes, including poor judgment.

Smokers and individuals exposed to secondhand (or sidestream) smoke can also develop chronic headaches due to a buildup of carbon monoxide and carboxyhemoglobin in their blood. Carbon monoxide, which makes up about 4 percent of the typical burning cigarette, aggressively displaces oxygen from its receptors, denying the brain its vital supply of oxygen. Again, an oxygen-starved brain undergoes abnormal brain wave patterns, and the individual can experience the symptoms mentioned above. Carbon monoxide also is a potent blood vessel dilator, another mechanism which causes headache. Formaldehyde and the litany of other chemicals in tobacco may also be headache triggers.

ALCOHOL

Excessive alcohol consumption has been shown to cause flare-ups of migraine and cluster headaches in susceptible sufferers.[21] Alcohol in all forms can trigger headaches through multiple mechanisms, not the least of which has to do with the fact that it contains a number of migraine-provoking chemicals. Even nonalcoholic beer, which contains no ethanol, contains these chemical triggers.

Alcohol dilates blood vessels throughout the body, reducing blood flow to vital organs such as the kidneys and brain. Some forms of alcohol contain sulfites, tyramine, and histamine that can trigger headaches by dilating blood vessels. Alcohol also contains *cogeners,* the substances that give each liquor its color and flavor, which can trigger headache. The darkest alcohols, such as red wine, scotch, and brandy, contain more cogeners and are most often implicated in headache flare-ups.

Alcohol also lowers blood sugar levels (see page 38) by triggering insulin production, leading to headache pain. Bourbon, brandy, rye, gin, cognac, scotch, vodka, and whiskey are more likely to lead to hypoglycemia than are other forms of alcohol. Drinking alcohol on an empty stomach is more likely to cause hypoglycemia than drinking after consuming foods containing protein, carbohydrates, and fat.

The dehydrating effect of alcohol can lower spinal fluid pressure and can lead to headache. Beer in particular induces increased urination and loss of blood volume (dehydration). Alcohol may also trigger headaches by affecting brain serotonin levels.

MEDICATIONS AND RECREATIONAL DRUGS THAT CAN TRIGGER HEADACHES

When it comes to vascular headaches, drugs are a mixed bag. As we'll discuss in chapter 16, some agents employed to treat head pain—especially those that dilate the blood vessels—can themselves cause headaches. In this section, we'll turn our attention to painkillers, hormonal agents, diet pills, and decongestants that have been implicated as headache triggers in some persons with chronic headaches. Other categories of drugs associated with headache in nonsufferers include high blood pressure and anti-ulcer drugs, antibiotics, and antihistamines. Drugs most commonly associated with headache include those shown in table 3.3.

TABLE 3.3: DRUG-RELATED HEADACHE TRIGGERS

Indomethacin	Captopril
Nifedipine	Piroxicam
Cimetidine	Metoprolol
Atenolol	Diclofenac
Trimethoprim-sulfamethoxazole	Methyldopa
Zimeldine	Glyceryl trinitrate
Isosorbide dinitrite	Terfenadine
Zomepirac	Propranolol
Ranitidine	Benoxaprofen
Isotretinoin	Metronidazole

Modified from H. Askmark, P. O. Lundberg, and S. Olsson, "Drug-related headache," *Headache* 29 (1989): 441.

PAINKILLERS

Painkillers can trigger headache pain? Indeed, these headache treatments can be responsible for the very symptoms they aim to stop. For most chronic headache patients, painkillers or analgesics are godsends; but for a small percentage, these drugs can spell trouble. For example, the popular pain medicine indomethacin is a known headache trigger in both headache sufferers and nonsufferers alike. Indomethacin narrows the carotid arteries, setting off migraines. Some people who take this medication for a prolonged period can develop a condition called *analgesic rebound headache.*

The American Association for the Study of Headache reports that analgesic rebound headache is the most common cause of chronic daily headaches. This form of headache recurs as each dose of painkiller wears off, prompting the sufferer to take more and more medication, perpetuating a vicious cycle. As was discussed earlier in this chapter, similar rebounds can occur with withdrawal from caffeinated beverages. If you experience the following symptoms, you may be a victim of drug-induced headaches:

- The daily or almost daily use of headache pills.
- Headaches that awaken you in the early hours of the morning.
- Nausea, abdominal pain, cramps, diarrhea, sleep disturbance, irritability, increase in intensity of headache—all symptoms of drug withdrawal—after suddenly discontinuing daily headache medication.[22]

Painkillers most commonly implicated in medication-induced headache include ibuprofen, naproxen, indomethecin, and other nonsteroidal anti-inflammatory drugs.[23] In addition, narcotics such as codeine, hydrocodone, oxycodone, and meperidine can induce rebound headaches. The treatment is to withdraw the offending drug and use another type of analgesic, if needed. Obviously, this should only be done under physician supervision.

DIET PILLS

Most appetite suppressants, both prescription and nonprescription, contain either amphetamines or caffeine as their main ingredient. These drugs trigger migraines by stimulating the brain. The precise mechanism by which this happens is unknown, but many migraineurs who've taken diet pills report a connection between taking these drugs and a flare-up of their migraine headaches. Caffeine-containing diet pills can cause chronic daily headache when caffeine withdrawal causes the individual to use more caffeine (see page 36).

HORMONAL CHANGES

As we'll discuss in chapter 8, oral contraceptive pills (also called birth control pills, or simply "the pill") and other forms of hormonal drugs, as well as the hormonal changes that occur during menstruation and pregnancy, have been associated with vascular headaches. A large number of women develop migraines for the first time after they begin taking birth control pills, and the headaches promptly stop after they quit taking the pill. Such headaches may be related to the fluctuations in hormonal levels associated with the pill. Unless the benefits outweigh the risks, we recommend that you not take birth control pills if you have migraine headaches or if you develop migraines after starting the pill. However, consult your physician when making that decision.

After menopause, a woman's estrogen levels decrease, placing her at increased risk of developing heart disease, hot flashes, and bone fractures due to osteoporosis. Similar risks exist after the removal of a woman's ovaries due to pelvic diseases, which can induce premature menopause. An important strategy to combat these serious consequences is to replace estrogen and progesterone (referred to as hormone replacement therapy, or HRT) through daily intake of a pill or through a patch placed on the skin. Like the birth control pill, HRT causes migraines in some women. Some women may be able to use alternative strategies such as soy and soy products, which contain phyto-estrogens. We recommend that you have an honest discussion with your health care provider if you develop HRT-associated vascular headache.

DECONGESTANTS

Decongestants, which typically contain phenylephrine and phenyl-propanolamine, have been implicated as migraine triggers. These drugs work by constricting blood vessels and stimulating the central nervous system—two mechanisms that are likely to precipitate a migraine headache in suscep-tible individuals.[24] If you have migraine headache, you may want to avoid both prescription and over-the-counter decongestants. Ask your health care practitioner if there are alternative agents that you may be able to take.

CARDIOVASCULAR DRUGS

Cardiovascular drugs, which are used to treat high blood pressure and other heart and blood vessel conditions, have been connected to headache flares.[25] As we discussed earlier, nitroglycerin, an effective medication for angina, induces migrainelike headache in the majority of users, as do the blood pressure drugs hydralazine and reserpine.

RECREATIONAL DRUGS

Like nicotine and caffeine, cocaine can narrow blood vessels and trigger migraine headache.[26] On the other hand, marijuana has been shown to both treat and cause headache.

JENNIFER'S STORY

Jennifer, a thirty-year-old successful businesswoman, began experiencing recurrent headaches at the beginning of the summer following her twenty-third birthday. During that summer, she began dating a French exchange student from a well-to-do background. During their dates at high-priced French restaurants, Jennifer would drink red wine with her meals.

Once the exact triggers were identified, Jennifer set about developing a plan for avoiding red wine and its components. Four months later, Jennifer's chronic headaches were reduced to an occasional, mild, nondescript head pain that occurred every three months on average.

MICHAEL'S STORY

A struggling twenty-two-year-old writer, Michael became increasingly frustrated with vicious headaches that seemed to come in regular cycles. His headaches began at age sixteen. They were severe, pounding, and located around his left eye socket. The headaches seemed to have a seasonal pattern and would wake Michael in the middle of the night. After undergoing his fourth medical evaluation, Michael wasn't any closer to controlling his pain than when he visited the first doctor.

Fortunately, the fifth time seemed to be the charm. After questioning him and performing a thorough physical examination and a few laboratory and X-ray studies, the fifth doctor diagnosed him with cluster headaches. The doctor prescribed sumatriptan self-injections and recommended that Michael stop drinking alcohol. Within three months, Michael's headaches were less frequent and his writing productivity dramatically increased. A best-selling novel is predicted in his near future.

IN SUMMARY

- Migraine, cluster, and other forms of headache can be triggered by a number of factors, including environmental factors (noise), foods (chocolate), drugs (birth control pills), and social habits (drinking alcohol).
- Environmental factors that can trigger headache include bright lights, high altitudes, and changes in the weather.
- Foods and food additives associated with headache flare-ups include chocolate, ice cream, caffeine, MSG, amines, nitrites and nitrates, sulfites, nuts, GABA, salt, and artificial sweeteners. Vitamin and mineral deficiencies have been anecdotally linked to headache.
- Social habits, including smoking and alcohol, can trigger headaches in some persons with migraine.
- Drugs such as painkillers, hormones, diet pills, and decongestants have been implicated as migraine triggers.

CHAPTER FOUR

Tension-Type Headaches

Tension-type headaches (formerly called *muscle contraction* or *tension headaches*) account for 90 percent of all forms of chronic, primary head pain reported in the United States.[1] In one survey, 63 percent of men and 86 percent of women reported suffering at least one tension-type headache episode within the past year.[2] During their lifetimes, 63 percent of men and 88 percent of women will experience this type of headache. Additionally, 80 percent of nontension-type headache sufferers, especially those with migraine and cluster headaches, experience tension-type headaches from time to time.

People who suffer from migraine headaches, the second most common type of all headaches, frequently seek health care for their headaches. In contrast, most tension-type headaches are amenable to treatment with over-the-counter medicines, and individuals who suffer from these headaches rarely seek physician care for them. In their book *Headache Relief,* headache specialists Drs. Alan Rapoport and Fred Sheftell report that tension-type headaches are usually not disabling, allowing sufferers to continue their normal activities.[3]

WHAT CAUSES TENSION-TYPE HEADACHES?

If you've ever observed a passenger on a bus holding his head in apparent pain, chances are he was experiencing a tension-type headache. Why do so many people get tension-type headaches? Why is it that only 1 percent of the population gets cluster headaches and a whopping 90 percent gets occasional tension-type headaches? What causes these headaches?

Unlike migraine headaches, there is no genetic or familial basis for tension-type headaches. Many tension-type headache sufferers, however, have observed someone with chronic headaches, usually at a young age. At least 40 percent of tension headache sufferers report that their recurrent headache pattern began before age twenty.[4] Some researchers believe that, in some cases, chronic tension-type headache suffering may be a learned behavior. The location of the pain (in the scalp and neck) leads scientists to believe that tension-type head pain results from abnormal stimulation of the arteries and veins, the muscles, and the nerves in the scalp and neck that sense pain.

What stimulates these pain receptors, and why? Tension-type headaches used to be called muscle contraction headaches because it was thought that muscle tension brought on by stress and other factors was the basis for them. However, recent research has failed to completely support this theory. That tight scalp and neck muscles result in a headache is no longer the prevailing theory. True, many tension-type headache sufferers report that their head pain often occurs during or following periods of heightened emotions, such as anger, irritability, anxiety, and stress. Anxiety about a variety of life issues, such as relationships, work, school, finances, and the future, is also associated with tension-type headaches. Patients with chronic depression sometimes experience tension-type headaches shortly after awakening. Whether these emotions trigger headaches or simply contribute to them is not entirely clear.

Headache researchers are now beginning to believe that tension-type head pain may result from the same biochemical changes in the brain and impaired blood flow in the scalp and neck that lead to migraine headaches. Scientists now believe that these headaches have to do with suppression of serotonin, the substance in the brain that controls sleep, emotions, and pain. Therefore, the muscle tightness in the sufferer's neck and scalp may be a result of chemical changes that brought on the headache, not the cause of the headache.

There are some cases of tension-type headaches that are related to poor posture. Holding one position for a long period of time can put undue strain on the muscles in the neck and shoulders. Tight muscles and associated tissues impede the free flow of blood and oxygen, resulting in the secretion of chemicals such as prostaglandin and serotonin. These chemicals irritate the surrounding nerves, which send a pain signal to the brain, and a headache ensues. If you've ever worked at your computer for many hours at a time, you know how you tend to hunch your shoulders and how stiff your neck can get.

> Lord, how my head aches! What a head have I! It beats as it would fall in twenty pieces.
>
> **William Shakespeare**

Some people with arthritis of the neck and inflammation of the shoulder joints develop stiff neck and shoulder muscles as they attempt to protect the diseased joints. A ruptured disc between the vertebrae in the neck can press on a nerve (this is what a pinched nerve is) that can also lead to recurrent headaches.

WHO GETS TENSION-TYPE HEADACHES?

Who suffers from tension-type headaches? Stressed-out people? Flat-out relaxed folks? Perfectionists, or slobs? The answer is people from all walks of life get these headaches. Rich and poor people, African Americans and Asian Americans, bankers and farmers—absolutely no one is spared. As we mentioned earlier, epidemiological surveys show a gender difference in tension-type headache sufferers; these headaches have a slightly higher incidence among women. Among chronic tension-type headache sufferers, 6.1 percent of males and 14 percent of females will have four or more headaches each month.

As we mentioned in chapter 1, headache researchers believe that most people who suffer chronic tension-type headaches were exposed to a parent, sibling, or relative who had recurrent headaches in response to daily stress.[5] Therefore, these headaches have deep roots in a learned behavior. Although tension-type headaches may begin in adulthood, between 10 and 20 percent of people with this type of headache started getting them as children or teenagers.[6]

HOW DO YOU KNOW IF YOU HAVE TENSION-TYPE HEADACHES?

As we wrote earlier, the majority of tension-type headache sufferers have never seen a health care provider for their head pain. Instead, they successfully treat themselves with over-the-counter drugs such as ibuprofen, acetaminophen, and ketoprofen. As a chronic tension-type headache sufferer, could you have misdiagnosed yourself? Could your headaches be caused by another problem? What are the symptoms of tension-type headaches? How do these headaches differ from, for instance, caffeine withdrawal headaches? If you recognize your symptoms after reading this section, we suggest you ask a qualified health care professional to confirm your impression.

The pain of tension-type headaches is identified by its location in the head and neck, and its severity, mode of onset, and duration. The Headache Classification Committee of the International Headache Society (HIS) defines tension-type as "an ache or sensation of tightness, pressure, or constriction, widely varied in intensity, frequency, and duration, sometimes long-lasting and commonly suboccipital (in the area between the neck and the back of the head)."[7] Most sufferers experience pain in the temples, forehead, back of the head, neck, and shoulders. Some report feeling knots in the neck and shoulder muscles. Typically, the pain originates in the back of the head and neck and radiates to the forehead. Unlike migraine headache pain, the pain of tension-type headache is commonly located on both sides of the head. Sufferers often report the sensation of their heads being "held in a vise," or having a "headband around it." A small number of tension-type headache sufferers experience pain behind their eyes.

The severity of the pain of tension-type headaches varies from person to person and from episode to episode in each person. Most headache episodes start out with mild pain that gradually intensifies over time. Even at the height of the pain, most sufferers rate their pain as mild (between 1 and 3 on a rating scale from 1 to 10), which explains why most people with this form of headache can continue their normal activities. Terms used to describe the severity of tension-type headaches include nagging, boring, and dull. Some patients report pressure rather than pain. (See Appendix A.)

Tension-type headache sufferers typically report that the pain sometimes starts upon waking or early in the day (although they are never wakened by their headaches). In contrast to some forms of migraine headaches, tension-type headaches are never preceded by an aura (characterized by visual disturbances, such as blind spots or flashing lights), weakness or numbness on one side of the body, or slurred speech. (See chapter 5.) If you experience any of these symptoms before your headaches, check with your health care provider to see if you might have migraines or both migraines and tension-type headaches. Also unlike migraine sufferers, tension-type headache sufferers do not report nausea, vomiting, and abdominal pain. Some people with tension-type headaches report sensitivity to light and sound, but these are not common symptoms of this form of headache. Other associated symptoms include fatigue, loss of appetite, and sleepiness.

The IHS identifies two kinds of tension-type headaches: episodic and chronic. Episodic or acute tension-type headaches are brief, lasting a few minutes to a few hours. The pain is present fewer than fifteen days each month. On the other hand, chronic tension-type headaches, which affect an estimated 2 to 3 percent of Americans, occur at least fifteen days a month for at least six months. In fact, chronic tension-type headaches are often referred to as chronic daily headaches.

Signs and symptoms of tension-type headaches include:

- Mild to moderate pain in back of the head, around the eyes, or in the temple
- Feeling of a tight band around the head
- Sensitivity to light and sound
- Fatigue
- Loss of appetite
- Sleepiness

Conditions that can mimic tension-type headaches include:

- Migraine headache
- Trigeminal neuralgia
- Temporal arteritis
- Pheochromocytoma

DIAGNOSING TENSION-TYPE HEADACHES

Unfortunately, there are no laboratory or X-ray tests for tension-type headaches. Physicians and other providers who evaluate headache patients must rely on a thorough history of the symptoms the sufferer experiences. Therefore, the accuracy of your answers during an exam counts. You can help your provider arrive at the correct diagnosis by keeping a diary of your headache and associated symptoms for a few weeks. (See Appendix A.) The diary allows you to record your symptoms and dispenses with the need to memorize them. It also provides a visual account of the pattern of your symptoms: what time they start, where in your head the pain is located, and what measures were successful in treating the headaches.

During the initial headache interview, your provider may ask you about the mode of onset (gradual or sudden); the location, severity, and duration of your headaches; and exacerbating and relieving factors. Are your headaches relieved by rest and neck massage, as is typically the case? Additionally, your provider may want to know if there are other symptoms associated with your head pain. Symptoms such as preheadache aura, nausea, and vomiting may indicate migraines or other forms of headaches rather than tension-type headaches. If you drink lots of caffeinated beverages or take lots of caffeine-containing drugs, you may be experiencing caffeine-rebound headaches rather than tension-type headaches.

During your visit, your provider will also want to know about your family history: whether or not your parents, siblings, and grandparents get headaches and, if so, what type. You'll also be asked about your social history. Are you married or divorced? Do you have children? Has there been a recent change in your financial status? Has there been a recent change in your relationships? How's your job, and how's your relationship with your coworkers and your supervisor? These questions are important in determining whether some aspects of your social support structures are contributing to your symptoms and whether you can rely on these support systems to help you manage your headaches.

Your diary will also help your clinician with the next aspect of your evaluation: the physical examination. Few physical clues (besides a voluntary wrinkling of the forehead, the universal "I have a headache" sign) help in the diagnosis of tension-type headaches. After reviewing your vital signs (your blood pressure, temperature, pulse, and weight), your provider will examine you to rule out signs of secondary headaches, such as meningitis or a brain tumor.

If your provider uncovers evidence that other conditions need to be ruled out, she may order the appropriate laboratory or X-ray studies. (See chapter 12.) For example, if your doctor feels that a chronic sinus condition might be the cause of your recurrent headaches, she might order X rays of your sinuses. Similarly, if a brain tumor or blood vessel abnormality is suspected, a brain imaging study such as a CT or MRI scan will be ordered. Also, psychological testing, such as the Zung Anxiety Scale or Beck Depression Inventory, may be helpful if you suffer from anxiety or depression.

Laboratory and X-ray evaluations of tension-type headache include:

- Complete blood count
- Thyroid function tests
- Chemistry panel tests

If diagnosis is still not certain, additional studies may include:

- MRI scan
- CAT or CT scan
- EEG
- ENG

HOW TO TREAT AND PREVENT TENSION-TYPE HEADACHES

Successful management of tension-type headaches, as in other forms of chronic headaches, requires a committed collaboration between the patient and the health care team. Once the diagnosis is confidently made, a treatment plan should be drawn up that addresses pain control and other contributing issues, such as excessive stress and poor posture. A typical treatment plan involves the primary care provider, the patient, and when appropriate, ancillary health professionals such as an optometrist (to evaluate the eyes) and a chiropractor (to evaluate the alignment of the spine). Other health professionals who may be involved in the management of recurrent headaches include psychologists, psychiatrists, dietitians, physical therapists, occupational therapists, and acupuncturists. (See chapter 13.)

All tension-type headache treatments can be placed into one of two management categories: nonpharmacologic (drug-free) and pharmacologic (drug) measures. Drug-free treatments, such as stress management, regular exercise, adequate sleep, and massage therapy, represent the cornerstone of management of all types of chronic headaches. (See chapter 15.) Even when drugs are necessary, nonpharmacologic measures should be fully and constantly exploited. Episodic or acute tension-type headaches usually respond well to over-the-counter painkillers. Some individuals require stronger painkillers and muscle relaxants that have to be prescribed by a health professional.

On the other hand, chronic tension-type headaches often require medications to kill the pain as well as a prophylactic drug to reduce the frequency and severity of the head pain. Clinicians today have a wide array of pharmacologic agents to employ in the treatment of tension-type headaches. (See chapter 16.) The choice of drug therapy is very individualized; drugs that may work well for one person may be ineffective for someone else. Most chronic tension-type headaches can be effectively managed with over-the-counter drugs such as ibuprofen (Advil), ketoprofen (Orudis), and acetaminophen (Tylenol). Prescription medications, such as butalbital, codeine, and isometheptene, require close follow-up by a physician, physician assistant, or nurse practitioner.

Drugs used as abortive therapy for tension-type headaches may include:

- NSAIDs (e.g., ibuprofen, naproxen)
- Muscle relaxants (e.g., flexeril, orphenadrine)
- Isometheptene
- Acetaminophen

Drugs used as prophylactic therapy include:

- NSAIDs (e.g., ibuprofen, naproxen)
- Tricyclic antidepressants (e.g., amitriptyline, nortriptyline)
- Selective serotonin reuptake inhibitors (fluoxetine, paroxetine)

JUAN'S STORY

A third-generation cattleman and farmer in a small western Texas town, Juan had seen a drastic decline in both the farming and cattle industries. He often wondered if his increasingly narrow profit margin justified staying in the business. Juan was torn between his moral obligation to carry on the rich tradition started by his great-grandfather in the late 1800s and the current economic reality that threatened to starve his family. His forefathers would have turned over in their graves if he had abandoned this rich family legacy. But then again, he had to feed his family and educate his children.

Over the past five years, this dilemma had weighed heavily on Juan's mind. Not a day went by that he didn't worry. His worrying led to a buildup of pain and tightness in his forehead and the back of his head and neck. Sometimes the pain felt like a tight band around his head. Worried about a serious medical problem, Juan sought medical help. "It feels like my head is held in a vise," Juan told his doctor. He recalled stressful days when his head would pound all day until he went to bed. The headaches didn't disturb his sleep, but they did affect his daytime functioning.

After a thorough evaluation, Juan's doctor diagnosed him with tension-type headaches and prescribed a pain-relief medication for him. The doctor also prescribed a regular aerobic exercise program and a balanced diet, and recommended that Juan get plenty of rest. Additionally, Juan was referred to a stress management course offered by the local Red Cross. Within three months, despite falling cattle and cotton prices, Juan managed his stress, developed a positive outlook about his life, and became headache free. He developed a creative scheme (aided by his relaxed attitude) whereby he sublet part of his farmland, reduced the size of his cattle holdings, and began working part-time in the booming real estate business. He grew confident about his future as his income soared.

IN SUMMARY

- Tension-type headache is the most prevalent of all types of headaches, accounting for 90 percent of all reported headaches. Approximately 63 percent of all men and 86 percent of all women have experienced at least one tension-type headache episode within the past year.
- In some cases, chronic tension-type headache suffering may be learned behavior; as youngsters, many such headache sufferers observed someone with chronic headaches.
- These headaches affect both adults and children, as well as both men and women, with a slightly higher incidence among women.
- Sufferers typically experience pain in both temples, the forehead, the back of the head, the neck, and the shoulders, with a sensation that their heads are being "held in a vise."
- There are no laboratory tests or X rays for tension-type headache, but your diary and description of your headaches will help your health practitioner diagnose it.
- Chronic tension-type headaches are managed with nondrug (stress management and regular exercise) as well as drug (over-the-counter and prescription drugs) therapies, with nondrug therapy as the cornerstone of management.

Migraine Headaches

Most people know someone, be it a friend, relative, neighbor, or coworker, who suffers from migraine headache. This is not surprising, because about twenty-five million Americans experience these harrowing headaches on a recurrent basis. Migraine headaches have been infamous since the early years of human existence. As we said in the preface, the name *migraine* is derived from the term *hemikrania* (meaning "half a head") used by Greek physician Galen in the second century A.D. to describe the devastating, one-sided head pain experienced by many migraine sufferers he treated.

When it comes to migraine's effects on lifestyle, today's migraineurs don't fare any better than did their second-century counterparts. Compared to other types of headaches, migraine headache accounts for the greatest number of health care visits. People who suffer from tension-type headaches, which are the most common type of headache, most often treat themselves with over-the-counter drugs such as aspirin and ibuprofen and seldom require medical attention. In contrast, the severity, frequency, and persistence of migraine headaches force most migraineurs to seek a physician's help to obtain prescription drugs and nondrug strategies to allay their suffering and to rule out secondary causes of their condition.

WHAT CAUSES MIGRAINE HEADACHES?

As a migraine sufferer, you know intimately what your headache feels like, but do you know what causes it? Why do so many people suffer from migraines? Do abnormal levels of brain chemicals, a personality flaw, or genetic defects have anything to do with migraines? What roles do stress, certain types of foods, lack of sleep, caffeine, alcohol, and nicotine play in the development of migraines? Is your headache life-threatening or completely benign?

Many sufferers of nonmigraine headaches label any head pain "migraines," using the word to indicate severe head and neck pain. Often, the statement "I had a bad migraine last night" in fact refers to a severe tension-type or other form of head pain. Migraine, however, is not just a name for any severe pain in the head; it's a specific type of headache with specific diagnostic criteria established to guide clinical doctors and researchers in the diagnosis and management of this type of head pain.

Migraine headaches are vascular headaches, because they involve changes in the diameter or size and chemistry of the blood vessels that supply blood to the brain. Headache researchers now believe that the blood vessel changes are a secondary phenomenon and do not cause the migraine itself. The throbbing head pain, however, is due in large part to the distended blood vessels surrounding the brain that press on adjacent nerves.[1] Exactly how and why these blood vessels dilate is a matter of conjecture, but a number of recent findings may shed light on this complicated process. It seems that some kind of chemical signal activates the pain sensors in the trigeminal nerve that runs from a spot near the center of the skull up and over the eyes and toward the forehead. The activated nerve fibers release protein fragments called *neuropeptides,* which cause the blood vessels to expand. The widened blood vessels further irritate the trigeminal nerve, resulting in head pain.

One chemical that has been commonly implicated in the migraine headache chain of events is serotonin, a neurotransmitter that helps relay messages among cells in the brain. Serontonin is normally present in the brain, blood vessels, and gastrointestinal system. During the 1960s, researchers discovered increased levels of the chemical 5-hydroxyindole acetic acid, a by-product of serotonin, in the urine of migraineurs at the onset of a migraine attack.[2] The changes in brain serotonin levels may account for the nausea, vomiting, and mood changes that characterize a migraine attack.

Nearly 15 percent of migraineurs experience an aura prior to developing their head pain. Typically, an aura involves visual disturbances, such as blind spots or flashing lights; weakness or numbness on one side of the body; or slurred speech. In most cases, the aura heralds an impending migraine attack, giving the sufferer time to take a painkiller. Scientists now believe that the aura represents a brief constriction (narrowing) of the blood vessels as a result of a signal from the brain stem, spreading across the brain. This results in a reduction of blood flow to certain parts of the brain causing the temporary sensory, motor, and visual disturbances that characterize an aura.

THE HEMICRANIA, OR PAIN OF ONE HALF OF THE HEAD, WAS VERY EARLY DISTINGUISHED BY MEDICAL WRITERS FROM THE OTHER SPECIES OF HEAD-ACHES: BUT WE HAVE NOT YET ADVANCED MUCH IN KNOWING HOW THIS DIFFERS FROM OTHER PAINS IN THE HEAD.

WILLIAM HEBERDEN

Another neurotransmitter, noradrenaline, is believed to play a large role in migraine attacks.[3] Migraineurs who experience auras show changes in noradrenaline activity that slows brain activity. This depressed brain activity results in reduced blood flow to some areas of the brain. These neurochemical and blood flow changes are believed to be the basis for the visual, sensory, motor, language, and cognitive disturbances that precede a migraine headache in some sufferers.

Among women migraine sufferers, hormonal variations, particularly of estrogen, have been found to play a role in migraine attacks. (See chapter 8.) After menopause, when estrogen levels markedly drop, migraine headaches disappear in a large percentage of women with hormone-associated migraines.

Whether there is a genetic basis for migraine headaches is unclear. Observational studies reveal that between 70 and 80 percent of migraineurs had at least one parent with the condition.[4] This finding, however, does not necessarily indicate a migraine/genetic linkage; it could also mean a common environmental influence.

COMMON TYPES OF MIGRAINE

Naming migraine headaches has been the subject of great controversy. In past years, various American medical organizations have been unable to reach a consensus on migraine classification. Regional terms such as "complicated migraine" and "migraine equivalent" had different meanings to different observers. Health committees in other countries had similar problems. Obviously, this level of confusion served only to stymie effective headache research and clinical practice.

In stepped the International Headache Society (IHS), whose membership agreed on a standardized glossary of headache terminology and diagnostic criteria in 1988. The IHS identified fourteen different types of migraine headaches.[5] Each type of migraine was assigned specific diagnostic criteria. Although these criteria were geared more for headache researchers, they have helped standardize clinical practice.

TYPES OF MIGRAINE HEADACHES

MIGRAINE WITH AURA

This type of migraine, previously referred to as *classic migraine*, accounts for about 15 percent of all migraine headaches. The one in six migraine sufferers who experience auras report a bizarre series of visual, motor, and speech disturbances prior to developing their head pain. Visual auras may involve flashes of light, spots of different shapes and colors, or only half of objects being visible. Motor auras sometimes produce weakness or numbness on one side of the body. People with speech auras can have slurred speech.

The aura phase of a migraine typically lasts from ten to thirty minutes, after which the headache phase begins. Approximately 40 percent of patients who have migraine with aura will often have an aura without an accompanying headache, a condition sometimes referred to as *migraine equivalents.* We'll discuss the features of the headache phase of migraine on pages 68 to 71.

MIGRAINE WITHOUT AURA

An estimated 80 percent of migraine sufferers have migraines without aura (previously called common migraine). This type of migraine usually lasts from four to seventy-two hours, is most often one-sided, and is commonly accompanied by nausea and vomiting. Sufferers characterize the pain as throbbing or pounding and moderate to severe in intensity.

UNCOMMON MIGRAINE VARIANTS

In this section, we'll discuss four uncommon types of migraine headaches, often referred to as *migraine variants, atypical migraine,* or *complicated migraine.* Most of these headaches are variants of migraine with aura.[6] Less than 2 percent of migraine sufferers experience these headaches. Other migraine variants include migraine aura without headache and retinal migraine.

HEMIPLEGIC MIGRAINE

This migraine variant is more common in children than adults. (See chapter 9.) It produces slurred speech and a temporary paralysis on one side of the body, or *hemiplegia,* reminiscent of a stroke. The hemiplegia may occur on the same side as the headache. Other symptoms of hemiplegic migraine include *vertigo,* or the sensation of one's surroundings spinning, and blurred vision.

These symptoms are followed by a headache about ten to ninety minutes later. Understandably, sufferers and family members become very anxious during an attack. In very rare cases, the paralysis is permanent.

Ophthalmoplegic Migraine

This form of migraine headache is caused by dysfunction of the occulomotor and abducens nerves, the nerves that control vision. Like hemiplegic migraine, it occurs most commonly in children. (See chapter 9.) During an attack, the pain is centered around the eye and is associated with a droopy eyelid, enlarged pupil, and double vision, which can last a few days to a few weeks.

Basilar Artery Migraine

This type of migraine headache is induced by dilation of the basilar artery, the blood vessel that supplies blood to the brain stem. Basilar artery migraine begins with loss of balance, difficulty speaking, double vision, transient blindness, poor muscle coordination, confusion, and in rare cases loss of consciousness. These symptoms, which typically last up to forty-five minutes, are followed by a severe headache at the base of the skull.

This form of migraine headache occurs mainly among children, adolescents, and young adult women, and often appears during the week leading up to the menstrual bleed. (See chapter 9.) Basilar artery migraineurs are slightly predisposed to migraine-related stroke. It is unclear how and why this happens and who is disposed to this migraine complication, although smoking and the birth control pill might be contributing factors.

ABDOMINAL MIGRAINE

This rare form of migraine also mostly affects children. (See chapter 9.) In abdominal migraine, all the usual migraine symptoms occur except the head pain. Instead, the sufferer experiences abdominal pain.

STATUS MIGRAINOUS

This rare complication of migraine can last seventy-two hours or longer—sometimes weeks. It can be triggered by certain pain medications. Individuals are often hospitalized to help combat the severe accompanying nausea and vomiting, are rehydrated via intravenous fluids, and are given drugs to halt the attack.

WHO GETS MIGRAINE HEADACHES?

Who is a typical migraineur? Why is it that you, like your mother, get migraines, and your sister or your best friend doesn't? Migraine headaches tend to run in families, but researchers aren't sure if there is a genetic or common-environment connection. At any rate, between 70 and 80 percent of migraineurs have family members who also suffer from the condition.

A noteworthy feature of migraine headache is that it is more prevalent among women than men, by a ratio of three to one. An estimated 18 percent of American women, 6 percent of men, and about 12 percent of the population as a whole, get migraines. The peak age for migraines to occur is thirty to forty years, but many children and some elderly people suffer migraines as well. One survey showed that about 75 percent of all migraineurs developed their first headache by age thirty, and 90 percent by age forty.[7] In Canada, an estimated 23 percent of women and 9 percent of men suffer from migraines.

The majority of women with migraines are plagued during the hormonally active years between adolescence and menopause. Like Emily, featured in the preface, many female migraineurs develop their headaches at the onset of their first period or sometime during their early teen years. A small number of women develop their first migraines around the time of menopause. If it weren't for the role of female hormones in the development of migraines, the prevalence of migraines would be equal in men and women.

ANATOMY OF A MIGRAINE ATTACK

What common symptoms do migraineurs experience and how long do they last? What part of the head hurts? Are there usually warning signs that signal the onset of a migraine episode? Are there additional symptoms associated with a migraine attack? The symptoms of a migraine attack vary from person to person (see table 5.1), but we'll describe the most common sequence of events.

THE TRIGGERS

Some migraine headaches are set off by dozens of triggers, or factors that may influence the secretion of biochemical substances that lead to the

TABLE 5.1: SYMPTOMS OF A MIGRAINE ATTACK

Prodrome	Fatigue, irritability, and food cravings.
Aura	Vision disturbance (seeing flashing lights or blind spots), numbness or weakness on one side of the body, slurred speech, and sensitivity to light and sound.
Headache	Throbbing headache (in 60 percent of cases, headache on one side of the head); lasts four to seventy-two hours.
Associated symptoms	Nausea and vomiting, diarrhea, lightheadedness, dizziness, and ringing in the ears (tinnitus).
Postdrome	Fatigue, euphoria, surge in energy, increased appetite, and confusion.

headache. About 10 percent of migraineurs have identifiable headache triggers, which may include certain foods, changes in the weather, changes in sleep patterns, exposure to bright lights, and psychological factors. One very common migraine trigger is changes in the sleep/wake cycle, either sleep deprivation or getting too much sleep. Medical scientists aren't sure why this is so but speculate that the hormonal changes that occur during the different stages of sleep may be responsible.

Stress, frustration, anger, depression, and other emotional factors are also common migraine triggers. It isn't unusual to see attacks triggered by certain fragrances, such as perfumes. Some triggers work in tandem with other triggers. For example, some women who suffer stress-induced migraines are only affected by stress during the premenstrual phase of their menstrual cycle. Caffeine withdrawal is a very common migraine precipitant; this tends to be more noticeable on weekends, when people are less dependent on coffee to get through the day. Some migraineurs report that caffeine worsens their migraines (oddly, several antimigraine drugs contain caffeine).

THE PRODROME

Some migraine sufferers experience *prodromal,* or preheadache, symptoms that may precede the headache by hours or days. Prodromal symptoms are somewhat vague and may include fatigue, irritability, and food cravings, often for carbohydrates and chocolate.

THE AURA

As we said earlier, 15 percent of migraine sufferers experience auras in the form of visual, sensory, cognitive, motor, or speech disturbances twenty minutes to an hour prior to the development of head pain. Visual auras may involve flashing lights, zigzag lines, bright spots of different shapes and colors, or loss of vision in one or more quadrants of the visual field. Motor

There is a dimness of sight in which dark spots float before the eyes, or only half, or some part of all objects appear, which continues for twenty or thirty minutes, and then is succeeded by a head-ach lasting for several hours, and joined sometimes with sickness.

William Heberden

auras sometimes produce weakness or numbness on one side of the body. People with speech auras can have slurred speech. The aura phase of a migraine typically lasts ten to thirty minutes, after which the headache phase begins.

THE HEAD PAIN

Migraine headaches are typically severe, throbbing, sometimes disabling head pain, although some sufferers experience milder degrees of pain. Approximately 60 percent of people with migraines report a pain on one side of the head, often behind or around one eye. The frequency of attacks varies widely, from two or three attacks a week to two or three attacks a year. The pain can last anywhere from four to seventy-two hours, feels sharp "like a knife" or "pressurelike," and is "made worse with each heartbeat." The headache can also worsen with exposure to noise, light, or any body movement; this explains why it is virtually impossible for some sufferers to go to work during an attack. Usually, all the sufferer wants to do is go to a quiet, dark room, and remain still, hoping to sleep off the head pain.

ASSOCIATED SYMPTOMS

Besides the head pain, most migraineurs report associated symptoms such as nausea and vomiting, dizziness, increased urination, and even diarrhea. Others report pain in the hands and feet, probably caused by changes in blood circulation to the extremities. Other associated symptoms include tingling or numbness in the lips, tongue, or face, or in the fingers on the same side as the headache. Family and friends often report that migraine attacks change the sufferer's personality.

THE POSTDROME

After the headache pain and associated symptoms clear up, it is not uncommon for sufferers to feel fatigued and prefer to be left alone. (Unfortunately, friends and family members often make the situation worse by insisting on helping the migraineur during an attack.) Some migraineurs experience a surge of energy, euphoria, and increased appetite up to twenty-four hours after an attack. Other postheadache symptoms include confusion, loss of memory, and difficulty performing common physical tasks.

THE HEALTH RISKS ASSOCIATED WITH MIGRAINE HEADACHES

Are migraine headaches associated with anything more than disabling head pain? How many migraineurs develop other, migraine-induced health problems? Are you at risk for these problems, and if so, how much? In recent years, migraine researchers discovered that migraine headaches are not completely benign head pain. A small number of sufferers may be at risk for other medical conditions. Calgary headache specialist Dr. Werner J. Becker, the president of the Canadian Headache Society, reassures sufferers that migraineurs who are otherwise healthy have nothing to worry about.

As we said earlier, during the early stages of a migraine attack, the blood vessels to the brain transiently narrow, reducing blood flow to the brain. A drop-off of blood to the brain accounts for the visual disturbances, weakness or numbness on one side of the body, and slurred speech reported by migraineurs who experience auras and the uncommon migraine variants. Some experts view these cognitive and physical deficits as strokelike events. In fact, both male and female migraine sufferers on average have a slightly higher risk than do their nonmigraineur peers of developing a stroke.

The likelihood of developing a stroke is further enhanced if you smoke or if you take birth control pills, especially if your headaches have worsened since you started taking the pill. Theoretically, a similar but lower risk exists for women who take hormone replacement therapy (HRT) to combat the effects of a postmenopausal drop in blood-estrogen levels. If you are a woman with migraines (especially an atypical variant), smoke, and take birth controls pills or HRT, you may be at increased risk of developing a stroke. Ask your doctor to help calculate your risk level and prescribe a course of action.

Like the blood vessels to the brain, if the blood vessels to the heart muscle are transiently narrow, blood flow to the heart can be compromised. A drop-off of blood to the heart can induce angina in migraineurs with coronary artery disease, which itself causes reduced blood flow to the heart muscle.

DIAGNOSING MIGRAINE

There is no blood test for migraine. It is diagnosed through clinical features, along with laboratory and radiological testing to rule out other medical conditions that can mimic migraines. There is symptom overlap between migraines and quite a few other medical conditions. Health care providers get many hours of training and many years of clinical experience in the evaluation of migraine patients, learning to recognize common features migraine sufferers report, such as auras, headache patterns, and light sensitivity. But even the most astute clinician is helpless without the headache patient's help. In fact, the smartest headache diagnostician is only as good as the level of cooperation he receives from his headache patient allows him to be.

Some conditions that can mimic migraine headaches include:

- Cluster headache
- Tension-type headache

- Trigeminal neuralgia
- Tumor
- Epilepsy

One of the best things you can do to help your doctor diagnose your migraine headache is to keep a diary of your headaches and associated symptoms for a few weeks. (See Appendix A.)[8] Your diary need not be elaborate or scientific. It only needs to describe what you felt, where in your head you felt it, what time of day you felt it, how long it lasted, and what you did to make your symptoms go away. For women, other information such as the dates of your last menstrual period may also be helpful.

During your visit, your provider will also want to know about your family history: whether your parents, siblings, and grandparents get headaches and if so, what type. You'll also be asked about your social history: are you married or divorced? Do you have children? Has there been a recent change in your financial status? Has there been a recent change in your relationships? How's your job, and how's your relationship with your coworkers and your supervisor?

Your diary will go a long way in helping your clinician plan her next move. It will give her valuable clues during the physical examination, which involves looking into your eyes, ears, nose, and throat and evaluating the nerves that feed your eyes, head, and neck. The physical examination allows your health professional to look for clues (such as red eyes) that may point to the problem at hand. During the neurological examination, your provider may test your memory; evaluate your peripheral vision; check the sensory stimuli and muscle strength in various parts of your head, neck, and extremities; and check your reflexes, coordination, and ability to sense vibrations at your wrists and ankles.

After the physical examination, your doctor might order selected laboratory tests and X-ray studies, depending on what she gleans from the examination. (See table 5.2 and chapter 12.) For example, if your doctor feels that a thyroid condition might be the cause of your recurrent headaches, she might order thyroid function tests to rule this possibility in or out.

TABLE 5.2 TOOLS FOR DIAGNOSING MIGRAINE HEADACHE

- Headache diary
- Detailed questioning by the health care provider
- Complete physical examination by the health care provider
- Complete blood count
- Chemistry panel
- Thyroid function tests
- MRI scan
- CAT or CT scan
- EEG
- ENG

Similarly, if a brain tumor or blood vessel abnormality is suspected, a brain-imaging study such as an MRI or CT scan will be ordered.

HOW TO TREAT AND PREVENT MIGRAINES

Migraine headaches are managed with nondrug strategies and drug therapy. (See table 5.3 and chapter 15.) For migraineurs with identifiable triggers, such as foods, noise, or hormonal changes, avoidance is an obvious solution, if at all possible. For example, if tyramine is the offending agent, you should avoid red wine, cheddar cheese, and other tyramine-containing foods. When avoiding migraine triggers is not enough, medications should be considered.

The last ten years have seen a tremendous leap in the management and prevention of migraine headaches. Specifically, the discovery of some of the underlying mechanisms involved in the development of migraine head pain has led to the discovery of drugs that work to reverse the basic aberrations. (See chapter 16.) One such drug introduced in 1993, sumatriptan (Imitrex), revolutionized the way migraines are treated. Sumatriptan, clas-

TABLE 5.3 MANAGEMENT OF MIGRAINE HEADACHE

Nondrug Strategies
Identify and eliminate dietary, environmental, and other headache triggers
Regular aerobic exercise
Acupuncture
Stress management
Biofeedback
Yoga
Transcendental meditation
Psychological counseling

Abortive Drug Therapy
NSAIDs (aspirin, ibuprofen, and naproxen)
Acetaminophen (Tylenol)
Ergotamines (Cafergot, DHE-45)
Sumatriptan (Imitrex)
Isometheptene (Midrin)
Narcotics (codeine)
Barbiturates (Fioricet, Esgic-Plus)

Prophylactic Drug Therapy
Tricyclic antidepressants (amitriptyline, doxepin, and desipramine)
Beta-blockers (propranolol and timolol)
Antiserotonergics (methysergide)
Anticonvulsants (valproic acid)
Selective serotonin reuptake inhibitors (fluoxetine and paroxetine)
Other agents (clonidine and cyproheptadine)

sified as a triptan, binds directly to receptors on the trigeminal nerve, shutting down the inflammation and transmission of pain. Post-marketing surveys show that between 70 and 80 percent of patients treated with sumatriptan report significant improvement in their symptoms.

Other drugs of the triptan class recently added to the migraine armamentarium include zolmitriptan (Zomig), naratriptan (Amerge), and rizatriptan (Maxalt). More pharmaceutical agents are predicted to come on the market in the near future. In the meantime, see your health care provider for a thorough evaluation.

MADELINE'S STORY

As the senior purchasing agent for a major garment manufacturer in New York City, Madeline was responsible for procuring all materials needed to manufacture her company's line of clothing. She oversaw a forty-million-dollar budget and a cadre of 120 workers that includes purchasers, accountants, stylists, and attorneys. To be sure, tremendous demands were placed on her time. Deadlines had to be met. Problems had to be solved immediately.

Like her mother, Madeline developed chronic headaches at age twelve. Her head pain predictably followed the appearance of a "blind spot" in her peripheral vision. Her headaches were characterized by a throbbing pain in either her left or right temple, lasted from four to seventy-two hours, and were always accompanied by nausea. When the headaches became severe, Madeline would prefer to lie still in a darkened room, but this was impossible while she was at the office. She therefore settled for partially effective painkillers and struggled to finish her work.

On the insistence of a friend, Madeline sought medical care. On her third office visit, Madeline's physician assistant confirmed that she was suffering from migraine headaches with an aura and her headaches were without a doubt triggered by workplace stress. The provider suggested that she might do well with a number of pain medications, but if she wanted to have a long and successful career, she would have to practice daily stress management techniques. The clinician referred her to a local American Heart Association sponsored stress management class, where she learned how to manage her time, delegate tasks to her subordinates, and develop the right expectations, as well as how to say "no" and develop a healthy way to look at the world around her.

Within six weeks of practicing what she learned from the class, Madeline was almost headache free and required only occasional pain medications for her headache. In the ensuing twelve months, her productivity, and that of her staff, skyrocketed.

IN SUMMARY

- Migraines affect an estimated twenty-three million Americans, but it is not a modern disease; references to migraines date back to the second century A.D.
- Migraine headaches represent a distinct syndrome of which the exact cause is not known. The pain appears to be related to dilated blood vessels pressing on adjacent nerve fibers.
- About 15 percent of migraineurs get an aura characterized by visual, sensory, or motor disturbances caused by a brief constriction of the blood vessels.
- Migraineurs who have atypical migraine syndrome, who smoke, or who take hormones may be at slightly higher risk for developing a stroke.
- There is no blood test for migraine headaches, but an accurate description of your symptoms (aided by a headache diary) will help your provider make a diagnosis.
- A new group of drugs called triptans have helped revolutionize the treatment of migraines by directly attaching to receptors on the trigeminal nerve and shutting down inflammation and transmission of pain.

CHAPTER SIX

Cluster Headaches

OTHELLO: I HAVE A PAIN UPON MY FOREHEAD HERE.

DESDEMONA: FAITH, THAT'S WITH WATCHING; 'TWILL AWAY AGAIN.

LET ME BUT BIND IT HARD, WITHIN THIS HOUR IT WILL BE WELL.

WILLIAM SHAKESPEARE

There are nearly two million cluster headache sufferers, and they are easy to spot during a painful episode. Famed headache specialists and clinicians Drs. Fred D. Sheftell and Alan M. Rapoport, codirectors of the New England Center for Headache, feel that cluster headaches are the easiest of all headaches to recognize and diagnose.[1] These headaches present with a distinct and unique set of symptoms that set them apart from other headaches (although some symptoms do overlap between cluster and migraine headaches). In this chapter, we'll describe the most common features of cluster headache syndrome and how doctors recognize and manage it.

The classification committee of the International Headache Society defines cluster headaches as head pain on one side of the head, usually around the orbit of one eye or the temple area, that lasts from 15 to 180 minutes and occurs at intervals ranging from once every other day to eight times a day.[2] Known by many pseudonyms in medical circles, including Horton's headache, atypical facial neuralgia, sphenopalatine neuralgia, and histamine cephalgia, cluster headache is a poorly understood syndrome with well-recognized features.

These headaches are notoriously cyclic, striking only during susceptible (or cluster) periods, during which the sufferer can experience multiple headaches that wax and wane for a period of days, weeks, or even months. Fortunately, cluster headaches are far less common than migraines; clusters affect an estimated 1 percent of the population while migraine and tension-type headaches strike 12 and 90 percent of the population, respectively.

There are two types of cluster headaches, differentiated by their frequency of recurrence and length of remission: the episodic and chronic types. The former is characterized by a cluster period that can last from four to twelve weeks, followed by a headache-free period of six months to a few years. Chronic cluster headaches, which affect about 20 percent of cluster sufferers, allow a cluster-free period of less than one week in twelve months. Chronic cluster headaches persist despite pain medicines and prophylactic drugs, all the while throwing the sufferer's life into a dizzying tailspin.

WHAT CAUSES CLUSTER HEADACHES?

What exactly happens in the brain and surrounding structures that causes a cluster sufferer to hold his head and scream in agony? Like migraines, cluster headaches are vascular headaches. So far, the precise mechanisms behind cluster head pain (the pertinent biochemistry, anatomy, and physiology) remain a total mystery. Based on the symptoms of cluster headaches, however, many theories have been advanced to attempt to explain the enigma.

The symptoms associated with cluster headaches are well recognized. Current cluster headache theories involve the disruption of the circadian rhythm (the body's twenty-four-hour clock that regulates its sleep/wake cycle and its responses to daylight and night) and alterations in a number of biochemical substances such as histamine and serotonin. Recent research into the body's circadian rhythm shows that its interruption, whether by certain medications or amount of daylight, can affect the body's immune system, blood pressure, hormonal levels, and seizure and pain thresholds. That clusters strike at near-specific times of the day and during the spring and fall seasons (as daylight increases and decreases drastically) lends credence to the theory that interruptions in the sufferer's biological clock play a role.

While the tearing and runny nose that most cluster sufferers experience may point to an allergic (hay fever) phenomenon—at one time a popular theory— it is no longer widely acceped. The seasonal patterning did not lend enough support to the theory that cluster head pain is somehow related to allergies. Some cluster sufferers also have a rise in histamine levels during a cluster attack. While these levels also rise during hay fever attacks, cluster headaches and hay fever do not have common origins.

For some time now, researchers have suspected that cluster headaches result from abnormal reaction of blood vessels that supply blood to the head. Apparently, these blood vessels constrict and dilate for unknown reasons. Many chemicals that precipitate cluster attacks, such as alcohol and nicotine, are known to narrow blood vessels. On the other hand, oxygen, which successfully aborts cluster attacks in a large number of cluster sufferers, dilates blood vessels. Thus, mechanisms that change the size of the blood vessels that feed the brain may be the root cause of cluster headaches.

Many cluster sufferers have reported a connection between certain factors (triggers) and the onset of their headaches. These triggers set off cluster headache pain only during the cluster period; the same factors will not set off headaches during the remission period. Common cluster headache triggers include alcohol, nicotine, strong sunlight, and emotional stress. Other cluster triggers include physical exertion, nitrites in foods and medications, and weather changes. See chapter 3 for a complete discussion of headache triggers.

THE CLUSTER HEADACHE SUFFERER

Why do some people get cluster headaches while others don't? Why do more men than women suffer cluster headaches? Why are these headaches so severely painful?

A distinguishing feature about cluster headaches is that, unlike migraine headaches, they affect more men than women. In fact, men are six times more likely to suffer cluster headaches than are women. Headache researchers have observed that the few women who get cluster headaches often have a some-what masculine appearance. However, a variant of cluster headaches known as *chronic paroxysmal hemicrania,* which is even more enigmatic than regular cluster headache syndrome, is more common in women than in men.

The typical cluster sufferer is a Caucasian man with a rugged, mascu-line appearance, leonine features, and hazel or blue eyes. Unlike migraine headaches, cluster headaches don't seem to have a familial connection. Some clinicians have observed that cluster sufferers are often ambitious perfectionists who display hypochondria. Additionally, cluster sufferers sometimes possess poor strategies for coping with anger and stress.

HOW DO YOU KNOW IF YOU HAVE CLUSTER HEADACHES?

What do cluster headaches feel like? When do they occur and how long do they last? Are there lifestyle factors that can precipitate clusters? Some clus-ter headache sufferers will have many of the symptoms listed below, while others will have only a few of them. These headaches are so complicated, only medical providers are qualified to diagnose them.

Signs and symptoms of cluster headache include:

- Severe pain around one eye or temple
- Tearing
- Redness in eyes

Conditions that can mimic cluster headache include:

- Migraine headache
- Tension-type headache

- Trigeminal neuralgia
- Temporal arteritis
- Pheochromocytoma

Three types of cluster headaches are recognized: episodic, subchronic, and chronic types. Episodic clusters, which affect between 80 and 90 percent of cluster sufferers, are characterized by multiple episodes of daily headaches for a period of four to six weeks. This is followed by a period of remission lasting from five months to one year. In subchronic cluster headaches, the remission period lasts less than six months. Chronic cluster headache sufferers get headaches several times a week without a remission period. Fortunately, only a few cluster sufferers experience the chronic form of the headache.

Cluster sufferers often implicate alcohol and nicotine as triggers during the cluster period. When the cluster period ends, the sufferer feels perfectly normal and can resume his usual activities and diet. This headache-free period can last for months to years before the next cluster period.

During an attack, cluster sufferers typically look gaunt, confused, and angry. A noteworthy feature of cluster headaches is their severity. Cluster headaches are regarded as the most painful of all headaches, and sufferers often describe the pain in graphic terms: "It feels like a hot poker pushing out my eye." The pain is commonly described as piercing or stabbing (hence one of its pseudonyms, "ice-pick headache"), causing most sufferers to scream aloud, pace back and forth, and in some cases even bang their heads against a wall in frustration. In direct contrast, migraineurs prefer to remain still, balled up in a darkened room during a migraine attack. The pain of cluster headaches is always located around the eye on one side of the head during an attack, but in 10 to 15 percent of patients, the headache moves to the other side of the head during subsequent clusters.[3] On the other hand, approximately 30 percent of migraine headaches occur on both sides of the head.

Cluster attacks are invariably associated with a runny nose and nasal congestion, as well as constriction of the pupil, drooping of the upper eyelid, and redness and tearing in the eye on the same side as the headache. Cluster attacks usually last from fifteen minutes to two and one-half hours and occur at intervals ranging from once every other day to eight times a day, often at the same time of day. Many persons with cluster headaches report attacks during sleep, specifically between the transition from REM to non-REM sleep. In fact, this is the only type of headache that typically awakens the sufferer.

DIAGNOSING CLUSTER HEADACHES

Knowing what to expect from your doctor's evaluation of your headache will help prepare you mentally, physically, and emotionally for the process. It is helpful to know what questions your provider is likely to ask, so that you can try to find the answers beforehand. For example, knowing that your health care provider is likely to ask when the headaches first started will let you think about that before your office visit, rather than spending valuable time during the visit trying to rack your brain for an approximate start date. Also, knowing that the workup of cluster headaches usually does not involve a spinal tap can help you relax during the interview.

Unfortunately, there is no single diagnostic test that signals the presence of cluster headaches. Unlike diabetes, which is diagnosed by a blood test, there is no biologic marker for cluster headaches. Cluster headache is instead diagnosed based on its clinical features and the exclusion of other conditions such as seizure disorders.

To diagnose your headache, your health care provider will likely employ the standard four components of a medical evaluation: the history, physical examination, selected laboratory tests, and appropriate radiographic imaging. (See chapter 12.) How much your doctor employs each of the four diagnostic approaches depends largely on the pattern of your headache. For instance, if after thorough questioning and examination, your symptoms show an unquestionable pattern of cluster headaches, your doctor may choose to forgo laboratory and radiographic tests and concentrate his efforts on developing an appropriate cluster treatment plan.

Laboratory and X-ray evaluations of cluster headaches may include:

- Complete blood count
- Thyroid function tests
- Chemistry panel tests
- MRI scan
- CAT or CT scan
- EEG
- ENG

THE HEALTH RISKS OF CLUSTER HEADACHES

In chapter 5, we said that migraineurs have a slightly increased risk for developing strokes and angina when compared to their peers without a history of migraine. So far, however, no studies have demonstrated any long-term health risks associated with cluster headaches.

HOW TO TREAT AND PREVENT CLUSTER HEADACHES

The only positive thing about the cyclic nature of cluster headaches is that most sufferers know when they are in a cluster period. After a few attacks, most people can mark the beginning and the end of the time they are liable to get those characteristic piercing headaches. Knowing that the next six weeks will be marred by cluster head pain motivates most sufferers to stick to their prescribed treatment and to stay away from the factors that aggravate or trigger their head pain.

The management of cluster headaches involves three treatment strategies: avoiding known triggers, taking prophylactic drugs (to reduce the frequency and severity of the pain), and taking abortive medications (to treat an acute attack). We'll offer a brief discussion here of the common drugs used to treat these headaches. (For a detailed discussion on these drugs, turn to chapter 16.)

As we discussed earlier, during the cluster period, certain factors such as alcohol and nicotine trigger cluster attacks. During the cluster period, you should completely avoid all tobacco and alcohol products. Not only do these products incite cluster head pain, they prevent cluster painkillers from deadening the headache. Bright lights and excessive glare may also set off or worsen your headaches during the cluster period.

Some cluster sufferers respond to inhaled 100 percent oxygen, and many emergency room physicians prescribe it as first-line therapy during an acute attack. As we'll discuss in chapter 16, doctors prescribe sumatriptan, indomethacin, prednisone, and methysergide to alleviate or abort cluster headache. Chronic cluster headache is also treated with prophylactic drugs, such as prednisone, calcium channel blockers, methysergide maleate, and lithium, to prevent or reduce the number of flare-ups. Common drugs used for controlling cluster headaches can be found in table 6.1.

GARY'S STORY

A tall, athletic man with rugged, leonine features and hazel eyes, Gary could easily have been mistaken for a Hollywood star; with a distinct dimple in his chin and his square, jutting jaw, he bore a striking resemblance to Kirk Douglas. At age thirty-three, this well-dressed, intensely ambitious corporate lawyer was well on

TABLE 6.1 DRUGS USED TO TREAT CLUSTER HEADACHE

Abortive Therapy
Oxygen
Sumatriptan (Imitrex)
NSAIDs (Indomethacin)
Corticosteroids (Prednisone)
Methysergide maleate (Sansert)

Prophylactic Therapy
Prednisone
Calcium channel blockers (verapamil, diltiazem)
Methysergide maleate (Sansert)
Lithium carbonate

his way up the corporate ladder of his Washington, D.C., law firm. Gary came to work early and left late, and had been successful in 99 percent of his cases. He was in high demand once client companies heard of his track record.

Gary was dependable to a fault, except during the four or so days a month when he stayed home nursing a debilitating headache. This accomplished legal eagle with measured confidence became a feeble kitten when his headaches struck. Coworkers wondered aloud how such a tough guy with great athletic prowess could succumb to something as trivial as a headache. How could a simple pain in the head overpower a man who epitomizes self-control and toughness? After all, most of the firm's sixty employees experienced stress headaches from time to time, but none regularly stayed home because of headache pain.

After Gary's seventh absence, during which he failed to show up in court for the firm's biggest client, Gary's boss confronted him, hoping to get an honest answer. "Gary, I'm sure you suspect that we are concerned about your monthly absences," he said. "I know your private life is none of my business, but please level with me: Do you have a gambling problem? A problem with alcohol? Are you having an affair, and trying to conceal it? You are our star, Gary, the fastest-rising star in this firm's ninety-year history! How do you logically explain this?"

Looking guilty, Gary described his monthly headaches, which were so severe he often contemplated suicide: "I consider myself very rational, but when these headaches hit, I can't think logically. I sometimes bang my head in disgust. My performance since joining this firm speaks for itself. Only something of extreme urgency will keep me from coming to a job I adore, trust me. These headaches are devastating. I have to admit that I haven't followed up with my doctor as she recommended, but I will."

Gary and his boss agreed on a timetable for conquering his runaway headaches. First, he agreed to see his primary care doctor for a firm diagnosis and to establish a treatment plan. His boss gave him a leave of absence to seek a complete evaluation of his headache. Then Gary planned to devote the time needed to learn everything he could about chronic headaches.

After a two-week comprehensive workup, Gary returned to his job, armed with a definite treatment plan and newfound confidence in his health. He jumped right back into the role as a brilliant corporate lawyer. Four months later, free of headaches, he was spotted at a lively cocktail party drinking only fruit juice—unusual for a guy who loved red wine. One of the things Gary learned during his evaluation was that alcohol was a common cluster headache trigger. If he wanted to remain headache free, he had to give up drinking alcoholic beverages.

IN SUMMARY

- Cluster headaches are relatively uncommon but are regarded as the most painful of all headaches. The pain of cluster headaches is striking, usually located on one side of the head, around one eye, and in the temple on the same side.
- Scientists are unsure of the root causes of cluster headaches, but theories to explain the causes of clusters include allergies, disruption of the body's circadian rhythm, and changes in the levels of biochemical substances, such as serotonin.
- Effective management involves three approaches: avoiding headache triggers, taking prophylactic drugs, and taking abortive drugs.

CHAPTER SEVEN

Mixed Headaches

In recent years, clinicians have come to recognize that some patients experience a combination of tension-type headaches, migraines, and other vascular headaches. Although not formally classified by the International Headache Society (IHS), physicians and other health care providers refer to these headaches as *mixed headache syndrome, tension-vascular headaches, combined headache,* or *chronic daily headaches.* Headache specialist Dr. Ninan Mathew criticizes the IHS headache classification for ignoring the significant clinical relationship between migraines and tension-type headaches.[1] Dr. Mathew feels that the mixed forms of headaches should be recognized as a distinct headache entity.

Mixed headache patients describe an alternating or simultaneous constellation of headache symptoms with features of both chronic tension-type headaches and migraines. For example, persons with mixed headaches experience the aura, light sensitivity, nausea and vomiting, and one-sided head pain of a migraine along with tightness in the back of the head and stiffness in the shoulders consistent with tension-type headaches. In one study, the majority of chronic headache patients attending a headache clinic required up to four diagnoses when the IHS criteria were employed; in other words, they had mixed headache syndrome.[2]

WHAT CAUSES MIXED HEADACHES?

People with mixed headaches have the biochemical dysfunction present in those with tension-type and migraine headaches. But what causes a strictly migraine or tension-type headache to transform into mixed headache?

WHEN YOUR HEAD DID BUT
ACHE, I KNIT MY HAND-
KERCHER ABOUT YOUR BROWS.

WILLIAM SHAKESPEARE

The most common reason a person develops mixed headaches is overuse of headache medications, as in regular daily intake of simple painkillers; the use of barbiturates or sedatives (see chapter 16) more than four times a week; or the use of narcotics or ergotamine more than twice a week.[3] As we discussed in chapter 3, frequent drug use leads to rebound headache as each dose of painkiller wears off, prompting the sufferer to take more and more medication, perpetuating a vicious cycle. In addition, pain medications can suppress the brain's production of endorphins, natural morphinelike painkilling chemicals. The same phenomenon can occur with prophylactic drugs used to prevent the frequent recurrence of headache and to reduce the severity of each flare-up. (See chapter 16.)

WHO GETS MIXED HEADACHES?

The mixed headache sufferer is typically someone who has suffered years of chronic headache—frequently migraine headaches—before developing a second type of headache. Most people who develop mixed headaches are in their thirties and forties. The mixed headache sufferer usually has a history of migraine and tension-type headaches. Eventually, she develops both types of headaches simultaneously.

WHAT DO MIXED HEADACHES FEEL LIKE?

A typical mixed headache attack begins with what seems like one headache—say, a tension-type headache—and then develops into a full-blown migraine flare-up. Alternatively, a migraine flare-up may subside, only to be replaced by protracted tension-type head pain. People with mixed headache often report daily, chronic tension-type headaches, as well as a recurrent hard, or "sick," migrainelike headache. Some sufferers experience all the symptoms they usually get with their vascular headache plus those present with tension-type headache; others experience only some of the symptoms of their usual and new headache syndromes. In other words, a migraineur who normally experiences sensitivity to lights may not have this associated symptom when she develops a mixed headache.

DIAGNOSING MIXED HEADACHES

Like other primary headaches, there is no blood test for mixed headaches; they are diagnosed by their clinical features and laboratory and radiological testing to rule out other medical conditions that can mimic mixed headache.

There is symptom overlap between mixed headache and quite a few other medical conditions. One of the biggest contributions you can make to the diagnostic workup is to keep a diary of your headache and associated symptoms for a few weeks. (See Appendix A.) In your headache diary, describe what you felt, where in your head you felt it, what time of day you felt it, how long it lasted, and what you did to make your symptoms go away. And again, in the case of women, information regarding your last menstrual period may also be helpful.

Signs and symptoms of mixed headaches can be a combination of tension-type headache symptoms and migraine headache symptoms.

Conditions that can mimic mixed headaches are migraine headache, trigeminal neuralgia, temporal arteritis, and pheochromocytoma.

Mixed headache is recognized by the combined features of tension-type and migraine headaches. Your provider may ask you about the location of your pain (the bandlike pain of tension-type headaches), any prodrome (the aura that precedes a migraine attack), and associated symptoms (the light sensitivity and nausea that accompanies migraines).

During your visit, your provider will also want to know about your family history: whether your parents, siblings, and grandparents get headaches, and if so, what type. You'll also be asked about your social history: Are you married or divorced? Do you have children? Have there been recent stressors in your life, such as unreasonable deadlines and loss of financial security? Has there been a recent change in your relationships? How's your job, including your relationship with your coworkers and your supervisor?

Your diary will help your health practitioner plan his next move. It will give him valuable clues during the physical examination, which involves looking into your eyes, ears, nose, and throat, and evaluating the nerves that feed your eyes, head, and neck. During the physical examination, your doctor will look for clues, such as red eyes, that may point to the problem at hand. During the neurological examination, your provider may test your memory; evaluate your peripheral vision; check the sensory stimuli and muscle strength in various parts of your head, neck, and extremities; check your reflexes and coordination; and test your ability to sense vibration at your wrists and ankles.

After the physical examination, your doctor might order selected laboratory tests and X-ray studies, depending on what is gleaned from the examination. (See chapter 12.) For example, if your doctor feels that a thyroid condition might be the cause of your recurrent headaches, he might order thyroid function tests to rule this possibility in or out. Similarly, if a brain tumor or blood vessel abnormality is suspected, a brain imaging study such as an MRI or CT scan will be ordered.

Laboratory and X-ray evaluations of mixed headache may include:

- Complete blood count
- Thyroid function tests
- Chemistry panel tests
- MRI scan
- CAT or CT scan
- EEG
- ENG

HOW TO TREAT AND PREVENT MIXED HEADACHES

Headache specialists Drs. Alan M. Rapoport and Fred D. Sheftell recommend relaxation techniques or biofeedback for mixed headache sufferers.[4] They also recommend a vigorous, regular aerobic exercise program, a balanced diet, and stable sleep patterns.

Because a common reason for developing mixed headache is overuse of analgesics, mixed headache sufferers should guard against overreliance on pain medication. The majority of individuals who suffer from coexisting migraine and tension-type headaches respond to simple pain medications, discussed in chapter 16. Overall treatment for mixed headache is presented in table 5.3 on page 75.

MARGARET'S STORY

A long-time migraine sufferer, Margaret, a homemaker and self-employed interior decorator, began having a slight variation in her usual headache pattern during the spring following her thirty-eighth birthday. The pain was located in the back of her head and neck and in both temples. The pain was dull, and felt like a tightness or pressure around her head, giving the sensation of "my head [is] being held in a vise or having a headband around my head."

Margaret was puzzled by having both the new headache and her usual migraine symptom complex simultaneously. She remembered from her reading and from her doctor's explanation that any change in headache pattern should be thoroughly investigated. Accordingly, she promptly made an appointment with her doctor, who diagnosed her with mixed headache. "Mixed headache?" she inquired. "I haven't seen such a syndrome discussed in any of my readings."

Margaret's doctor explained that some migraineurs go on to develop tension-type headaches, in addition to their migraines. These individuals experience features of both types of primary headache. After a thorough review of her medication profile, Margaret's physician felt that she was using painkillers too frequently, and that this may have triggered her mixed headache pain. Margaret was prescribed the drug propranolol (see chapter 16) and Tylenol for mild to moderate pain, was encouraged to practice biofeedback, and was told to return for reevaluation in one to two months. Six months later, Margaret reported having only one episode of migraine flare-up, and her tension-type headache had disappeared.

IN SUMMARY

- Mixed headaches (also called *tension-vascular headaches,* among other terms) are a combination of tension-type and vascular headaches, usually migraine.
- Mixed headaches result from the same biochemical aberrations present in tension-type and vascular headaches and are often triggered by overuse of headache medications.
- Migraineurs succumb to mixed headache more often than sufferers of other primary headaches.
- Mixed headaches are diagnosed via a thorough history, a complete physical examination, and when indicated, laboratory and radiographic studies to exclude other conditions.
- The treatments for mixed headache include regular, aerobic exercise; a balanced diet; stable sleep patterns; and relaxation and biofeedback techniques. When medications are needed, simple analgesics work well in the majority of cases.

CHAPTER EIGHT

Headaches in Women

Why are we devoting a separate chapter to headaches in women? Because compared to men, children, and adolescents, there are unique biological factors involved in women headache sufferers.

A large body of information gathered in the past few decades shows that the hormonal milieu in women creates an environment ideal for the development of certain types of headaches. As noted in chapter 3, the hormonal changes during menarche (the start of a girl's very first menstrual period), menstruation, pregnancy, and menopause, as well as taking birth control pills and other forms of hormones, have been associated with vascular headaches in some women. A significant number of adolescent girls and adult women develop migraines for the first time at menarche or after starting on birth control pills. According to neurologist Dr. Christina Peterson of the National Headache Foundation, the onset of menstruation is the single most significant trigger for female migraineurs.[1]

In this chapter, we'd like to explain why and how being female places one at risk for primary headaches. We'll examine headaches, especially migraines, associated with menstruation, pregnancy, menopause, and the use of birth control pills and hormone replacement therapy. First, we will look at how headache syndromes differ among women, men, children, and adolescents.

As we said in chapters 5 and 6, there are marked gender differences in prevalence within the various types of primary headache syndromes. More women than men report tension-type headaches (86 versus 69 percent), and approximately three times more women than men get migraine head

MAN ENDURES PAIN AS AN
UNDESERVED PUNISHMENT;
WOMAN ACCEPTS IT AS A
NATURAL HERITAGE.
ANONYMOUS

pain. On the other hand, men experience a sixfold greater incidence of cluster headaches than do their female counterparts. Most authorities believe that the observed gender differences may be partly explained by the cyclic hormonal changes that occur in women.

Among prepubescent children, more boys than girls experience migraines; after puberty, the trend reverses and more girls than boys suffer from migraines. Most experts believe that the reversal in incidence is largely related to the difference in hormonal changes, especially estrogen fluctuations, that occur in girls compared to boys at the time of puberty. Medical scientists, however, know very little about the biology of hormonal changes and how these changes lead to head pain.

With regard to headache management, the vast majority of men with headaches respond to standard medications. In contrast, many female headache sufferers often fail to respond to standard headache remedies, particularly women with atypical headache syndromes.

WHAT KINDS OF HEADACHES DO WOMEN GET?

As we've been saying all along, with the exception of cluster headaches, women suffer the lion's share of all types of primary headaches. Women suffer from tension-type, migraine, and mixed headaches. Among male and female migraineurs, women experience a higher incidence of atypical migraines (hemiplegic migraines, ophthalmoplegic migraines, and basilar artery migraines), compared to their male counterparts. Women even get cluster headaches, which are largely the domain of male vascular headache sufferers.

THE MENSTRUAL CYCLE IN REVIEW

A series of complicated secretions of hormones and neurotransmitters originating in the brain, the ovaries, and the uterus comprise a woman's menstrual cycle, the continuous biological changes that prepare a woman for conception. As a continuous cycle of events, the menstrual cycle doesn't have a starting and stopping point. For practical purposes, however, medical authorities use the first day of the menstrual bleed to mark the first day of the menstrual cycle.

Signs and symptoms of hormonally related headaches include severe pain around one eye or temple, tearing, and redness in the eyes.

Conditions that can mimic hormonal headaches include migraine headache, trigeminal neuralgia, temporal arteritis, and pheochromocytoma.

The entire cycle is driven by a series of hormones that work together to prepare the uterus for implantation of a fertilized egg. Hormones involved in the complicated chain of events include serotonin and noradrenaline, which influence an area in the brain called the hypothalamus.

Under hormonal instructions, the hypothalamus secretes gonadotropin-releasing hormone (GnRH), which influences the release of leutinizing hormone (LH) and follicle-stimulating hormone (FSH) from the pituitary gland.[2] FSH peaks at midcycle (ovulation), stimulating the ovary to release an egg into the fallopian tube. In the meantime, the inner lining of the uterus thickens to accommodate and nourish a fertilized egg.

Estrogen levels rise before ovulation, fall after ovulation, rise again slightly in the days between ovulation and menstruation, and fall sharply just before menstruation. Progesterone levels rise at ovulation and fall sharply before menstruation. If no egg is fertilized, the inner lining of the uterus sloughs, leading to the menstrual bleed. At this point the process starts over again.

THE MENSTRUAL CYCLE AND HEADACHES

The majority of female migraineurs, both adolescents and adults, trace the onset of their headaches to menarche. Surveys have shown that up to 60 percent of female migraineurs who keep a headache diary identify a relationship between their menstrual cycle and their headache flares.[3] Headaches associated with menstruation result from changes (either an increase or decrease) in the level of estrogen during the menstrual cycle. Estrogen levels directly affect the brain's endorphin and serotonin levels. As we discussed in chapter 1, serotonin, a major brain neurotransmitter, is responsible for the development of headaches.

Is there a difference between premenstrual migraine and menstrual migraine? By definition, premenstrual migraine begins from the seventh to the third day before a woman's period and improves or resolves with the onset of the menstrual flow.[4] Women who experience true menstrual migraine headaches experience recurrent head pain a week or so before the menstrual bleed, during the menstrual period itself, and up to three days after the menstrual bleed. Women who experience midcycle headaches are said to have "menstrually related" migraines. A small number of women suffer migraine attacks at ovulation, coinciding with a midcycle surge in estrogen.

During the premenstrual phase of the menstrual cycle, water retention caused by elevated estrogen levels influences the headache of premenstrual syndrome (PMS). Other symptoms of PMS include fatigue, crying spells, depression, anxiety, cyclic weight gain, breast swelling and tenderness, and food cravings. A number of theories have been advanced to explain the mechanisms involved in PMS-associated headaches. The most plausible explanation has to do with widening of blood vessels triggered by hormonal fluctuations.[5]

The treatment of menstrual migraine should begin during the premenstrual phase of the menstrual cycle. The headache is best treated with ergotamine (see chapter 16), avoidance of headache triggers, proper nutrition, regular aerobic exercise, and practice relaxation strategies such as biofeedback (see chapter 15). After menopause, when estrogen levels decline dramatically, menstrual migraines disappear or subside in most women. Unfortunately, some women experience a worsening in their menopausal years related to hormonal fluctuations during the "change of life."[6]

PREGNANCY AND HEADACHES

Pregnancy is usually a time of joy for an expectant mother and her family and friends. However, chronic headache sufferers' headache experiences vary during pregnancy. The majority of pregnant migraineurs report a worsening of their headaches during the first trimester, when estrogen levels rise dramatically.[7] More troubling, the majority of migraine medications are contraindicated during pregnancy. Fortunately, about 70 percent of headache sufferers experience a lessening or complete resolution of their headache symptoms during the second and third trimesters, when hormone levels don't fluctuate as much. Some women experience a complete loss of headache pain for the entire nine months of their pregnancies, only to have headaches return shortly after delivery.

There's no shortage of theories to explain the relationship between pregnancy and recurrent headaches. One theory blames the escalating levels of estrogen during the early months of pregnancy for worsening headaches, but offers no clear explanation how.[8] Other theories blame prostaglandins, hormonelike chemicals that increase our sensitivity to pain. To explain why headache improves in a number of pregnant women, some authorities theorize that endorphins, the body's natural morphinelike painkillers, may play a role.

During the postpartum period, migraines are apt to return to prepregnancy levels, and in some cases to worsen. However, migraineurs who opt to breast-feed their newborns may continue to see a reduction or temporary resolution of their attacks, probably due to the stabilization in estrogen levels that occurs with breast-feeding. Remember that these head pain patterns are not the same for all women. Even in the same woman, things are unpredictable; a woman can have nearly opposite experiences during two different pregnancies.

If you are not pregnant now and are contemplating pregnancy in the future, we recommend you learn to control your headaches through non-drug strategies such as biofeedback and relaxation therapy. (See chapter 15.) Pregnant migraineurs should avoid nicotine, alcohol, caffeine, and refined sugars—substances that may trigger migraines.

During pregnancy, your choices of safe painkilling drugs decrease. However, if painkilling drugs become necessary, acetaminophen (Tylenol), acetaminophen with codeine, and meperidine (Demerol) are safe during pregnancy.[9] For pregnant sufferers who need to take headache prophylactic drugs, the beta-blocker metoprolol (Lopressor) and the selective serotonin reuptake inhibitor fluoxetine (Prozac) appear safe. (See chapter 16.) However, it is best to check with your health care provider first.

MENOPAUSE AND HEADACHES

Menopause is not a sudden event but a two- to three-year–long process during which a woman makes the transition from the biological ability to bear a child to the biological inability to do so. The "change of life" process leading up to menopause is marked by various degrees of hormonal and other changes and is referred to as the perimenopausal period. Menopause is characterized by a physiological drop and stabilization in the levels of estrogen in a woman's body. Similarly, premature menopause due to the surgical removal of a woman's ovaries results in a drop in estrogen levels. Research during the past thirty years has conclusively linked a drop in estrogen to disconcerting "hot flashes," emotional lability, and an increased risk for heart disease and osteoporosis (thinning of the bones).

Like pregnancy, menopause and the period leading up to it affect women differently. For most female migraineurs, increased headache flares mark the perimenopausal period.[10] Menopause is a welcomed relief for most women because their migraine attacks invariably subside or disappear. This continues for most women headache sufferers, by and large, through the postmenopausal years. Unfortunately, however, the drug treatment for postmenopausal "hot flashes" and other medical problems referred to as hormone replacement therapy, or HRT, can mean a revisit of migraines (see our discussion on HRT on pages 104 and 105.)

No one really has a clear answer for why, like pregnancy, menopause affects headaches. Perhaps the falling and fluctuating estrogen levels during early menopause trigger headaches similar to the rise of estrogen levels early in pregnancy.[11] In some women, the deeply emotional state associated with the inability to bear a child, especially for women without children or those who wish they had had more children, may trigger headache pain.

Treatments of postmenopausal headaches include painkillers and prophylactic drugs (see chapter 16), proper nutrition, avoidance of headache triggers, a regular aerobic exercise program, and relaxation measures such as biofeedback. (See chapter 15.)

BIRTH CONTROL PILLS AND HEADACHES

Most birth control pills available in the United States contain either a combination of synthetic forms of the hormones estrogen and progesterone or progesterone only. Also available are progesterone tablets and progesterone injections administered every three months, as well as progesterone implants that are placed under the skin every five years. Additionally, there is a morning-after pill that contains the hormone diethylstilbesterol (DES), an estrogenlike hormone.

Birth control pills are prescribed cyclically to prevent ovulation. As we said earlier, ovulation signals the release of an egg from an ovary into the fallopian tube to be fertilized. Combination birth control pills suppress this process at the ovarian level. Progesterone-only pills and injections suppress ovulation by inhibiting the pituitary gland in the brain from releasing the hormones that drive the menstrual cycle.

Most women take birth control pills without any side effects. The main side effect of the progesterone-only birth control method is irregular menstrual bleeding. Unfortunately, for a few women, birth control pills can bring on or exacerbate migraine and other types of headaches.[12] These headaches may be related to the fluctuations in hormonal levels associated with the pill. In addition, DES can cause endometrial cancer in postmenopausal women exposed to the drug for more than one year. Female children of women who used DES during pregnancy are at risk for vaginal and cervical cancers later in life.

We recommend that, unless the benefits outweigh the risks, you not take birth control pills if you have preexisting migraine headaches or if you develop migraines after starting the pill. As we said in chapter 5, migraineurs who smoke and take birth control pills are also at increased risk of stroke. However, your physician is best positioned to help you make that decision.

HORMONE REPLACEMENT THERAPY AND HEADACHES

Like birth control pills, HRT involves manipulating the hormonal levels in the body for a specific purpose. HRT involves taking a pill each day, cyclically on certain days of the month, or wearing a hormone patch on the skin in order to alleviate the "hot flashes" resulting from falling estrogen levels and to reduce the incidence of osteoporosis and heart disease. (Recent studies raise a big question about previous studies showing that HRT reduces the incidence of heart disease in postmenopausal women.)

HRT can start or worsen migraines in some women; other women experience no change. As was noted in chapter 5, HRT, like birth control pills, can place a small fraction of female migraineurs, especially women who smoke and suffer from variant migraines, at a slightly increased risk for stroke. Some women may be able to use alternative strategies such as soy and soy products, which contain phytoestrogens. We recommend that you have an honest discussion with your health care provider if you develop HRT-associated vascular headaches.

Other strategies for managing postmenopausal headache include proper nutrition, a regular aerobic exercise program, and relaxation measures such as biofeedback. (See chapter 15.)

BARBARA'S STORY

Like her forty-something-year-old peers, Barbara, a manager at a taxi company, was faced with a litany of health dilemmas, including reproductive and preventive health issues. She was in the very early stages of menopause and was starting to experience the physical effects of falling estrogen levels, such as decreased vaginal lubrication and the socially disruptive "hot flashes." Barbara also had a history of migraine with aura that began at menarche. She had a strong family history of heart disease and stroke. Barbara was slightly overweight, had a slightly elevated lipid (cholesterol and triglycerides) profile, and smoked a half pack of cigarettes each day.

At a recent "women-only" group discussion, the topic was as close to home as it could have been for Barbara: how to avoid pregnancy during the perimenopausal years? In light of two recent studies showing that HRT can increase the risk of breast cancer, what were her remaining options? A doctor who moderated the group discussion recommended that Barbara talk with her health care provider about the best way to approach her menopausal symptoms in light of her risk factors for heart disease and stroke.

Barbara had a long talk with her family nurse practitioner regarding the risks and benefits of taking HRT. Because she was at high risk for stroke and other health problems, Barbara's health care provider suggested that she start a regular walking program, consult a dietitian about a low-fat diet, and attend a tobacco cessation program offered by the local chapter of the American Red Cross. Faced with tough decisions, Barbara realized the need for major lifestyle changes, and she began to follow the advice of her nurse practitioner.

DONNA'S STORY

Donna, the principal owner of a popular diner in the middle of town, and her spouse have to make a family planning decision. As an ophthalmoplegic migraine sufferer, Donna's obstetrician recommended that she not take birth control pills, and the low efficacy of condoms ruled out their use as a primary birth control method. The logical choices were thus reduced to tubal ligation and vasectomy. After much discussion, Donna's husband decided that he'd have a vasectomy.

IN SUMMARY

- Hormonal changes unique to women at menarche and during menstruation, pregnancy, and menopause, along with the use of birth control pills and hormone replacement therapy, account for the gender differences prevalent within different types of primary headache sufferers.

- With the exception of cluster headache, women suffer the lion's share of all types of primary headaches.
- About 60 percent of female migraineurs report a definite relationship between their menstrual cycles and headache flare-ups.
- The majority of pregnant migraineurs experience a worsening of their headache during their first trimesters and a lessening or temporary resolution of their head pain during the second and third trimesters.
- Premenopausal and perimenopausal women frequently report a worsening of their migraine symptoms; after menopause, the majority will have a marked reduction or complete resolution of their condition.
- Birth control pills and hormone replacement therapy often exacerbate headaches. Female migraineurs who smoke and take birth control pills or HRT are also at increased risk for stroke.

CHAPTER NINE

Headaches in Children and Adolescents

Kids suffer severe headaches, too. Twelve-year-old Jean Marie, a sixth grader who makes straight A's in school, has suffered from chronic headaches since she was eight. At a time when girls her age are etching out identities for themselves relative to their peers and learning new social skills, Jean Marie spends a lot of her time learning to live with recurrent headache pain. She says, "Almost every day, no matter where I'm at or what I'm doing—in school, playing with my friends, or doing my homework—my head pounds. I have to take lots of medicines that make me drowsy, and my mom has to massage my head and neck to make me comfortable. In the third grade, I missed a lot of school because I was always sick with my headaches; many of my friends thought I was weird and different."

If you are a parent, your child or children have complained or will complain at some time or other to you about having a headache. As a concerned parent, you probably wonder whether your child's headaches signal a functional problem, a curable illness, or an ominous condition. Is he trying to avoid a schoolyard bully? Does he have a chronic sinus infection? Or does he have a brain tumor or brain infection?

In most cases, the pain disappears before you come up with answers, because the vast majority of headaches in children are acute and clear in a few hours. There are cases, however, where the headache persists, requires painkillers, disrupts normal day-to-day activities, and may require medical evaluation and intervention. School attendance, social well-being, and self-esteem may suffer.

CHILDREN ARE NOT SIMPLY MICRO-ADULTS, BUT HAVE THEIR OWN SPECIFIC PROBLEMS.

BELLA SCHICK

In this chapter, we'll enumerate the features of the various headaches that children and adolescents get and discuss which are primary headache disorders, which result from an acute problem (viral illness), and which ones are serious and require prompt evaluation by a doctor. We'll suggest ways of helping your child cope with a problem that can potentially unravel the basic fabric of his psychological and social existence.

HOW COMMON ARE CHILDHOOD HEADACHES, AND WHO GETS THEM?

The fact is a lot of kids get headaches, and some start getting them at a very early age. Dr. Irving Fish, who runs the pediatric neurology department at New York University Medical Center in New York, estimates that almost 85 percent of children have had significant headaches by the time they're seventeen years old. Another study revealed that 70 percent of children had had at least one headache, and 30 percent reported having headaches at least once a month by age fourteen.[1]

Like adults, children and adolescents with headaches suffer tremendous physical and psychological, as well as social, disability. An estimated 10 to 15 percent of childhood headache sufferers miss school due to disabling head pain. In one study, children with migraines missed over seven days of school a year compared with the less than four days missed by their peers with other medical problems.[2]

Although there's no consensus, one survey of a cross-sectional population showed that approximately 5 percent of children suffer from migraines, 15 percent from tension-type head pain, and 30 percent from nonmigraine, or simple headaches.[3] Over 90 percent of children who suffer from migraines have a family history of similar headaches. Among prepubescent migraine sufferers, boys slightly outnumber girls; however, after puberty, migraine is two to three times more common in girls, a shift apparently related to the start of menstruation.[4]

Experts tell us that many cases of headaches in toddlers and young children go unrecognized because they are unable to say, "My head hurts." As you'll learn later, toddlers and young children who get headaches often get abdominal migraines, which manifest as stomachaches, vomiting, and periods of dizziness. Fortunately, children under the age of five rarely develop primary headaches.

IS HEADACHE IN CHILDREN AND ADULTS THE SAME DISEASE?

Many adult headache sufferers began having headaches during childhood and adolescence. For example, statistics show that 50 percent of adult migraineurs have a history of childhood migraines. So, what's the difference? Although children suffer the same types of headaches as adults, childhood headaches have physiological and psychological features that are different from those in adults.

Children and adolescents with migraine headaches have auras that are slightly different from those that adults get.[5] Auras in children frequently include confusion, hallucinations, dilated pupils, or difficulty speaking; auras in adults commonly are visual auras and involve flashing lights, zigzag lines, and bright spots of different shapes and colors. In contrast to their adult counterparts, young migraineurs experience headaches on both sides of the head. Children and adolescents also get more migraine flare-ups than adult migraineurs.

Children and adolescents get more migraine variants than adult migraineurs. Thus, during the headache phase of a migraine flare-up, some children with migraine may experience severe abdominal pain (abdominal migraine or migraine equivalent) instead of the throbbing head pain experienced by adults.[6] The mechanism for this is uncertain, but childhood migraineurs as a result may be subjected to extensive and expensive testing to rule out abdominal disease while migraine syndrome goes unrecognized.

WHAT KINDS OF HEADACHES DO CHILDREN AND ADOLESCENTS GET?

As a parent, when your child falls ill, the worst-case scenario invariably comes to mind. In the case of recurrent headaches, the nagging question invariably is: Does my child have a brain tumor? Such fears can be further confounded if your child gets a migraine-associated aura, such as confusion, difficulty speaking, and hallucinations.

There is no question that children do get brain tumors, but how common is this condition among children? You may have seen newsmagazine shows such as *20/20* and *60 Minutes* present one or two cases of bad outcomes in children with headache, but be reassured that, like those in adults, the vast majority of childhood headaches are not life threatening and do not pose the risk for permanently debilitating disease.[7] Indeed, children suffer the same types of headaches as do adults, but the prevalence of the types of headaches may be different between the two age groups. As we said earlier, approximately 5 percent of children suffer from migraines, 15 percent from tension-type head pain, and 30 percent get nonmigraine, or simple headaches. Less than 5 percent of children with headaches suffer from serious illness (i.e., secondary headaches).

MIGRAINE HEADACHES

If your child has migraine headaches, chances are you are intimately familiar with the syndrome because you are likely to also be a migraine sufferer. Indeed, 90 percent of children who suffer from migraines have a family history of similar headaches. This vantage position allows you to empathize with your child's suffering and prepares you to offer solid advice and comfort.[8]

Most children and adolescents who get migraine headaches do so without aura. As was discussed earlier, auras in children commonly involve confusion, hallucinations, dilated pupils, and difficulty speaking. Migraine triggers are similar in both adults and children; however, unlike most adult migraineurs, children with migraines usually experience the pain on both sides of their heads. Children also have more frequent flare-ups than their adult counterparts.

Children migraineurs experience the same associated symptoms, such as nausea, vomiting, and photophobia, as do adults. And like their adult counterparts, children prefer to find a quiet, dark room to fall asleep in during an attack. Some children run low-grade fevers, and most become agitated and temperamental.

Compared to adults, children suffer a higher prevalence of the migraine variants discussed in chapter 5. The four types of migraine variants, often referred to as atypical migraine or complicated migraine, are hemiplegic migraine, opthalmoplegic migraine, basilar artery migraine, and abdominal migraine.[9]

Hemiplegic Migraine

This migraine variant is more common in children than in adults. It produces slurred speech and a temporary paralysis on one side of the body, known as *hemiplegia,* which is reminiscent of a stroke. The hemiplegia may occur on the same side as the headache. Other symptoms of hemiplegic migraine include vertigo (sensation of one's surroundings spinning) and blurred vision.

These symptoms are followed about ten to ninety minutes later by a headache. Understandably, sufferers and family members become very anxious during an attack. In very rare cases, the paralysis is permanent.

Ophthalmoplegic Migraine

This form of migraine headache is caused by dysfunction of the nerves that control vision (the occulomotor and abducens nerves). Like hemiplegic migraine, it occurs most commonly in children. During an attack, the pain is centered around the eye and is associated with a droopy eyelid, an enlarged pupil, and double vision, which can last a few days to a few weeks.

Basilar Artery Migraine

This type of migraine headache is induced by dilation of the basilar artery, the blood vessel that supplies blood to the brain stem. Basilar artery migraines begin with loss of balance, difficulty speaking, double vision, transient blindness, poor muscle coordination, confusion, and in rare cases, loss of consciousness. These symptoms, which typically last up to forty-five minutes, are followed by a severe headache at the base of the skull.

This form of migraine headache is more common among girls than boys and often appears during the week leading up to the menstrual bleed. Basilar artery migraineurs are slightly predisposed to migraine-related stroke. How and why this happens, as well as who is predisposed to this migraine complication, is unclear, although smoking and the use of birth control pills might be contributing factors.

Abdominal Migraine

This rare form of migraine affects mostly children. In abdominal migraine, all the usual migraine symptoms occur except head pain. Instead, the sufferer experiences abdominal pain, which sometimes lasts several hours. These migraines, which can affect small children and toddlers, are often diagnosed retrospectively, after a child with recurrent stomachaches, vomiting, and motion sickness is found to have no organic problems after repeated tests and numerous visits to the doctor.

TENSION-TYPE HEADACHES

An estimated 15 percent of children suffer tension-type headaches from time to time. The majority of these sufferers experience episodic headaches; fewer children than adults get chronic tension-type headaches.

CLUSTER HEADACHES

Children get cluster headaches. You may recall from our discussion in chapter 6 that cluster headaches are probably the most painful and easily the most enigmatic of all headache syndromes. Among children and adolescents who suffer from cluster headaches, as among adults, males outnumber females by a ratio of seven to one.[10]

During an attack, cluster sufferers typically look gaunt, confused, and angry. The pain of cluster headache is commonly described as piercing or stabbing (hence one of its pseudonyms, the "ice-pick headache"), causing most sufferers to scream aloud and pace back and forth in frustration. In direct contrast, migraineurs prefer to remain still, balled up in a dark room during a migraine attack. The pain is located around the eye on one side of the head during an attack, but in 10 to 15 percent of patients, the headache moves to the other side of the head during subsequent clusters.[11] On the other hand, approximately 30 percent of migraine headaches occur on both sides of the head.

Cluster attacks are invariably associated with a runny nose and nasal congestion, as well as constriction of the pupil, drooping of the upper eyelid, and redness and tearing in the eye on the same side as the headache. Cluster attacks usually last from fifteen minutes to two and one-half hours, occur at intervals ranging from one every other day to eight times a day, and often occur at the same time of day. Many persons with cluster headaches report attacks during sleep, specifically between the transition from REM to normal sleep. This is the only type of headache to typically awaken the sufferer.

LIFE-THREATENING HEADACHES

In chapter 11, we discuss the various types of life-threatening headaches. As a concerned parent, it's natural to worry about the unknown: Does your child's recurrent headache—something you can't see or feel—represent a life-threatening condition? Despite the odds that the vast majority of headaches are primary, benign headaches, your fears may be made worse if no one else in the family suffers from chronic headaches.

As you'll learn in chapter 11, chronic headaches that have not changed over time are less likely to be due to a brain tumor or some other life-threatening condition. However, headaches that change, in terms of severity, location, duration, and associated symptoms, are troubling. In fact, changes of headache pattern in children are more troubling than those seen in adults. Other "red flags" that warrant immediate medical attention to rule out life-threatening conditions are:

- New-onset seizures
- Disturbances in speech, balance, or vision
- Memory loss, confusion
- Partial or complete loss of control in a limb
- Sudden onset of "the most painful headache"
- Headache that is worse upon awakening
- Recurrent vomiting

COPING WITH SCHOOL AND CHRONIC HEADACHES

In our society, as in most others, going to school is more than about learning math, reading, and writing. The experience of going to school helps students develop social and physical skills, build confidence and self-esteem, and learn to make the transition from one stage of life to another. This is a tall order to fill, even without distractions like a chronic health problem that is painful, academically distracting, and emotionally devastating.

Children with recurrent headaches report significant depression and anxiety. They are depressed that their peers consider them "weird," "different," "weak," and "undependable." Missing school, getting poor grades, and possibly flunking out add to the sufferer's misery. Anxiety stems from the uncertainty of not knowing when an excruciating episode, including vision disturbance, difficulty speaking, and vomiting, will strike. Small wonder many childhood headache sufferers miss lots of school and usually lag behind their peers in schoolwork. What can parents, educators, peers, family, and friends do to help the preteen or teenager suffering the effects of repeated headache?

Besides a comprehensive medical evaluation and medication and other treatments, young headache sufferers should strive to maintain the same social structure as their nonsuffering peers. This starts with thoroughly educating peers, teachers, family, and friends. As we discussed in chapter 2, myths about headaches abound. A complete explanation of migraine headaches, as well as its prevalence, effects, treatment, and prognosis, will likely help others understand and empathize with the young sufferer.

For young headache sufferers, maximum school attendance is very important. Missing school due to prolonged illness—not sharing in the activities of peers—can result in reduced self-esteem.[12] Frequent absences can inadvertently reinforce "school phobia" and create a vicious cycle of pain-dread-pain. During an especially disabling bout of attacks, the child can still return to school for short, defined periods of time. For example, she may return for three hours and gradually return to a full schedule over a five-day period.

Another strategy parents and children can use for dealing with this problem is to develop a specific plan for coping with an attack. The plan should address the following issues: who to tell, where the child should be taken during an attack, who will pick up the child and when, and what the family will do for the child on returning home.[13] After the plan has been carried out, parents and children should together reevaluate its efficacy and make any necessary changes. This type of elaborate plan inspires confidence in both parent and child and may help the child overcome "school phobia."

DIAGNOSING CHILDHOOD HEADACHES

As we've said in previous chapters, there is no blood test for diagnosing primary headaches; they are diagnosed based on clinical features. Primary care clinicians are trained to rule out secondary causes of headaches by taking a thorough history, performing a complete physical examination, and ordering appropriate blood tests and radiographic imaging. Table 9.1 summarizes the signs and symptoms of headache in children and adolescents.

Pediatricians, family physicians, and other health care providers learn to recognize the common clinical features of primary headache syndromes, such as the aura, nausea, and vomiting that occur with migraines. They are also aware of symptoms and signs such as personality changes, slurred speech, swelling in the nerves that lead to the eyes, and fever that can signal brain infections and other forms of secondary headaches.

Even the most astute clinician is helpless without the headache patient's help, however. The smartest headache diagnostician is only as good as the level of cooperation she receives from her headache patient. The following conditions can mimic headache in children:

- Trigeminal neuralgia
- Temporal arteritis
- Pheochromocytoma

An important role for a parent of a child or adolescent with headaches is to help your child articulate the symptoms he experiences. In the case of a child with recurrent headache, you may want to help him or her keep a headache diary for a few weeks. (See Appendix A.) The diary need not be elaborate or scientific. It only needs to describe what your child felt, where in his head he felt it, what time of day he felt it, how long it lasted, and what you or he did to make the symptoms go away.

TABLE 9.1 SIGNS AND SYMPTOMS OF HEADACHE IN CHILDREN AND ADOLESCENTS

Migraine headache
> Nausea and vomiting
> Sensitivity to lights

Atypical migraine headache
> Slurred speech
> Temporary paralysis on one side of the body
> Vertigo
> Blurred vision
> Double vision
> Loss of balance
> Confusion
> Loss of consciousness
> Abdominal pain

Tension-type headache
> Mild to moderate pain in back of the head or around the eyes or temple
> Feeling of a tight band around the head
> Sensitivity to light and sound
> Fatigue
> Loss of appetite
> Sleepiness

Cluster headache
> Severe pain around one eye or temple
> Tearing
> Redness in eyes

During the medical office visit, the health care provider will also want to know about the family history on both sides of the family: whether parents, siblings, or grandparents get headaches and if so, what type. The clinician may also be interested in recent changes in relationships, school attendance, or grades.

The diary will go a long way toward helping your child's doctor plan her next move. It will give her valuable clues during the physical examination, which involves looking into your child's eyes, ears, nose, and throat; listening to the heart and lungs; examining the abdomen; and evaluating the nerves that feed the child's eyes, head, and neck. A health professional uses the physical examination to look for clues, such as red eyes, that may offer valuable diagnostic information. During the neurological examination, the provider may test your child's memory, evaluate his peripheral vision, and check the sensory stimuli and muscle strength in various parts of his head, neck, and extremities. In addition, she will check your child's reflexes and coordination and his ability to sense vibrations at the wrists and ankles.

After the physical examination, the doctor might order selected laboratory tests and X-ray studies. For example, if your child's doctor feels that a thyroid condition might be the cause of his recurrent headaches, a thyroid function test may be ordered to rule this possibility in or out. For acute headaches with features of meningitis, a complete blood count and spinal tap may be done. If a brain tumor or blood vessel abnormality is suspected, a brain imaging study such as an MRI or CT scan will be ordered.

Laboratory and X-ray evaluations of headaches in children can include the following:

- Complete blood count
- Thyroid function tests
- Chemistry panel tests
- MRI scan
- CAT or CT scan
- EEG
- ENG

TREATING AND PREVENTING CHILDHOOD HEADACHES

Childhood headaches are managed with nondrug strategies and drug therapy. An active lifestyle can help relieve stress and contribute to overall well-being. Biking, walking, and swimming are good aerobic activities. Playing sports is a good way for your child to stay active as well as learn social and athletic skills and strengthen emotional and psychological health.

For migraineurs with identifiable triggers, such as foods, noise, or hormonal changes, removal of the cause or avoidance, if at all possible, is the obvious solution. For example, if tyramine is the offending agent, your child should avoid cheddar cheese, liver, and other tyramine-containing foods.

When avoiding migraine triggers is not enough, medications should be considered; chapter 16 lists the drugs commonly employed in the management of migraines in adults and children. The last ten years have seen great improvements in the management and prevention of migraine headaches. (See table 5.3, page 75.) However, the discovery of some of the underlying mechanisms involved in the development of migraine head pain has led to the discovery of drugs that work to reverse the basic aberrations. Unfortunately, many of the newer antimigraine medicines are contraindicated in persons younger than age eighteen. More child-friendly pharmaceutical agents are predicted to come on the market in the near future. In the meantime, see your child's health care provider for a thorough evaluation.

TOMMY'S STORY

By all accounts, Tommy was a good boy. His teachers praised his diligence in school, friends loved him for his congeniality, and his personality immediately attracted people. At fourteen, this honor student and baseball team captain was a well-adjusted teenager and the pride and joy of his parents. But Tommy had a dark secret. He suffered from the type of migraines that cause severe abdominal pain.

Fortunately, after an extensive medical workup when he was ten years old, he was accurately diagnosed with transformed migraine. Most of Tommy's difficulties stemmed, not from his illness, but from trying to convince skeptics that migraines can cause abdominal pain and not head pain.

IN SUMMARY

- According to one study, 85 percent of children and adolescents have had significant headaches by age seventeen.
- The prevalence of headaches among children and adolescents are as follows: 5 percent get migraines; 15 percent get tension-type headaches; and 30 percent get simple headaches. As in adults, the majority of headaches in children and adolescents are primary headaches.
- Auras in children often include confusion, hallucinations, dilated pupils, or difficulty speaking; adults experience flashing lights, zigzag lines, and bright spots of different colors and shapes.
- Children and adolescents experience more migraine variant episodes than do adults.
- Life-threatening headaches are rare and usually present with dramatic associated symptoms, such as a new onset of seizures, memory loss, and recurrent vomiting.
- Parents can help their children adjust to recurrent headaches by having a detailed plan for headache flare-ups and by educating teachers and peers about the implications of chronic headaches.
- A detailed headache diary will help your child's pediatrician accurately diagnose and effectively treat her headaches.
- Childhood headaches are managed by avoiding known headache triggers and by taking painkillers and prophylactic drugs as prescribed.

CHAPTER TEN

Medical Conditions That Cause Headaches

In chapter 1, we defined a secondary headache as one that results from an identifiable cause such as a sinus infection or a brain tumor. In contrast, primary headaches, such as cluster and migraine, have no clearly identifiable cause. Secondary headache sufferers have untreated or undertreated medical or organic conditions, such as high blood pressure, chronic eyestrain, and untreated respiratory allergies, producing headaches that can mimic migraines and other forms of primary headaches. The treatment for these headaches is the appropriate treatment of the underlying medical problem. For example, headaches caused by a bacterial sinus infection are best treated with antibiotics, nasal decongestants, and increased fluid intake.

SECONDARY HEADACHES

In this chapter, we'll discuss the most common forms of secondary headaches, which make up less than 5 percent of all headaches in adults and children. Secondary headaches include those caused by allergies, sinus problems, high blood pressure, vision problems, and temporomandibular joint (TMJ) syndrome. Additionally, many people experience both acute and chronic headache after head trauma. Hormonal imbalance in some women can manifest as headache. Temporal arteritis (inflammation of the artery in the temple and scalp) can produce severe pain as can pseudotumor cerebri and cervicogenic disease, as well as withdrawal from drugs and excessive stress.

Medical conditions that cause headaches include:

- Allergies
- Sinus problems
- High blood pressure
- Vision problems
- Temporomandibular joint (TMJ) syndrome
- Posttraumatic headaches
- Hormonal imbalance
- Temporal arthritis
- Pseudotumor cerebri
- Cervicogenic headache
- Drugs such as painkillers, antibiotics, and high blood pressure pills
- Dehydration
- Alcohol overindulgence
- Post–spinal tap headache
- Physical exertion
- Carbon monoxide poisoning
- Fever
- Stress

ALLERGIES

Allergies, a term used loosely to refer to hay fever or hypersensitivity to pollen, house dust, animal dander, and other allergens, refers to one of the most common conditions affecting humans.[1] The medical term for the condition is *allergic rhinitis,* and individuals with this condition experience either seasonal (usually spring and fall months) or perennial (year-round) symptoms. Allergic rhinitis frequently runs in families.

The most common symptoms of hay fever are repeated sneezing, runny nose, and headache located in the forehead, between the eyes, and below the eye sockets. Sometimes the only symptom of allergies is a dull,

nagging chronic headache. Many people with primary headache have allergy-induced headaches, and
sometimes it is difficult to distinguish among
headache types.

Avoidance of the irritant is the best way to prevent
and treat allergies. Antihistamines and decongestants,
discussed in chapter 16, are the mainstays of drug
therapy for hay fever. Sometimes migraine headaches improve with decongestants because these drugs constrict blood vessels, including those associated with migraines.[2]

> "I'M VERY BRAVE GENER-
> ALLY," HE WENT ON IN A LOW
> VOICE: "ONLY TO-DAY I HAP-
> PEN TO HAVE A HEADACHE."
> **LEWIS CARROLL**

SINUS PROBLEMS

The sinuses are air-filled cavities within the bones of the skull. A relatively
rare form of headache called *sinus headaches* affect an estimated 2 percent
of the population. Most problems within the sinuses occur when the membranes lining the sinus cavity produce excess mucus and the tissues become swollen and inflamed. Those foods most commonly implicated in
the triggering of sinus troubles are dairy products.

Infection of the sinuses, called *sinusitis,* can cause localized, dull
headaches in the forehead, behind and between the eyes, or in the cheeks.
The pain can radiate to the temples or to the top or back of the head and
can become worse when bending forward. Thick, yellowish-greenish nasal
drainage often occurs. Sometimes sinusistis is accompanied by teeth pain.
Fever is often present.

The headache of sinusitis is commonly mistaken for migraine or cluster headaches. This is especially true when the individual has chronic sinusitis. The sinus blood vessels are some of the vessels involved during a
migraine attack, but the other symptoms produced by sinusitis, such as
fever and yellowish nasal discharge, can help rule out primary headaches.

Sinus headaches clear up after the underlying sinusitis is successfully
treated, usually with antibiotics if bacteria are the culprits. Other commonly

used medications include decongestant tablets and short-term use (a three-day course) of nasal decongestants via a nasal spray. If you have recurrent sinus trouble, you may get prolonged reprieve from the problem by staying away from milk, cheese, and ice cream. Remember that other foods, too, can be sources of the problem.

HIGH BLOOD PRESSURE

High blood pressure, also called *hypertension,* is higher-than-normal pressure within the blood vessels as the blood circulates throughout the body. Hypertension affects an estimated fifty million American adults and two million American children and adolescents. Normal blood pressure is defined as pressures less than 140/90 mm Hg. Mild and moderately elevated blood pressures (up to 160/100 mm Hg) rarely cause headache symptoms. However, severely elevated blood pressure (over 180/120 mm Hg), referred to as *malignant* or *accelerated hypertension,* can produce a pounding headache along with a feeling of giddiness.

Unfortunately, hypertension is twice as likely to occur in migraineurs as nonmigraineurs.[3] Headache secondary to high blood pressure is relieved when the blood pressure is brought under control. Unfortunately, some high blood pressure medications can cause headache in a small percentage of people who take them. The most notable of these medications are reserpine, prazosin, hydralazine, and nifedipine and other calcium channel blockers. (See chapter 16.)

VISION PROBLEMS

Eyestrain, uncorrected vision loss, glaucoma, and other conditions of the eyes are common causes of chronic headache. Using a video display terminal (VDT), such as a computer screen, with uncorrected vision loss can cause you to squint, placing strain on the muscles in and around your eyes. Eyestrain is a common reason for chronic headaches in persons with this frequent eye problem.

Individuals with normal vision who stare at a VDT for extended periods of time can also experience eyestrain headaches. Factors contributing to eyestrain include glare, poor lighting, and improper workstation ergonomics. Visual-associated headaches may have the following pattern:

- They occur most often toward the end of the day.
- They aren't present upon awakening.
- Unlike migraine headaches, they aren't associated with auras, light sensitivity, or nausea.
- They often occur in a different pattern, or not at all, on weekends.

The best strategy for avoiding eyestrain is to have your eyes checked on a regular basis and to wear corrective lenses if needed. If you have normal vision and work at a VDT for prolonged periods, take a five-minute break from your work each hour.[4]

Glaucoma refers to a buildup of pressure on the optic nerve, the nerve that controls vision. This pressure comes from poor drainage of the fluid inside the inner eye. Symptoms of glaucoma include blurred vision, halos around lights, nausea and vomiting, and diffuse, daily headache. Only an eye care specialist such as an optometrist or ophthalmologist is qualified to diagnose and manage glaucoma. Untreated glaucoma can lead to permanent blindness.

TMJ SYNDROME

Dental malalignment, gum disease, cavities, and teeth clenching place extreme strain on the temporomandibular joint (TMJ), the joint between the jaw and temple located in front of the ear, and on surrounding muscles, resulting in recurrent pain. TMJ syndrome is very common, affecting an estimated ten to fourteen million Americans.[5] In addition to pain, TMJ syndrome is characterized by clicking of the joint with jaw movement, limitation of jaw movement, and locking of the jaw joint that is aggravated by chewing.

TMJ syndrome can be managed by a number of dental, medical, and alternative medical strategies. For example, nighttime teeth clenching (usually a result of stress) can be remedied by wearing a mouth guard and by stress management techniques. Check with your dentist. If you have a problem that requires surgical intervention, you may be referred to an oral or plastic and reconstructive surgeon.

TMJ syndrome may also be amenable to osteopathic manipulation. Ask your primary care provider for referral to an osteopathic physician. Allopathic physicians often prescribe relaxation exercises and nonsteroidal anti-inflammatory drugs, such as ibuprofen and aspirin, for TMJ syndrome. (See chapter 16.)

POSTTRAUMATIC HEADACHES

A large percentage of people develop recurrent headaches following a head, face, or neck injury. Posttraumatic or head injury headaches can start twenty-four to forty-eight hours after the injury and can last for weeks, months, or even years. The severity of the head pain and associated symptoms does not correlate with the severity of the trauma.[6] The exact causes of posttraumatic headaches are largely unknown, but a few theories have been proposed. The most common theory has to do with the bruising of the brain against the bony skull. This bruising, called a *contusion*, may disrupt the activity of neurotransmitters, the chemical messengers that facilitate communication among brain cells.

Posttraumatic headaches may also result from whiplash injury, a sudden jerky movement of the head and neck. It is felt that whiplash somehow disturbs the connections among the nerves, muscles, tendons, and ligaments in the head and neck. For example, trauma to the nerves in the inner ear, which monitors body position and balance, may produce the dizziness often reported by individuals with posttraumatic headaches.

Besides moderate to severe daily headaches and dizziness, some individuals also experience mental confusion, insomnia, and blurred vision. Other symptoms include ringing in the ears, vague blurring of vision, reduced libido, and alcohol intolerance. Some sufferers experience sleep disturbance, anxiety, and depression. Posttraumatic headache can be made worse by sneezing, coughing, and physical exertion. If you've suffered head trauma, especially if the pain gets progressively worse, go to your health care provider to rule out serious injuries to the brain and surrounding tissue.

HORMONAL IMBALANCE

Some women have recurrent headaches brought on by the imbalance of the female hormones estrogen and progesterone that occurs during the menstrual cycle. As we discussed in chapter 8, these headaches typically occur a week or two before the menstrual bleed or during the menstrual period itself. About 60 percent of female migraineurs experience headache flare-ups during the menstrual cycle, and many flare-ups are exclusively associated with the cycle.[7]

Like the menstrual cycle, menopause is characterized by hormonal changes. The falling and fluctuating estrogen levels during the premenopausal period can trigger headaches. As noted in chapter 8, these biological changes affect women differently. For most female migraineurs, more headache flare-ups mark their perimenopausal period.[8] Others get fewer headaches. Fortunately, most female headache sufferers will have less headaches during their postmenopausal years.

Women prescribed HRT to prevent pregnancy and to replace a drop in estrogen levels are also prone to getting repeated headaches. Again, migraineurs probably should not be presribed birth control pills or HRT.

TEMPORAL ARTERITIS

Temporal arteritis, also called *giant cell arteritis,* results from thickening of the walls of the superficial arteries that feed the temples and the eyes. The cause is unknown, but affected persons invariably have another condition called *polymyalgia rheumatica.* (See the glossary.) These two conditions rarely affect persons younger than fifty years of age and are three times more common in men than in women.

The headaches associated with giant cell arteritis are typically located on one side of the head and produce scalp sensitivity, altered vision, and pain in the jaw. Moreover, there is a risk of permanent blindness. The diagnosis is made by examining a sample of the affected artery under a microscope, and treatment includes the steroid drug prednisone and physical therapy.

PSEUDOTUMOR CEREBRI

This rare condition, also called *benign intracranial hypertension,* is characterized by abnormally high pressure in the cerebrospinal fluid that bathes the brain and spinal cord. The exact cause of this condition is unknown, but it is associated with some conditions (i.e., head injury, pregnancy, vitamin A deficiency, and obesity) and some medications (tetracycline, sulfonamides, and indomethacin, for example).[9]

Signs and symptoms of pseudotumor cerebri include vomiting, swelling of the optic nerve that serves the eye, and headache. The condition is treated with periodic removal of spinal fluid to lower the fluid volume in the brain.

CERVICOGENIC HEADACHE

This condition, sometimes referred to as *vertebrogenic headache,* is due to arthritis of the joints in the neck.[10] Clinical experts and researchers are divided over the significance of neck conditions on chronic headache.

DRUG-INDUCED HEADACHES

Medications are a common source of recurrent headaches. As hard as it is to believe, headache therapy can cause the very symptoms it is supposed to treat and prevent. Painkillers, hormonal agents, diet pills, and deconges-tants have been implicated as headache triggers in some persons with chronic headache. Other categories of drugs associated with headaches in previous nonsufferers include high blood pressure and antiulcer drugs, an-tibiotics, and antihistamines.

The most commonly implicated category of drugs includes painkillers or analgesics. The American Association for the Study of Headache reports that analgesic rebound headaches are the most common type of chronic daily headache. This form of headache recurs as each dose of painkiller wears off, prompting the sufferer to take more and more medication, lead-ing to a vicious cycle of headache-painkiller-headache-painkiller. If you ex-perience the following symptoms, you may be a victim of drug-induced headaches:[11]

- The daily or almost daily use of headache pills
- Headaches that awaken you in the early hours of the morning
- Nausea, abdominal pain, cramps, diarrhea, sleep disturbance, irritability, increase in intensity of headache—all symptoms of drug withdrawal—after suddenly discontinuing daily headache medication

The painkillers most commonly implicated in medication-induced headaches include narcotics, such as codeine, hydrocodone, oxycodone, and meperidine. In addition to indomethecin, other nonsteroidal anti-inflammatory drugs that can cause rebound headaches include ibupro-fen and naproxen. The treatment is to withdraw the offending drug and use another if needed. Obviously, this should be done under physician supervision.

STRESS

As we said in chapter 3, stress and other emotional factors can trigger headache flare-ups in people with chronic headaches.

OTHER MEDICAL CAUSES OF HEADACHES

Besides the conditions discussed above, many other medical conditions can present with headaches. These conditions include post–spinal tap headache, alcohol overindulgence, physical exertion, dehydration, and carbon monoxide poisoning. Additionally, a fever often causes headaches.

Ominous conditions can also cause acute and recurrent headaches. These conditions include brain tumors, brain infections, and aneurysm and brain hemorrhage. (See chapter 11.) People with headaches secondary to these conditions have severe and progressive symptoms.

IN SUMMARY

- A litany of identifiable medical conditions, such as eyestrain and allergies, can cause head pain, referred to as secondary headache. Treatment of these headaches involves treating the underlying medical condition. Hay fever typically causes sneezing and a runny nose and is treated with antihistamines and decongestants.
- Sinus headaches result from excess mucus and swelling in the sinus cavities and is treated with decongestants and antibiotics when indicated. Dairy products and other foods can be sources of sinus headache.
- High blood pressure, blood pressure exceeding 140/90 mm Hg, can cause headaches, as can some drugs used to treat the condition.

- Visual disturbances such as eyestrain and glaucoma can cause re-current headache pain.
- TMJ syndrome affects an estimated ten to fourteen million Americans, often due to undue stress on the muscles and joints between the temple and jaw.
- Posttraumatic headaches may start within twenty-four hours after trauma to the head, face, and neck and can last for days, weeks, months, or even years. These headaches are probably due to bruising of the brain as it hits the bony skull and from a disruption of the nerves, muscles, tendons, and ligaments in the head and neck.
- The menstrual cycle, menopause, and hormone pills (whether as a birth control measure or to replace falling estrogen levels after menopause) can be associated with chronic headache.
- Temporal arteritis usually causes one-sided headaches, scalp sensitivity, and fever.
- Signs and symptoms of pseudotumor cerebri include vomiting and swelling of the optic nerve.
- Cervicogenic headaches result from arthritis of the joints in the neck.
- Painkillers, some antibiotics, antihistamines, and high blood pressure drugs can cause headache.
- Other causes of headaches include stress, alcohol overindulgence, dehydration, drug withdrawal, and fever.

CHAPTER ELEVEN

Life-Threatening Headaches

This chapter has not been included to frighten you or cause needless worry. Rather, our hope is that the information presented here will reassure you and ease your fears. If, after reading this chapter, you are concerned that your headaches may fit the description of a serious, underlying medical condition, seek medical help immediately.

Many serious conditions can cause headaches. More often than not, these conditions cause more than just headache; they produce numbness, weakness, speech difficulty, and other troubling problems. In this chapter, we'll discuss headaches that result from life-threatening disorders. These conditions include brain tumors, meningitis, and ruptured aneurysm and stroke.

TWO TYPES OF HEADACHES

Practically speaking, there are two types of headaches: the type that's not life threatening (over 95 percent of all headaches) and the type that's potentially life threatening (less than 5 percent of all headaches). Although both types of headaches are painful, disruptive, and sometimes disabling, life threatening headaches such as those caused by brain tumors, meningitis, and severe high blood pressure are the most urgent. Let's again emphasize that no book can diagnose headaches caused by life-threatening conditions. Only physicians or clinicians working under physician supervision are adequately trained and qualified to determine whether meningitis or other life-threatening problems are causing your headaches.

Generally speaking, chronic headaches that have not changed over time are less likely to indicate a brain tumor or some other urgent or emergent condition. However, acute and chronic headaches that change in severity, location, duration, and associated symptoms may represent a serious condition. If your headache pattern changes, you should immediately contact your health care provider, even if you've suffered from chronic headache for several years. As discussed in chapter 9, changes of headache pattern in children are more troubling compared to adults.

The following list includes some common features or "red flags" of life-threatening headaches such as those caused by brain infections and severe high blood pressure. See a doctor immediately if your head pain has any of these features:

- Headaches that begin and persist after trauma to the head, neck, or back
- Disturbances in your speech, balance, or vision (blurred or double)
- Memory loss and/or confusion
- Headache that awakens you from a deep sleep
- Partial or complete loss of control in a limb
- Coordination or balance problems with or without a headache
- Sudden onset of "the most painful headache" you've ever had
- New onset of headaches after age forty-five
- Headaches associated with fever or shortness of breath
- Headaches associated with neck stiffness
- Headache triggered by cough, bending over, straining, sexual activity, or other exertion

BRAIN TUMORS

Ask people who recently began having headaches (or some who have had headaches for years) what they dread most about their head pain, and they'll tell you they worry that their headaches may stem from a brain tumor. Even patients who've suffered years of a well-defined and effectively diagnosed primary headache syndrome worry about brain tumors.

Although their incidence has increased in recent years, however, brain tumors are still a rare occurrence. The National Center for Health Statistics estimates that less than 0.5 percent of all headaches result from brain tumors. And only 50 percent of brain tumor patients experience headaches related to their tumor, and those are usually mild in severity.

Because the brain has no pain receptors, brain tumors themselves do not result in headache pain. However, these tumors produce headaches by causing the displacement or impingement of pain-sensitive blood vessels and nerves. Less than 8 percent of brain tumor patients experience headaches as their only symptom. Tumors in the brain are most likely to cause seizures and disturbance in vision, speech, coordination, and cognition. Headaches due to brain tumors worsen as the tumor grows and are aggravated by coughing, sneezing, bending over, straining during a bowel movement, or any other activities that increase pressure in the skull.[1] Brain tumor headaches are often worse in the morning and are associated with nausea and vomiting.

Signs and symptoms of brain tumors can include:

- New-onset seizures
- Disturbances in your speech, balance, or vision
- Memory loss and/or confusion
- Partial or complete loss of control in a limb
- New onset of headaches after age fifty
- Headache that is worse upon awakening
- Recurrent vomiting

Only a physician or clinician working under physician supervision is qualified to make a definitive diagnosis of a brain tumor. If you're worried about whether your headaches are caused by a tumor, check with your primary care provider or hospital emergency department at once. If your doctor is concerned, a computed axial CT or MRI scan will be ordered. (See chapter 12 for a discussion of CT and MRI scans.)

Not all brain tumors are cancerous. Noncancerous tumors are surgically removed if the location allows surgery, followed by an observational period. Cancerous lesions are also surgically removed if the location allows for surgery, which is followed by radiation therapy or chemotherapy, depending on the type of cancer.

MENINGITIS AND ENCEPHALITIS

Plain and simple, meningitis and encephalitis are potentially life-threatening medical emergencies, requiring immediate physician attention. Meningitis refers to an infection or inflammation of the membranes covering the brain and spinal cord. Encephalitis is infection or inflammation of the brain itself.

Many organisms (bacteria, viruses, fungi) can cause meningitis and encephalitis. Viral meningitis is often a self-limited condition, rarely requiring hospitalization. Meningitis can also result from noninfectious causes such as tumors and chemical irritation. Encephalitis can also be caused by lead poisoning and is always a serious condition, with a potential for brain swelling, coma, and other serious consequences.

Signs and symptoms of meningitis and encephalitis include a bad headache, fever, nausea, vomiting, and pain and stiffness in the neck. Undiagnosed and untreated, meningitis and encephalitis can quickly lead to seizures, coma, and death. Only a physician or clinician working under physician supervision is qualified to make the definitive diagnosis of meningitis and encephalitis.

The treatment of meningitis and encephalitis depends on its cause. Bacterial meningitis, for example, is treated with antibiotics, while antifungals are used to manage fungal meningitis. Lead-induced encephalitis is treated with drugs that bind, or *chelate,* to the mineral, and steroids are used to reduce brain swelling.

RUPTURED ANEURYSM

An aneurysm is an area of weakness in a vein or artery due to thinning in the vein's walls. This weak spot tends to bulge under the pressure of circulating blood. Over time, this aneurysm can rupture or burst, resulting in a sudden leakage of blood, or hemorrhage, into the brain and spinal fluid. When this happens in vital blood vessels, such as those that feed areas of the brain that control speech and coordination, sensitive regions of the brain are denied oxygen and other nutrients normally brought in by the blood. The ultimate result is a stroke or brain attack, similar to a heart attack caused by disruption of blood flow to vital parts of the heart muscle. In about 50 percent of cases, a warning headache occurs before the rupture.

Aneurysms rupture due to a variety of triggers, including severely high blood pressure, illicit drug use (for example, cocaine), and strenuous physical activity. The symptoms of a ruptured aneurysm are variable. One of the most common symptoms a ruptured aneurysm produces is a sudden, violent headache, often referred to as a "thunderclap" of head pain. Other common symptoms include slurred speech, weakness, poor coordination, and loss of consciousness.

Obviously, a ruptured aneurysm is not a self-diagnosis. It is an emergency, requiring prompt physician assessment. Don't drive yourself or have anyone drive you; dial 911 and ask for an ambulance to take you to the emergency room.

STROKE

A stroke, or a cerebrovascular accident (CVA) in medical terms, is a lack of oxygen and other nutrients to parts of the brain resulting from interruption of blood flow. There are two broad reasons for lack of blood flow: a blood clot from an embolus or thrombus or a rupture of a blood vessel causing bleeding. Medical professionals recognize two types of strokes: one type resulting from blockage of the blood vessel (embolic and thrombotic strokes) and a second type caused by bleeding (hemorrhagic stroke).

Embolic stroke typically occurs when a blood clot breaks off from somewhere else in the body and travels to the tiny arteries that supply blood to the brain. If the blockage originates due to fatty deposits in the lining of the arteries in the neck and brain, this is called a *thrombotic stroke.* *Hemorrhagic stroke* commonly occurs when the arteries are unable to tolerate the pressure exerted by the circulating blood.

All strokes can cause headaches, but the highest incidence of stroke-induced headache occurs among individuals suffering from a hemorrhagic stroke. In addition to headaches, strokes usually cause vomiting as well as weakness and numbness in the arms and legs. As was discussed in chapter 5, migraineurs with aura are at a slightly higher risk for stroke, especially those who smoke and use birth control pills. If you have no symptoms other than headache, it is unlikely that you are suffering from a stroke.[2] Remember, however, only physicians or other health care professionals are qualified to determine if you are having a stroke. If you are worried about having a stroke, seek professional medical help immediately.

IN SUMMARY

- Brain tumors produce headaches by causing the displacement or impingement of pain-sensitive blood vessels. Symptoms include seizures and disturbances in vision, speech, coordination, and cognition.
- Meningitis is an infection or inflammation of the membrane covering the brain and spinal cord. Encephalitis is an infection or inflammation of the brain itself. These conditions are always medical emergencies that, if untreated, can lead to severe consequences.
- An aneurysm or weak spot in a blood vessel can burst, causing bleeding into the brain. Slurred speech, "thunderclap" headaches,

and loss of consciousness are commonly encountered symptoms. It is an emergency; an ambulance should be called.

- A stroke results from a clot or bleeding that interrupts blood flow to a part of the brain.
- These life-threatening conditions are true medical emergencies that can only be diagnosed by a physician or clinician working un-der physician supervision.

CHAPTER TWELVE

Medical Evaluation of the Headache Patient

What should you expect when you go to a clinician for evaluation of your headache? What laboratory tests, X-ray studies, and procedures are typically ordered? Do these tests and procedures hurt? What is your role in the evaluation process?

As for other medical problems, doctors diagnose headache disorders based on a thorough headache history, a complete physical examination, ordering appropriate laboratory and X-ray testing, and performing some diagnostic procedures.[1] You need not be a passive recipient while undergoing medical testing; ask what the tests are for, how much they cost, and whether they are necessary. The more you know about the evaluation process and the more active a participant you become, the quicker and easier the process will proceed. As an active participant, you may even save time and money. Chapter 13 lists helpful tips for working with your health care team.

In this chapter, we'll help you uncover the mystery behind the process involved in arriving at a headache diagnosis. We'll describe a typical headache history, physical examination, laboratory and radiographic testing, and diagnostic procedures.

THE HEADACHE HISTORY

Initially, your health care provider will want to know why you've come in for the visit. He will likely ask you the following questions about your headaches: How long have you been getting them? How often? What time of day do they usually start? Where in your head or neck are they located? In addition, you'll be asked: What do your headaches feel like? How intense are they? How long do they last? What triggers them? What treatments have you received so far?

Your physician may also want to know about associated symptoms such as nausea and vomiting and whether your head pain was preceded by an aura (for example, zigzag lines or loss of vision). If you have kept a headache symptom diary (see Appendix A), this is the time to review it with your clinician, because it can be extremely helpful in identifying the type of headache syndrome you have and any headache triggers you're sensitive to, and even determining what treatment is likely to help you.

Because many types of headaches run in families, the questions will likely shift to a detailed family history. Who in your family gets headaches, and what type of headaches do they get? At what age did their headaches start? Which treatments have proven effective? As we detailed in chapter 3, many psychosocial factors are known headache triggers. Your provider will also likely ask you the following: Are you married or divorced? Do you have children? Has there been a recent change in your financial status? Has there been a recent change in your social relationships? How's your job, and how's your relationship with your coworkers and your supervisor?

Finally, your clinician will want to know about your past medical problems so he can determine whether they could be contributing to your current problem. You should list for him any and all medical and surgical illnesses and the medications you take for them.

THE PHYSICAL EXAMINATION

After the medical history, your provider will examine you. This is the hands-on portion of the evaluation, in which physical findings (e.g., an enlarged thyroid gland) may offer clues as to what's going on in your body. The typical physical examination of the headache patient includes the following:

GENERAL OBSERVATION

This begins as you walk into the medical facility. Your gait, demeanor, and overall health are assessed.

VITAL SIGNS

Nurses or other support personnel usually take your temperature, pulse, respiratory rate, and blood pressure, and record them on your health record for the provider to evaluate.

VISION TESTING

This test, also done by support personnel, evaluates your uncorrected and, if applicable, your corrected vision. If you wear glasses or contact lenses, you will need them at this time.

HEAD

The head examination, done by your clinician, evaluates the general appearance of your head. Any unusual contours, tenderness, or rash is noted.

EAR, NOSE, AND THROAT

Handheld instruments are used to look for signs of infections, sores, or anatomical defects such as a deviated nasal septum.

NECK

The neck contains blood vessels, lymph nodes, and your thyroid. These structures are palpated and auscultated (listened to with a stethoscope) and evaluated for abnormal lumps and tenderness.

NEUROLOGICAL EXAMINATION

A complete neurological examination is imperative in the evaluation of the headache patient. This involves a series of basic questions to check your brain function and physical maneuvers to check the integrity of your nervous system. An important aspect of the neurological examination is evaluation of your cranial nerves, the twelve nerves that connect the brain to the head and neck regions. To laypersons, the examination of the cranial nerves may seem trivial; you'll be asked to "puff your cheeks," "wrinkle your forehead," "stick out your tongue," and so forth. Much vital information can be gathered during these maneuvers, however, such as whether you have a tumor pressing on the nerve that controls your vision or whether your facial nerves are affected by multiple sclerosis.

COMMON LABORATORY TESTING

If you've never been "worked up" for your headaches, your clinician may order selected laboratory tests. Laboratory studies are usually obtained to rule out conditions, such as anemia, sinus infection, and thyroid disease, that can present with recurrent headaches. Laboratory testing involves obtaining a sample of your urine, blood, spinal fluid, and other bodily fluids to check for abnormal levels. The typical laboratory evaluation of headache patients may involve a urinalysis, complete blood count, thyroid function tests, and a chemistry panel. Not all headache patients need to undergo laboratory testing, while others may need extensive testing.

URINALYSIS

The urinalysis (UA) measures pH and the concentration of your urine output and rules out kidney and other medical conditions that can cause headaches. Abnormalities of the UA include the appearance of sugar (indicating diabetes), white blood cells (indicating kidney infection), and protein or red blood cells (indicating kidney damage due to high blood pressure).

COMPLETE BLOOD COUNT

The complete blood count (CBC) measures the various components of the circulating blood, including white blood cells, red blood cells, and platelets. The CBC can detect conditions such as sinus infection and anemia.

CHEMISTRY PANEL TESTS

This battery of tests evaluates the levels of large numbers of chemicals in the body. The extent of these tests varies, but generally, the blood sugar, electrolytes (potassium and chloride), liver enzymes, and cholesterol are checked. The blood chemistry is ordered to rule out conditions such as low potassium (indicating a tumor in the adrenal gland) and high liver enzymes (indicating hepatitis) that can present with recurrent headaches.

THYROID FUNCTION TESTS

The thyroid gland modulates the function of almost all bodily processes, such as the rate of skin turnover and heart rate. Both hypothyroidism (underactive thyroid gland) and hyperthyroidism (overactive thyroid gland) can cause recurrent headaches.

COMMON X-RAY STUDIES

Radiographic studies are usually ordered to better evaluate unusual symptoms that can point to conditions such as tumors or abnormal blood vessel patterns within or outside the brain. If your head pain shows a pattern clearly consistent with a primary headache syndrome, your provider may elect to forgo radiographic testing. It's important to remember that radiographic studies don't prove or disprove the presence of a primary headache; they rule out tumors or other illnesses or problems that could be the source of your headache.[2]

COMPUTED AXIAL TOMOGRAPHY SCAN

A computed axial tomography (CAT) scan obtains three-dimensional X-ray images of the body by using computer-enhanced technology. Patients undergoing CAT scanning are placed in a cylindrical trough over which the CAT machine traverses. In the headache workup, the CAT scan is used to detect brain injury that may indicate tumors, infection, or stroke.

The procedure takes about thirty minutes, and some individuals experience claustrophobia while lying in the CAT scan's cylindrical tunnel. If you have a history of claustrophobia, your provider can prescribe a mild sedative for you to take prior to undergoing the study.

MAGNETIC RESONANCE IMAGING SCAN

A magnetic resonance imaging (MRI) scan obtains images of the body by placing it in a magnetic field. Patients undergoing MRI scanning are placed in a cylindrical tunnel containing a strong magnetic field. The magnet interacts with hydrogen atoms in the body to create an image of various body structures. A computer converts the images into a picture of the tissue being studied. Sometimes a dye is injected into the vein to help "light up" this area.

The procedure takes about thirty minutes, and again, you may experience feelings of claustrophobia while going through the MRI scan's cylindrical tunnel. In this case as well, your provider can prescribe a mild sedative. You cannot undergo MRI if you have metal implanted in your body such as orthopedic screws, braces, and metal plates, because these objects can damage the MRI equipment and distort the images. However, regular dental fillings pose no problem.

OTHER DIAGNOSTIC TESTING AND PROCEDURES

Occasionally, headache patients undergo other testing to rule out conditions not clearly delineated by the usual imaging studies. These studies include the positron-emission tomography (PET) scan, the electroencephalogram (EEG), the electroystagamogram (ENG), an angiogram or arteriogram, and a spinal tap.

PET SCAN

A PET scan is done to evaluate the brain's structure, activity, and blood vessel pattern. Individuals undergoing a PET scan are first injected with a compound containing relatively harmless radioactive isotopes that have an affinity for various chemicals in the brain (for example, glucose). The PET scanner measures particles called positrons, which are emitted as a radioisotope decays. The more positrons emitted from a specific part of the brain, the more activity is taking place there. PET scans are used primarily to diagnose strokes and other brain dysfunctions.

EEG

The EEG represents a recording of the brain's electrical impulses, akin to an electrocardiogram that records the electrical activity of the heart. The recording is obtained by attaching tiny electrodes to the patient's scalp, and the entire procedure is painless.

ENG

An ENG records the electrical impulses of the eye muscles. This study is ordered to rule out tumors on the cranial nerves located in the head and neck.

ANGIOGRAM

An angiogram, also called an arteriogram, is done to evaluate the patency and layout of specific arteries such as those that carry blood to the brain. This study is ordered when there is a strong suspicion of arterial narrowing. An arteriogram involves placing a catheter in an artery in your groin and advancing it to the carotid arteries in your neck. Contrast dye is then injected into the blood vessel and a series of pictures taken to map out the architecture and determine the health of the arteries.

SPINAL TAP

A spinal tap, also referred to as a lumbar puncture, involves placing a needle into the lumbar portion of the spinal canal to remove spinal fluid for analysis or to relieve pressure on the brain. This procedure is done if it becomes necessary to rule out a tumor or brain infection or if the spinal fluid is abnormally high (as in the condition called *pseudotumor cerebri*).

Lumbar puncture incurs the risk of infection. After the procedure, be sure to lie flat on your back for about four hours to prevent leakage of spinal fluid. A small percentage of individuals undergoing a spinal tap experience benign headaches for days or weeks afterward.

IN SUMMARY

- The headache workup involves a thorough headache history, a complete physical examination, select laboratory and X-ray studies, and certain diagnostic procedures.
- The headache history involves questions about your head pain, past medical conditions, and your family history.
- The typical physical examination checks your vital signs and vision; you may also receive a neurological and head-to-toe, hands-on evaluation by your health care provider.
- Laboratory testing includes urinalysis, complete blood count, chemistry panel, and thyroid function tests.
- Common radiographic testing includes CAT and MRI scans. Uncommon radiographs and procedures include PET scans, EEGs, ENGs, arteriograms, and spinal taps.

CHAPTER THIRTEEN

Working with Your Health Care Team

A study conducted by the National Headache Foundation found that the biggest obstacle to effective treatment for migraines was a lack of communication between health care providers and headache patients.[1] In the study, many physicians felt that in order to foster the efficacy of the interaction, patients should educate themselves before coming in for each health visit. Clinicians also believed that recording headaches in a diary was very beneficial to both patients and doctors.

WHAT TO EXPECT FROM YOUR HEALTH CARE TEAM

As a chronic pain sufferer, your immediate priority is to get rid of your nagging headache. An effective health care provider should also have this as her goal.[2] The clinician should be your ally, advocating on your behalf with all her effort. You should expect the following attributes and services from physicians and other clinicians taking care of you:

- Honesty. (You should also be honest.) Your provider should honestly tell you what she can do for you.
- A complete appraisal of your condition. You should be afforded a full explanation of what your physical examination showed, all laboratory and radiographic studies, and any prescribed medications.

- A reasonable amount of your provider's time. As you may be well aware, doctors and other health care employees are an overworked group of professionals. Enough time should be allotted, however, to allow you to ask your questions and get complete answers.

GETTING THE MOST OUT OF EACH HEALTH CARE VISIT

Because chronic headaches can be a complicated condition, the evaluation may take time. There are no blood tests to establish the diagnosis, so the evaluation focuses on ruling out other conditions and a trial of medications to determine the right ones. Avoid making an appointment for other health problems when you go in for evaluation of your head pain. With two minutes left during a visit for unrelated health problems, don't make the mistake of saying, "By the way, I also have been getting a lot of headaches for the past eight months." This is the best way to ensure a slipshod evaluation of your headache.

Other tips on getting the most out of your health care visit include:

- Prepare for the office visit. Do your research. Learn everything there is to know about your chronic condition. Write down all your questions before your appointment.
- Visit your doctor specifically for your headache. Headache evaluation is complicated, and trying to be seen for multiple problems during the same visit will likely result in substandard care for your headache.
- Be honest with your provider about your symptoms, your current medications, and your fears. He can help you much more if he knows your comments, concerns, and suggestions.
- Be proactive during the visit. Take notes. Remember, the wise medical consumer is a coequal partner with her health care practitioner.

- Be aware that primary headaches are a biological condition with no definite cure, but that the symptoms can be effectively controlled.
- Focus on solutions.
- Ask for detailed instructions on medication and nonmedication management of your condition.
- Follow up regularly with your doctor at recommended intervals.

KEEPING A HEADACHE DIARY

The success of the medical encounter depends greatly on the accuracy of the information the patient provides the clinician, because an evaluation and treatment plan are only as effective as the history you provide. The medical history should include what, where, when, and how severe, as well as previous self-management measures and how they worked.

Perhaps the most important tool in headache evaluation, treatment, and prevention is the headache diary. (See Appendix A.) Clinicians can glean valuable

IT IS OUR DUTY TO REMEMBER AT ALL TIMES AND ANEW THAT MEDICINE IS NOT ONLY A SCIENCE, BUT ALSO THE ART OF LETTING OUR OWN INDIVIDUALITY INTERACT WITH THE INDIVIDUALITY OF THE PATIENT.

ALBERT SCHWEITZER

information, such as the underlying causes of head pain and its patterns, from the diary. As we discussed in chapter 3, a number of internal and external factors and substances have been implicated in headaches. The best way to identify these factors and substances is to keep a diary of your symptoms, including the time of day the headache began, the weather conditions, where were you when the pain kicked off, and the relationship of the headache to your menstrual period, if appropriate.

Once headache triggers have been identified, some sufferers are able to conquer their chronic headache solely by avoiding them. Wouldn't it be nice to get rid of your debilitating head pain just by avoiding certain foods?

Obviously, this is the cheapest, safest, and most painless way to treat a chronic condition.

FORMING A PROVIDER/PATIENT PARTNERSHIP

Our premise from the outset of this book has been that the patient should be a comanager, along with the health care practitioner, in the treatment of his chronic medical problem. In our diverse and complex health care system, largely dominated by managed care, the success of the health encounter is a shared responsibility of the patient and provider. Becoming a partner with your health care team is the key to successfully managing your recurrent headaches.

JIM'S STORY

A shy and unassuming gentleman in his late thirties, Jim was well liked. He got along with everyone and could be counted on to support whatever position was presented to him. When Jim sought medical care for his chronic headache, he never questioned his diagnosis or treatment plan. He was a good patient. Deep inside, though, Jim was in turmoil. He was not getting better and was privately upset about his doctor's choice of treatment. He grew more and more frustrated with his reluctance to speak up and to "rock the boat."

At a retreat for men organized by his church, Jim was encouraged to talk about his fears, frustrations, and concerns. He was immediately relieved after discussing his uncontrollable chronic headaches.

IN SUMMARY

- Your health care practitioner should be honest with you, give you a reasonable amount of his time, and provide you a complete appraisal of your condition.
- To get the most from your medical evaluation, you should prepare for the visit, make an appointment specifically for your headache, be honest with your provider, be a proactive participant, accept the biological facts about your condition, focus on solutions, get written instructions, and follow up as recommended.
- Keep a headache diary; it's the best tool to facilitate the diagnosis and management of your headache.
- Form a coequal partnership with your health provider.

CHAPTER FOURTEEN

Which Practitioners Should Evaluate and Treat Your Headaches?

In this age of medical specialization and high-tech medical devices, it is hard to determine which health care provider is best suited to evaluate and treat which medical problem. Unfortunately, chronic headaches are often misdiagnosed as other head and neck disorders. For example, the tinnitus (ringing in the ears) of basilar artery migraines has been mistakenly linked to the tinnitus of hearing loss, prompting referral to a hearing specialist rather than to a headache specialist. In some cases, this has led to years of untreated headaches, while the frustrated hearing specialist searches in vain for a hearing disorder, sometimes prescribing a hearing aid as a last resort.

Understandably, most laypersons are confused about the role of, say, an internist or a neurologist in caring for people with recurrent headaches. After all, a neurologist is an internist with additional training in the evaluation and management of conditions of the nerves and brain, including headache. Would you be better off with the broad-based knowledge of an internist versus the narrow scope of a neurologist, or vice versa? Which providers are qualified to evaluate and treat your headaches? Who should you start with? Of all the qualified doctors, which one charges less? Would the less expensive family doctor be just as qualified as the more expensive neurologist in evaluating and treating your headaches? We'll answer these and other questions for you and provide practical guidance to help you understand the position each health care practitioner holds in the headache medicine hierarchy.

Because complementary and alternative medicine is fast becoming an accepted way to treat many conditions, you may hear about this form of treatment as you look for a cure for your chronic headaches. We'll discuss the merits of homeopathy, acupuncture, and massage therapy in the treatment of chronic headaches.

Many specialized headache clinics operate around the country; the famous Diamond Headache Center, the Jefferson Headache Center, and the New England Center for Headache are but a few such centers. In this chapter, we'll offer a brief discussion of these headache centers, including their strengths and weaknesses.

CONVENTIONAL PRACTITIONERS

PRIMARY CARE PHYSICIANS

The vast majority of patients seeking health care for chronic headaches consult primary care physicians. Most of these patients have primary headache syndromes that can be competently diagnosed and managed by primary care doctors and nonphysician practitioners, such as physician assistants and nurse practitioners, working under a doctor's supervision.

What is the extent of a primary care doctor's training, and is such a doctor qualified to manage recurrent headaches? The American Medical Association defines a primary care physician as one who provides general health care to patients with such self-limiting ailments as the common cold, gastrointestinal infections, vaginal infections, and headaches. These doctors include family physicians, pediatricians, and general internists.

Primary care doctors have a broad-based medical knowledge that also makes them good general medical diagnosticians and therapists. For example, their expertise allows them to recognize if a patient's headaches stem from dehydration, sinusitis, hay fever, or migraine syndrome, and to competently manage any of these conditions.

Family Physicians

The family physician practices the lion's share of primary care medicine. These versatile providers are well positioned to evaluate and manage most headache syndromes and to make referrals to specialists when indicated. Health maintenance organizations and other managed care organizations consider family medicine physicians "gatekeepers" who manage most medical problems and defer to specialists when indicated.

General Internists

Don't confuse the role and qualification of internists (doctors who specialize in internal medicine) with those of interns (recent medical graduates in the first year of post–medical school training). Internists or internal medicine physicians complete three years post–medical school training in the management of a variety of illnesses, such as high blood pressure, thyroid disease, arthritis, and headaches. The training and experience of internists allows them to recognize uncommon medical conditions, such as thyroid disease and high blood pressure, that can mimic primary headaches. Some general internists go on to subspecialize in specific internal medicine subspecialties such as cardiology, neurology, and rheumatology.

> TO ME THE IDEAL DOCTOR WOULD BE A MAN ENDOWED WITH PROFOUND KNOWLEDGE OF LIFE AND OF THE SOUL, INTUITIVELY DIVINING ANY SUFFERING OR DISORDER OF WHATEVER KIND, AND RESTORING PEACE BY HIS MERE PRESENCE.
>
> **HENRI AMIEL**

Pediatricians

Pediatricians are trained in the medical care of children. Like family physicians, pediatricians practice a broad range of medical care. Their training and experience provide them with the expertise to evaluate and treat a wide variety of childhood diseases, including headaches.

Osteopaths

Osteopaths are physicians trained in the medical model that the physical body, the mind, and the spirit are interdependent and inseparable.[1] Osteopaths undergo the same medical school training as their allopathic (medical doctor) colleagues, with additional training in manipulation of the musculoskeletal system. Today, most osteopathic physicians (D.O.s) practice in the same medical and surgical specialties as do their M.D. colleagues. A few D.O.s exclusively practice osteopathic manipulation (OM).

Osteopaths who use OM to treat some headaches perform OMs on applicable bones, joints, and muscles. OM aims to improve range of motion, restore joint mobility and alignment, stimulate body functions, and increase circulation.

Other Primary Care Providers

Other nonphysician primary care practitioners who care for headache patients include physician assistants and nurse practitioners. These providers work under the supervision of a physician to evaluate and manage medical conditions traditionally within the domain of a physician. Physician assistants and nurse practitioners are trained to take patients' histories; examine them; order appropriate laboratory, radiographic, and other studies; and develop and implement treatment plans. These clinicians consult with their physician preceptors for practice guidance.

SPECIALTY PHYSICIANS

Physician specialists specialize and practice in one narrow area of medicine. Specialists who care for headache sufferers include neurologists, headache specialists, and psychiatrists.

Neurologists

Neurologists are general internists who subspecialize in diseases of the nerves and brain. Therefore, they are the best-qualified doctors to diagnose and treat headaches. Because neurologists have specialized knowledge of the brain and nerves, they can recognize uncommon conditions, such as brain tumors and brain infections, that can present with headaches. Family physicians, pediatricians, and internists refer difficult headache cases to neurologists.

Headache Specialists

Headache specialists are physicians whose practice is largely devoted to the management of headaches. Technically speaking, headache management is not a distinct medical specialty, as is cardiology or orthopedics. Therefore, any physician can call herself a headache specialist. Most headache specialists, however, are neurologists, internists, and anesthesiologists.

The obvious advantage of being cared for by these clinicians is their advanced level of expertise in evaluating and managing recalcitrant headaches. Primary care providers can competently manage most people with straightforward headaches; only a small percentage of chronic headache sufferers ever need the expertise of a headache specialist.

Psychiatrists

These physicians specialize in the evaluation and management of mental, emotional, and behavioral disorders. If your headaches are caused by or result from psychiatric disorders, your primary care provider or headache specialist might suggest that you see a psychiatrist.

OTHER SPECIALISTS

Other specialists care for secondary headache patients, and although they usually take self-referrals, we recommend that you check with your primary care provider before seeking the care of a specialist. These practitioners can prove to be very expensive and you may go from specialist to specialist (for example, choosing a surgeon instead of an allergist), needlessly spending lots of money before finding the right professional.

If your headache is caused by a problem with your vision, you may be referred to an optometrist or ophthalmologist. If you suffer from severe allergies, you'll likely be seen by an allergist. A general dentist or oral surgeon may be consulted if a jaw joint problem is causing your head and face pain.

Otolaryngologists, commonly referred to as ENT surgeons, take care of ear, nose, and throat problems, such as sinus disease and tinnitus, that can manifest as chronic headaches. Finally, orthopedic surgeons and neurosurgeons evaluate and manage neck and spine problems such as arthritis and ruptured disks in the neck.

NONPHYSICIAN PRACTITIONERS

A number of nonphysician practitioners care for headache patients. These clinicians include chiropractors, physical and occupational therapists, and psychologists.

CHIROPRACTORS

Daniel David Palmer of Point Perry, Ontario, founded chiropractic medicine in the late 1800s. Palmer believed that diseases resulted from subluxed vertebrae impinging on spinal nerves, and that correcting the subluxation allowed the nerves to resume their normal function. Today's chiropractors are nonphysician providers who specialize in the treatment of disorders of the musculoskeletal system. These practitioners evaluate and manage a large variety of conditions such as low back pain, hip pain, and headaches related to malalignment of the neck.

Chiropractors take medical histories, perform physical examinations, and order X-rays to diagnose medical problems. In addition, they employ spinal manipulation, pressure, massages, and other maneuvers and special devices to restore the spinal vertebrae to their normal alignment.

PHYSICAL AND OCCUPATIONAL THERAPISTS

Chronic pain has a way of robbing you of your physical strength, endurance, and confidence. Physical therapists use heat, ice, special exercises, sound waves, and other means to treat disorders of the musculoskeletal system. (See chapter 15.) Occupational therapists focus on helping you develop proper physical dexterity and body posture to take on difficult day-to-day tasks at work and at home.

PSYCHOLOGISTS

Psychologists are nonphysician mental health practitioners who are trained to evaluate and manage mental, emotional, and behavioral disorders. If your headaches are psychologically based or have psychological components, such as anxiety, anger, and depression, your primary care provider or headache specialist might suggest that you see a psychologist. These practitioners teach self-improvement skills such as stress management and relaxation techniques.

COMPLEMENTARY AND ALTERNATIVE PRACTITIONERS

The practice of alternative medicine, sometimes called complementary therapy, is rapidly gaining popularity among Americans and Canadians. Physicians and other conventional practitioners on both sides of the border are gradually warming to acupuncture, homeopathy, naturopathy, and massage therapy as legitimate medical treatments.

ACUPUNCTURISTS

Acupuncture originated in China over 5,000 years ago and its popularity spread throughout Asia and eventually to Europe and the New World. During the 1900s, preeminent physician Sir William Osler endorsed the practice of acupuncture. Nevertheless, acceptance of the practice in the United States waned for the next fifty years, until the 1970s saw a resurgence of acceptance of acupuncture among Americans, probably aided by closer political and cultural ties between the United States and China. The American Medical Association and the World Health Organization endorse acupuncture as a legitimate treatment for a wide array of illnesses.

Today, American acupuncturists, many of whom are licensed physicians, are certified to practice in all fifty states and the District of Columbia. Acupuncturists see over twelve million patients for a variety of ailments ranging from irritable bowels to chronic headaches. Check with your health care provider to see if you are a candidate for acupuncture therapy, either as a supplement to other treatments or as a primary treatment. In chapter 15, we'll discuss in detail the basic philosophy behind acupuncture and the purported mechanism of efficacy as reported by proponents of acupuncture.

HOMEOPATHS

The practice of homeopathy dates back to the 1790s, when German physician Samuel Hahnemann reported success in prescribing small doses of natural substances that stimulated the immune system to protect the body.[2] Our current immunization program employs the same principle; we administer minute amounts of inactive parts of a virus or bacteria to stimulate the body's immune system to make antibodies to fight these germs.

Today, homeopathic physicians use a variety of substances derived from flowers, roots, berries, snake venom, and other sources to relieve epilepsy, diabetes, chronic pain, and other conditions. The basic philosophy of homeopathy is: "Treat like with like." Homeopaths prescribe diluted substances that cause the same symptoms as the ones of which the patient complains. For example, a small dose of belladonna, which causes a slight headache, is used to treat a throbbing headache.

According to noted physician, medical researcher, and author Dr. Isadore Rosenfeld of Cornell Medical Center in New York, questions remain about the ability of homeopathy to withstand the rigors of scientific testing.[3] Can the benefits of homeopathic medicines be counted on to provide across-the-board cures like those of penicillin and ibuprofen? Recently, Dutch researchers declined to lend legitimacy to over one hundred homeopathic studies submitted for conventional scientific scrutiny, finding fault with the basic scientific methodologies employed in these studies.

This finding, however, does not automatically dismiss the benefits of homeopathy. Dr. Rosenfeld believes that homeopathic therapy still performs better than placebo. He points to the multibillion-dollar homeopathic business and the anecdotal claims of thousands of people. As long as the condition is not life threatening, homeopathy appears to be a safe alternative when conventional medicine doesn't have a good answer. Our recommendation is that you examine your own condition with the help of your physician and decide whether the potential benefits will outweigh any possible harm.

NATUROPATHS

An American osteopathic physician, Dr. Randolph Stone, pioneered the practice of naturopathy in the 1900s. Naturopathy is based on the belief that when the human body gets ill, it's better to employ a proper diet, fresh air, exercise, and rest, as well as other natural modalities, to help the body reestablish its own state of good health. Unlike conventional medical practitioners, naturopaths don't believe in "finding a disease and killing it."

In addition to a proper diet, exercise, and rest, naturopathic practitioners employ herbal medicines, nutritional therapies, acupuncture, acupressure, and massage therapy to help restore good health. While acknowledging that conventional treatments are at times necessary, naturopaths believe that many conditions such as chronic headaches can be effectively managed through the principles of naturopathy.

MASSAGE THERAPISTS

Massage therapy is rapidly gaining popularity as a way to obtain total body relaxation and to feel rejuvenated. Fueled by the stress caused by the rat race of the 1980s and 1990s, massage spas are springing up everywhere in the United States. Industry analysts report a one-billion-dollar-a-year business, citing over 1,000 spas around the country—a 47 percent increase since 1997.

Massage therapists emphasize holistic health measures that include hydrotherapy, facial massages, skin exfoliation, reflexology, meditation, and aromatherapy. They use water, color, sound, light, aromas, and even herbs to appeal to their patrons' senses. Clients are served herbal tea and healthy foods in a delightful atmosphere. We doubt that massage therapy will completely replace your migraine medication, but it may be an excellent adjunct and may lessen your dependence on drugs.

CHRONIC PAIN AND HEADACHE CENTERS

Finding the right practitioner is one thing, but how about finding the right facility to care for your headaches? When do you need to go to a center that specializes in chronic pain or chronic headache pain?

As we said earlier, primary care physicians can effectively manage most primary headache sufferers. A small percentage of sufferers, however, have headaches that defy the best primary care efforts. They fail to respond to multiple drug regimens and develop drug dependency, become depressed and anxious, develop musculoskeletal deconditioning, have failed relationships, and lose their jobs. These individuals are certainly candidates for specialized centers and clinics that provide a comprehensive approach to chronic pain management.

The common philosophy of chronic pain centers is that chronic pain affects many aspects of your life (work, family, and physical and psychological health) and therefore requires a broad treatment approach.[4] Chronic pain centers and headache pain centers offer a multidisciplinary team of experts ranging from physician headache specialists to physical therapists. Some offer acupuncture, massage therapy, and dietary counseling. Some programs are affiliated with medical schools and large medical centers and have many diagnostic and therapeutic resources available.

What are the advantages and disadvantages of these specialized programs? First, chronic headache centers do nothing but take care of chronic headache sufferers. This narrow focus brings a high degree of headache expertise to bear and facilitates continuity of care. These centers have the resources to comprehensively address all aspects of chronic pain.

The biggest disadvantage of these specialized programs is that they are expensive; care can run into the thousands of dollars. Some insurance carriers may not pick up the entire bill for such in-depth evaluation and treatment of headache. Because no national standards dictate what constitutes a "headache treatment program," some poorly equipped and staffed clinics may pass themselves off as headache clinics.

Talk to your primary care physician or neurologist to see if you are a candidate for a headache treatment program. For more information, check with the American Council for Headache Education or the National Headache Foundation. (See Appendix B.) These organizations are dedicated to helping the headache consumer obtain good care to relieve unnecessary suffering.

IN SUMMARY

- Various primary care providers, including family physicians, physician assistants, and pediatricians, treat primary headache syndromes. Headache specialists, neurologists, and internists also treat primary headaches.
- Chiropractors, physical therapists, psychiatrists, and psychologists also provide primary and adjunctive care for headache disorders.
- Acupuncturists are licensed to manage a variety of ailments, including chronic headache.
- Homeopaths prescribe small amounts of natural substances that stimulate the body's immune system.
- Naturopaths recommend dietary and fluid strategies and preventive nutrition to treat recurrent headaches and other illnesses.
- Massage therapists use a variety of measures, including hydrotherapy, facial massage, and aromatherapy, to obtain total body relaxation and rejuvenation.
- Headache and chronic pain centers provide a multidisciplinary approach to evaluating and treating chronic headache. While these programs are very effective, they are also very expensive.

CHAPTER FIFTEEN

Managing Your Headaches Without Drugs

Does every headache sufferer need drugs to manage his head pain? Because headaches can be triggered by environmental and dietary factors, social habits, and medication use, might your headaches be kept at bay by avoiding these triggers? How about physical exercise, acupuncture, acupressure, massage therapy, and biofeedback when trigger avoidance is not possible or not enough?

Before introducing you to the drugs used to treat headaches, we'd like to review the many nondrug measures that you might be able to employ in your quest to become headache free. In recent years, more physicians have been emphasizing nondrug, or nonpharmacological, management—once considered unorthodox treatment—for patients with many chronic medical problems, such as high blood pressure, low back pain, and chronic headaches. Recent research has shown that lifestyle strategies such as a balanced diet, physiological therapies such as acupuncture and physical therapy, and mind/body strategies such as biofeedback can help relieve underlying conditions (for example, stiff muscles and emotional stress) that cause some types of headaches. Even when drugs are necessary, these various therapies can help medications work better.

In this chapter, we'll discuss the role of lifestyle modifications and physiological therapies in the management and prevention of chronic headaches. We'll also review the merits of so-called mind/body therapies such as stress management, biofeedback, transcendental meditation, yoga, and creative visualization. It is important to remember that only your health care provider can determine if these strategies and measures are right for you. If you plan to employ these approaches to enhance the management of your chronic headache, don't stop taking your medications without your clinician's blessings.

LIFESTYLE MODIFICATIONS

A large body of evidence shows that the way you live your life influences your chances of developing certain diseases, such as diabetes and high blood pressure, dubbed by many in medicine to be lifestyle-induced diseases. Even when a genetic predisposition exists, most lifestyle-induced conditions develop due to a sedentary lifestyle and a diet of high-fat, high-calorie foods. Eliminating these lifestyle factors under physician supervision is relatively safe, inexpensive, and easy to accomplish. Let's look at the merits and means of dietary modification and regular aerobic physical activity.

DIETARY MODIFICATION

In chapter 3, we talked about dietary factors that trigger headaches in susceptible individuals. According to physician and author Dr. Paula Maas, fully 10 percent of all migraine headache sufferers implicate certain foods, beverages, nutritional supplements, or food additives as triggers of their head pain.[1] The exact mechanisms by which foods trigger headaches aren't entirely clear. Nevertheless, the most common foods identified as triggers of migraine, cluster, and other forms of headaches include chocolate, monosodium glutamate (MSG), amines, nitrates, sulfites, artificial sweeteners, and nuts. Gamma-aminobutyric acid (GABA), salt, ice cream, and caffeine are additional culprits.

Like food triggers, vitamin and mineral deficiencies and hypoglycemia (low blood sugar) can lead to headache flare-ups. Most authorities agree that if you are unable to strictly stick to a balanced diet, you should take a daily vitamin and mineral supplement. Refined sugars, which can make your blood sugar level unstable, should be avoided at all costs.

REGULAR AEROBIC PHYSICAL ACTIVITY

If you don't exercise, you should set a date and start a regular aerobic exercise program after discussing your plans with your primary care provider. Many health education organizations, including the National Institutes of Health, recommend that all adults and children engage in thirty minutes or more of moderate-intensity physical activity on most days of the week. This recommendation is based on a large body of research that unequivocally shows that aerobic fitness improves overall health and increases longevity. In clinical studies, aerobic exercise has been shown to significantly reduce cluster headaches.[2]

Benefits of Exercise

Regular aerobic exercise, such as walking, biking, jogging, swimming, dancing, and hiking, increases blood levels of endorphins, the body's natural morphinelike chemicals. Persons with comorbid conditions such as high stress levels, diabetes, and elevated cholesterol may also benefit from regular physical activity. Other benefits of regular exercise include enhanced self-confidence, opportunity for socializing, better muscle tone and strength, increased lean body mass, improved digestion, improved sleep, and an overall healthy mind-set.[3] Remember, however, it will take time for you to realize these benefits. Don't give up after a few days if your headaches continue or your self-confidence fails to go through the roof.

Set Realistic Exercise Goals

If you haven't exercised for a while, you should start slowly and work your way up to your desired fitness level.[4] Set an achievable goal, and remember that incremental goal-setting is an advisable strategy. Doing too much too soon will likely result in fatigue, burnout, and possibly injury. If you choose walking, start with perhaps a moderately paced walk, and then increase the speed or distance based on your exercise tolerance and rate of improvement. Remember that progress may be just the incentive you need to stick to your exercise routine. A lack of progress provides the perfect excuse to conclude, "This is not working; it's been eight days and I still can't walk more than half a mile."

What's My Target Heart Rate?

You should exercise at a level of intensity that achieves between 60 and 80 percent of your target heart rate. You can calculate your target heart rate using the following formula: 220 minus your age in years, then multiply by 60 or 80 percent. If you are forty years old, you'd calculate your target heart rate as follows:

$$220 - 40 = 180 \times 0.6 = 108$$
(if you use the 60% rate)

or

$$220 - 40 = 180 \times 0.8 = 144$$
(if you use the 80% rate)

Thus, if you are forty years old, your pulse during exertion should be maintained between 108 and 144 beats per minute.

How About Isometric Exercises?

Lifting weights can be lots of fun if you use the proper technique. Poor technique can lead to serious injuries involving the neck, arms, back, knees, and ankles. If you are unfamiliar with weight-lifting procedures, you should seek help from people versed in the proper technique, such as athletic trainers or fitness instructors. If you have high blood pressure—especially if you are over forty years old—you should check with your health care provider before engaging in isometric exercises.

Barriers to Exercising

There are very few barriers to exercising, but many excuses.[5] Common excuses for not exercising include:

- "I'm too busy."
- "It's winter and dark during the time when I can exercise."
- "It's raining."
- "I have a physical impairment."
- "I'm too old for that."
- "I can't afford to buy expensive exercise gear."

It takes only 90 to 120 minutes each week to exercise. Whether it's less time watching television or talking on the telephone, everyone can find time to exercise. Walking at lunchtime is one way to get around the excuse of "not enough daylight time." You should have an indoor exercise program, such as a stationary bike, for days when the weather precludes outside activity.

Age and most physical impairments are not barriers to exercising. New research indicates that healthy people in their seventies and eighties can safely undertake physically appropriate exercise on a regular basis.[6] Even nursing home residents can benefit from modest forms of exercise. An effective exercise program need not be elaborate or expensive. For instance, walking requires a modest investment in shoes and clothing.

Exercise Under Advisement

If you are over age forty or if you have a personal or family history of cardiovascular disease, consult your doctor before engaging in vigorous physical activities. Discuss your training program and find out if your age or any conditions you may have may preclude certain activities.

PHYSIOLOGICAL THERAPIES

Except for physical therapy, most physiological therapies have their roots in ancient medical practices such as traditional Chinese medicine. Many chronic headache sufferers have benefited immensely from acupuncture, acupressure, shiatsu, physical therapy, and massage therapy.

ACUPUNCTURE

The American Medical Association, the largest and most prestigious physician-advocate group in the United States, recently endorsed acupuncture as an acceptable treatment for a number of medical conditions, including arthritis and headaches. As we said in chapter 14, acupuncture has its origins in China and has been used by Chinese health practitioners for over 5,000 years. Ancient Asian medical practitioners believed that our well-being is controlled by a life-force energy, called *ki* in Japanese, or *chi* in Chinese, that protects the body from disease. Opposing body forces, called *yin* and *yang*, must be in balance before chi can flow smoothly to ensure good physical, emotional, and spiritual health. The premise of acupuncture is that this life-force energy flows from head to toe via lines or *meridians*, with energy access points, called *tsubos*, to each meridian. The smooth flow of bioenergy through the meridians can sometimes become blocked due to stress or muscle tension. The acupuncturist manipulates the tsubos to restore balance to the flow of the body's energy and health to the organ system served by a given meridian.

Proponents of acupuncture believe that many medical problems, such as asthma and chronic headaches, have their origins in the altered flow pattern of chi. This leads to an imbalance between yin and yang and, in the case of headaches, stiff muscles lead to head and neck pain. Western scientists suggest a different therapeutic model to explain how acupuncture works. Many believe that needle stimulation of acupuncture points causes the release of morphinelike substances, called endorphins, by the brain. Endorphins kill pain and relieve backaches, headaches, and other forms of musculoskeletal pain. This might explain why some people feel euphoric for hours or even weeks after acupuncture treatment.

Acupuncture has enjoyed rising popularity in the United States since the 1970s, largely aided by the establishment of closer political and cultural relations with China. Today, many conventional physicians use acupuncture to supplement painkilling drugs, exercise, ice massages, and other pain therapy. Needle placement depends on the type of ailment being treated. For headache, needles are commonly placed in the middle of the web area on the hands between the thumb and index finger, points on either side of the nose, a point at the base of the skull, and a point between the large and second toes.[7] Acupuncture has proven effective in treating tension-type and migraine headaches, and headaches associated with TMJ syndrome.

Some of the most common conditions for which acupuncture has become first-line treatment, and for which the National Institute on Drug Abuse has endorsed its use, include drug, tobacco, and alcohol abuse. Alternative medicine researcher Dr. Isadore Rosenfeld recommends acupuncture for conditions such as asthma and back pain, but discourages its use as anesthesia during major surgery.

ACUPRESSURE/SHIATSU

Acupressure, also known as shiatsu, uses the same principles as acupuncture. Instead of needles, however, acupressurists use their fingertips, palms, elbows, knees, and feet to stimulate the acupuncture points to produce the same results as acupuncture.

The premise of acupressure is the same as that for acupuncture, in that energy flows throughout the body along meridians, and may become blocked due to stress or muscle tension. The accupressurist manipulates these access points to restore balance to the flow of the body's energy and health to the organ system served by a given meridian. Acupressure can successfully treat migraine, sinus, and tension-type headaches and TMJ syndrome.[8] Most individuals can easily learn to perform pressure-point self-treatments with little instruction. There are many books on the subject, but it is best to first consult an acupressurist.

PHYSICAL THERAPY

Physical therapy is a branch of rehabilitative medicine that employs a variety of therapeutic modalities to treat disorders of the musculoskeletal system. Licensed physical therapists use heat, ice, special exercises, sound waves, traction, and other means to relieve sprains, strains, and pain, including headache pain. Physical therapy aims to strengthen weak muscles, improve the range of motion of joints, increase body awareness, and ultimately to treat and prevent acute and chronic pain.[9]

In some states, physical therapists require a formal referral from a physician or other nonphysician provider in order to administer therapy. For headache pain, physical therapists perform manual manipulation of the head, neck, and shoulders and use transcutaneous electrical nerve stimulation (TENS). TENS is an effective modality that uses a pulsating electrical impulse to stimulate nerves in order to treat head and neck ache accompanied by poorly conditioned muscles and other connective tissue. TENS may interfere with pacemaker function and is therefore contraindicated in people who have these devices.

Physical therapists also apply traction to relieve shortened neck muscles that can cause headache. For home care strategies and body awareness, you may be instructed to consciously improve your posture and to do neck and shoulder exercises. Shoulder rolls take a few seconds and can be done a few times throughout the day, even at work. Standing with your arms hanging relaxed at your sides, make big circles with your shoulders by lifting them toward your ears. Next, push your shoulders forward, down, back, and up again in big circles for five to ten repetitions. Repeat this motion in the opposite direction.

MASSAGE THERAPY

Massage therapy is a popular alternative therapy in the United States. In fact, it is the third most popular form of therapy for musculoskeletal ailments, after relaxation techniques and chiropractic care. Today, massage therapists are licensed (in about twenty-five states) to treat a number of ailments, including low back pain, hamstring strain, and chronic headaches. Massage therapy encompasses a number of massage disciplines, including Swedish massage and reflexology.

The Swedish School

Swedish massage, developed by Peter Ling of Sweden in the late 1840s, uses stroking, kneading, tapping, and rubbing to release muscle tension and pain, including headache pain.[10] A Swedish masseuse or masseur utilizes oils to increase circulation, improve muscle tone, and bring about total body relaxation.

If you are considering massage therapy for your headaches, check with your primary care clinician before doing so. People with certain conditions, such as high blood pressure and circulatory problems, can be harmed during vigorous massages.

Reflexology

This popular form of massage therapy, performed by over 25,000 practitioners worldwide, aims to promote relaxation and energy balance through stimulation of pressure points on the soles of the feet, palms, and ears.[11] Originating in China about 5,000 years ago, this therapy was introduced to the West in the early 1900s by Dr. William Fitzgerald, an ear, nose, and throat surgeon, who applied these techniques to relax his patients during surgery. Fitzgerald's pioneering work spawned a large following, and over the years reflexology has become a popular form of relaxation therapy, with reflexologists working in many locations throughout the United States and Canada.

Reflexologists claim to be able to help a number of chronic conditions, including chronic constipation, asthma, and headaches. Exactly how reflexology works is still a matter of speculation, but reflexology proponents believe that pressure exerted at strategic points reduces the buildup of lactic acid (a by-product of muscle contractions that can cause discomfort in muscle tissue). Another theory holds that reflexology massages out calcium crystals that accumulate and irritate nerve endings; podiatrists and other conventional practitioners have dismissed this particular theory as science fiction.

Whatever its mechanism, reflexology appears to be a reasonable approach to managing most forms of chronic headaches. It is safe, but you should check with your doctor before pursuing it. You might want to avoid reflexology therapy if you have a foot or hand injury or if you have a history of blood clots in your lower legs. If you are pregnant, you may also want to avoid reflexology. More information on reflexology can be obtained from the International Institute of Reflexology. (See Appendix B.)

MIND/BODY THERAPIES

Few would disagree that the mind influences the way the body functions. Unfortunately, research in this area is sparse, and the little we do know is based on conjecture. The more common mind/body measures include stress management, biofeedback, transcendental meditation, yoga, and creative visualization.

STRESS MANAGEMENT

Everyone has to contend with some degree of stress. Whether stress damages a particular person depends on the intensity of the stress and the strength of that person's support network, her coping skills, and her personality. Numerous studies have shown that severe stress or distress (a situation where daily stressors outstrip a person's coping resources) can negatively affect a person's health. As we said in chapter 3, stress is a common trigger of migraines and other headaches. Stress management techniques have been shown to be very effective in relieving and preventing recurrent headaches.[12]

Common, everyday stressors include deadlines, unrealistic expectations, and disappointments. Headaches are a symptom that life stressors have outstripped a person's coping resources. The following strategies have been shown to reduce the effects of stress:

- Time management
- Delegation of tasks
- Realistic expectations
- Aerobic exercise
- Practicing mind/body therapy such as biofeedback, transcendental meditation, yoga, and creative visualization

BIOFEEDBACK

Biofeedback, probably the most studied mind/body strategy, grew out of the work of psychologist Dr. Neal Miller in the 1960s. It involves using audiovisual techniques (a beeper or flashing light) to help a person see or hear various bodily functions, such as heartbeat, respiration, skin temperature, or muscle tension, that are normally involuntary. The person can then learn to voluntarily moderate these physiological functions through operant conditioning.

People undergoing biofeedback are taught to use deep relaxation, self-suggestions, and other strategies to alter the body function in question. When the feedback light flashes or the beeper beeps too often, the biofeedback trainee must use the learned techniques to alter the audiovisual signals and along with them the body functions they monitor. In the case of tension headaches, the biofeedback trainee receives feedback about his amount of scalp muscle tension. He is then taught to use self-suggestions ("I'm totally relaxed") to lessen the tension of his scalp muscles. The result is increased blood flow to scalp muscles and a sense of calm.

Your provider can help you decide whether you are a candidate for biofeedback and refer you to a reputable certified biofeedback therapist. Learning biofeedback requires practice, so don't expect to significantly decrease your muscle tension and stress after two sessions of biofeedback maneuvers. Like any new skill, it will take lots of repetition to become effective.

TRANSCENDENTAL MEDITATION

In a study published in the American Heart Association's journal *Hypertension,* transcendental meditation (TM) techniques effectively lowered high blood pressure in a group of African American men and women with high stress and other risk factors for the disease.[13] TM can also be used to manage recurrent headaches.

This mind/body tool grew out of yoga and Zen meditation. The physiological changes caused by TM include a reduction in the rate of metabolism and production of alpha brain waves, the dominant brain waves during relaxation. TM involves sitting in a comfortable position and repeating a sound or word for twenty minutes, usually twice a day. The goal is to eliminate all distracting thoughts and gain a deep sense of restful alertness. TM might not work for everyone with chronic headaches, so check with your doctor before pursuing TM as a treatment.

YOGA

This form of relaxation has its roots in Hinduism, which stresses mind-over-body discipline. Yoga has helped reduce stress and blood pressure and stop headaches in anecdotal accounts, but has not been scientifically proven to do so. Originating in Asia over 6,000 years ago, yoga has enjoyed modest popularity in the West during the past four decades, mostly among alternative health advocates.[14]

Yoga practitioners, called yogis, tout its efficacy in relieving mental and physical stress. The various schools of yoga aim to achieve union and wholeness through harmony and control. According to alternative medicine researcher Dr. Isadore Rosenfeld, yoga employs three major components: posture, breathing, and meditation.[15] Yogis teach eighty-four different postures, called *asanas,* but five are particularly significant. An important objective is to learn to assume a given position that will improve your circulation, restore normal body alignment, and help other body functions. Once this position is mastered, the student practices proper breathing techniques that fill the lungs. Next comes meditation, made possible by proper posture and breathing, that helps remove you from your environment and brings peace, enlightenment, and tranquility.

On a practical level, if yoga helps you to relax and concentrate, improves circulation in your head and neck, and reduces your recurrent headaches, then it might be for you. See how your doctor feels about it. Appendix B lists resources that can help you obtain information on yoga.

CREATIVE VISUALIZATION

The human mind has a unique capacity to create both positive and negative feelings out of thin air. For example, you may be able to make yourself nauseated just by thinking of a gruesome movie scene or hungry by thinking about a scrumptious Italian meal.

This power of the mind can be harnessed to relieve headache pain in two ways: by achieving a sense of calmness and by influencing your behavior. You can use your thoughts to foster positive imagery, bringing you a sense of calmness that may relax your scalp muscles and improve blood flow to them.

Creative visualization can have a powerful effect on your behavior. When you think of yourself as a person without illness, you'll behave like a person free of illness. For example, if you have chronic headaches and see yourself without headaches, you'll likely be motivated to relax, even during stressful times.

You can come up with your own imagery. Create a pleasant scene in your mind or recall a happy event from your past. For instance, try to remember every detail of an exhilarating family picnic or camping trip: Who was there? What happened? What did you talk about?

Creative visualization can also be used to mentally rehearse future events. You can fill in the details of the way you would like the events to occur. If it involves a personal fitness goal, for example, you can imagine yourself getting started and building up to your target heart rate and exercise tolerance and finally reaching your ideal body weight.

IN SUMMARY

- Nondrug therapies, once considered unorthodox treatments, have been shown to effectively manage chronic headaches, either alone or in conjunction with drug therapy.
- Lifestyle modifications, such as a balanced diet, regular aerobic physical activity, and physiological therapies such as acupuncture and massage therapy, can effectively manage recurrent headaches, as can mind/body therapies such as stress management, biofeedback, transcendental meditation, yoga, and creative visualization.
- Check with your health care provider before starting any of these therapies.

CHAPTER SIXTEEN

Headache Drugs

Unfortunately, nondrug strategies don't always keep headaches at bay. Some headache sufferers need medications to treat and prevent their recurrent head pain.

The Headache Sourcebook is not meant to be an authority on headache medications. Pharmacology and drug prescriptions are a very technical aspect of medical practice. It is your health care team's responsibility to educate you about any drug you are taking: how much to take, when to take it, what side effects to expect, and how it can interact with other drugs. Drug therapy is constantly changing as new research and clinical trials are published. Your physician, physician assistant, nurse practitioner, pharmacist, and other health care team members are best suited to help you decipher the complexities of drug therapy.

In this chapter, we'll introduce you to some of the drugs commonly prescribed for the treatment for chronic headaches. We'll discuss their indications, side effects, and interactions with other drugs and medical conditions. Our intention in this chapter is only to describe in general terms the drugs commonly used to treat headaches, not to recommend specific drugs. We also avoid listing dosages because the effective dosages vary widely; we don't want to give you the impression that you are being poorly treated because your dose is higher or lower than the standard.

WHEN SHOULD YOU TAKE HEADACHE DRUGS?

The best person to answer this question is your primary health care provider. He knows your health history and current health status and can recognize the point at which nondrug therapy should no longer be the mainstay of your headache management. Moreover, your clinician knows which drug should be tried first, when multiple drug therapy is indicated, and how to monitor you for drug toxicity. Here we'll simply look at some general issues and guidelines sometimes used to determine the point at which drug therapy should be employed in the management of headache pain.

Acute pain is relatively simple to treat; it clears up quickly without recurrence. Chronic pain is another matter and requires a more involved approach. Many chronic headache sufferers do perfectly well with the intermittent use of analgesics or painkillers. Others need painkillers as well as prophylactic, or preventive, therapy. Your provider is the only person who can decide whether or not you need single- or multidrug therapy.

It is important to remember that even if you are prescribed both analgesics and prophylactic drugs, you should still continue to practice nondrug strategies such as stress management and a regimen of regular aerobic exercise. Nondrug therapy may reduce the amount of medication needed and may help your current medications to work better.

LEARNING ABOUT HEADACHE DRUGS

Using drugs to treat headache is nothing new. The Cherokee Indians practiced a ritual in which a headache patient chewed ginseng, the root of a plant with medicinal value, while her forehead was rubbed gently with the palm of the right hand and a mixture of water and ginseng juice was sprinkled over the painful area.[1] Today, conventional drugs are the most commonly used headache treatment modality. In recent years, however, herbal remedies such as feverfew, valerian root, and skullcap have become popular alternatives to conventional headache drugs.

The answer to the question, "What is the best headache drug for you?" is, "The one that works." There isn't one medication that works for every headache sufferer. When indicated, your provider will recommend you take either over-the-counter or prescription drugs to manage your recurrent headaches. All drugs, including over-the-counter medications, are chemicals and potentially dangerous. The FDA mandates that the more dangerous drugs be available only by prescription. Your health care practitioner will decide which drugs are indicated for your headaches and write you a prescription, and your pharmacist will dispense it. If you take over-the-counter drugs, you'll still need the help of your doctor or pharmacist.

DRUG EFFECTS

Before you put a drug into your mouth or rub it on your skin, make sure you know everything about it: what it is, how it works, how long it takes to work, whether it needs to be taken with food, and its common side effects. Additionally, you'll want to know if the drug interacts negatively with other drugs you might take and if there are alternative medications.

All drugs can cause side effects. Two important adverse outcomes from taking painkillers are drug addiction and rebound headaches. Generally speaking, narcotics are the painkillers to be concerned about, because narcotic addition is a common problem among individuals with chronic pain syndromes.

As we discussed in chapter 3, long-term use of painkillers can trigger headache pain, causing the very symptoms they aim to stop. Rebound headaches are actually very common; the American Association for the Study of Headache reports that painkiller rebound is the most common cause of chronic daily headache.

HEADACHE ABORTIVE
MEDICATIONS

As their name implies, abortive medicines are taken to stop a condition from continuing. In the case of headache pain, abortive drugs, most often painkillers like aspirin and ibuprofen, are used to reduce the intensity and duration of a headache flare-up, and in the best case to completely stop the pain. Some headache abortive drugs also relieve the inflammation associated with vascular headaches. You've probably heard aspirin referred to as a "pain reliever," "painkiller," "fever reliever," and an "anti-inflammatory drug"; this is why aspirin, ibuprofen, and similar compounds are prescribed for headaches, arthritis, and high fever. These drugs are very versatile, hence their popularity.

> I WILL LIFT UP MINE EYES UNTO THE PILLS. ALMOST EVERYONE TAKES THEM, FROM THE HUMBLE ASPIRIN TO THE MULTI-COLOURED, KING-SIZED THREE DECKERS, WHICH PUT YOU TO SLEEP, WAKE YOU UP, STIMULATE AND SOOTHE YOU ALL IN ONE. IT IS AN AGE OF PILLS.
>
> MALCOLM MUGGERIDGE

Other pain relievers include the ergotamines, the triptans, and the sympathomimetic agents. There are other pain relievers that are very effective but don't offer the versatility of aspirin and related compounds and may potentially cause problems like medication addiction. These painkillers include codeine and morphine; although these drugs are excellent painkillers, they are also addictive when taken for extended periods and can cause sedation in most users.

NONSTEROIDAL ANTI-INFLAMMATORY DRUGS

Nonsteroidal anti-inflammatory drugs (NSAIDs) were discovered in the 1960s as a substitute for steroids (or corticosteroids) that were found to produce a number of undesirable side effects. Today, there are over one hundred different NSAIDs on the market: some sold over the counter and others pre-

TABLE 16.1 NONSTEROIDAL ANTI-INFLAMMATORY DRUGS
(NSAIDS)

Over-the-counter NSAIDs
Aspirin (Bayer, Excedrin)
Ibuprofen (Advil, Nuprin, Motrin IB)
Naproxen sodium (Aleve)

Prescription-only NSAIDs
Naproxen sodium (Anaprox, Naprosyn)
Piroxicam (Feldene)
Ketoprofen (Orudis, Actron)
Nabumetone (Relafen)

scribed by a health care practitioner. Over-the-counter NSAIDs include aspirin, ibuprofen, and naproxen sodium; indomethacin, piroxicam, and nabumetone can only be obtained with a prescription. (See table 16.1.)

NSAIDs are the most commonly prescribed painkillers for all forms of mild to moderate pain, including arthritis, joint sprains, gout, and headaches. These agents are effective analgesics and don't have the addictive properties of narcotic painkillers. They block production of prostaglandins, hormonelike substances in the body involved in pain and inflammation responses.

The most common side effect of these agents is gastrointestinal irritation, which manifests as nausea and abdominal pain. These symptoms can be reduced or eliminated by taking NSAIDs after meals or with milk. Two potentially more serious side effects of NSAIDs are stomach bleeding and ulcers, but these generally occur with long-term use of high doses of these drugs. To reduce the likelihood of bleeding and developing ulcers, individuals who need to stay on these drugs for extended periods can be prescribed a drug called *Misoprostol*. Two newer NSAIDs, celecoxib (Celebrex) and rofecoxib (Vioxx), were developed to reduce the likelihood of developing ulcers and stomach irritation.

People with a history of peptic ulcer or any form of gastrointestinal bleeding should avoid all NSAIDs. Pregnant women should not take any type of NSAID, including aspirin. As discussed earlier, NSAIDs can induce rebound headaches with chronic use.

THE ERGOTAMINES

Ergotamine is one of the oldest and most frequently used treatment for migraines and cluster headaches. This drug is derived from the fungus *Claviceps purpura,* which grows on damp and moldy grains. Discovered in the 1920s and introduced in the United States in the early 1930s, ergotamine drugs can be taken by mouth, under the tongue, as a nasal spray, as a suppository, or by injection.

The ergotamines include:

- Ergotamine tartrate (Ergostat, Ergomar)
- Ergotamine tartrate and caffeine (Wigraine or Cafergot tablet; Cafergot rectal suppository)
- Dihydroergotamine (DHE-45 injection; Migranal nasal spray)

Ergotamine relieves migraine headaches by narrowing the blood vessels to the brain that are widened during a migraine attack. Studies show that these drugs are effective in 90 percent of migraine sufferers.[2] The injectable form of the drug works the fastest, within fifteen to thirty minutes. Ergotamines are also highly effective in aborting cluster headache flare-ups.

Used incorrectly, ergotamines can become toxic to the body and result in a group of symptoms collectively referred to as *ergotism.* These symptoms can include burning in the fingers and toes, disturbed vision, and weakness of the extremities. The most common side effects of ergotamine are nausea, vomiting, and a rapid heart rate. The nasal spray can cause burning in the nostrils and a transient sore throat.

People with high blood pressure, hardening of the arteries, angina, and disorders of the kidneys and liver should not take ergotamine derivatives. These agents are also contraindicated during pregnancy and in breast-feeding mothers. Ergotamines are not recommended for children.

THE TRIPTANS

The triptans, or selective 5-HT receptor antagonists, bind directly to receptors on the trigeminal nerve, shutting down the inflammation and transmission of pain. These drugs are specifically antimigraine and anti-cluster medicines; they work at the root cause of migraine and cluster pain. Marketing surveys show that between 70 and 80 percent of patients treated with sumatriptan report significant improvement in their symptoms.

The triptans include:

- Sumatriptan (Imitrex injection; Imitrex tablet; and Imitrex nasal spray)
- Zolmitriptan (Zomig tablet)
- Naratriptan (Amerge tablet)
- Rizatriptan (Maxalt tablet)

Available as an injection, oral preparation, and nasal spray, the triptans are probably the most effective treatment for migraine and cluster headaches. These drugs act quickly; the fastest acting is the injectable preparation. Like the ergot preparations, the triptans narrow blood vessels in the head and neck but are more effective and specific than the ergot preparations. The triptans are quite expensive.

The most common side effects of the 5-HT receptor antagonists are increased blood pressure, fatigue, and tingling in the hands and feet. Individuals with heart disease and those susceptible to developing strokes shouldn't use triptans. Because these drugs work by narrowing the blood vessels in the head and neck by as much as 10 percent, the fear is that they may also significantly narrow the arteries that feed the brain and heart muscle, reducing vital blood flow. Check with your health care provider regarding your risk when using this class of drug.

You shouldn't use the triptans within twenty-four hours of using ergotamine and shouldn't take them while taking methysergide (see page 194), the selective serotonin reuptake inhibitors (see page 200), or the monoamine oxidase inhibitors (see page 201). You should take a reduced dose of rizatriptan (Maxalt) if you take the migraine prophylactic drug propranolol (Inderal). The triptans are contraindicated during pregnancy and in breast-feeding mothers and are not recommended for children.

SYMPATHOMIMETIC AGENTS

Isometheptene mucate (Midrin) is a combination of a painkiller and sedative. This drug is flexible and is prescribed to treat both tension-type and migraine headaches.

The most common side effects of Midrin are drowsiness and dizziness, and people with glaucoma, kidney, heart, or liver disease should not use it if its concurrent use with the monoamine oxidase inhibitors is contraindicated.

BARBITURATE AND ANALGESIC COMBINATIONS

The barbiturates are used to treat tension-type and migraine headaches, and they are effective for the majority of people who take them. However, like most painkillers, these drugs can cause rebound headache.

Barbiturates and analgesic combinations include:

- Butalbital, acetaminophen, and caffeine tablet (Fioricet)
- Butalbital, acetaminophen, and caffeine tablet (Esgic-Plus)

- Butalbital, aspirin, and caffeine tablet and capsule (Fiorinal)
- Butalbital and acetaminophen tablet (Phrenilin)

The most common side effects of the barbiturate and analgesic combinations are drowsiness, dizziness, paradoxical excitement, and shortness of breath. Long-term use of these drugs can lead to dependence. Barbiturates can interact with antidepressants and should never be taken with alcohol.

NARCOTIC ANALGESICS

Some narcotic painkillers are natural compounds derived from opium. Others are synthetic agents that provide the same level of pain relief as the natural compounds. Narcotics are very effective at aborting headache flare-ups, but long-term use of these drugs can lead to dependency, addiction, and rebound headaches. In recent years, they have been used less frequently due to the advent of the nonaddicting agents such as the NSAIDs and vascular-specific medications such as the triptans.

Narcotic analgesics include:

- Acetaminophen, propoxyphene napsylate (Darvocet)
- Acetaminophen, codeine (Tylenon #3)
- Oxycodone (Percocet, Tylox, Roxicet)
- Meperidine (Demerol)
- Pentazocine (Talwin)
- Morphine (Duramorph, Roxanol)

Common side effects of narcotic painkillers include sedation, dizziness, and constipation. In addition, these agents can impair judgment and coordination. You should not take narcotics if you drive, operate dangerous machinery, or are required to remain alert.

Methysergide

Methysergide maleate (Sansert) has been used in the United States since the 1950s to treat cluster headaches and to prevent migraines. Because of its potential adverse effects (formation of scar tissue around the kidneys, in the lungs, or in the heart valves), this agent is reserved for use by individuals for whom all other preventive drug treatments fail.

The most common side effects of methysergide are nausea, drowsiness, dizziness, insomnia, muscle cramps, and pain or swelling in the extremities. The most troubling adverse effect, the accumulation of excess connective tissue, is less likely to occur if you take the drug for less than six months, stop for one month, and resume taking it for another six-month stretch. Your provider may also elect to monitor you by ordering a yearly MRI scan of your abdomen. You can't take methysergide and any of the triptans at the same time. If you take methysergide and the ergot preparations at the same time, your provider should reduce your methysergide dosage.

Corticosteroids

Corticosteroids or glucocorticoids are used to treat cluster and migraine headache flare-ups. The most common adverse effects of corticosteroids are ulcers and elevated blood pressure. Long-term use of steroids can suppress the immune system, making the user susceptible to infections, and over time these drugs can cause glaucoma and cataracts.

Corticosteroids include:

- Prednisone (Deltasone)
- Dexamethasone
- Prednisolone (Pediapred)

Miscellaneous Abortive Therapies

Oxygen and lidocaine are highly effective abortive treatments for cluster attacks, although the mechanism by which these strategies work is unclear. Oxygen is delivered via an oxygen mask and works within minutes. Lidocaine liquid, which is normally used as a local anesthetic, is dropped into the nostril on the side of the cluster headache. Like oxygen, lidocaine also works within minutes.

HEADACHE PROPHYLACTIC MEDICATIONS

Acute head pain management fails some chronic headache sufferers; their headaches require an additional class of medications. For these patients, doctors prescribe a wide range of prophylactic or preventive medications to relieve or reduce the frequency, intensity, or duration of headache flare-ups. Additionally, prophylactic medications help abortive drugs work better. Headache preventive drugs are not painkillers; rather, they work to stabilize the body's biochemical milieu.

Prophylactic drugs generally take a few weeks to build up in the nervous system, so don't get frustrated if you don't see improvement in your head pain after a few days of taking them. Successful prophylactic therapy is considered to be a 50 percent reduction in the frequency, duration, and intensity of your headache flare-ups.[3] Some headache sufferers may be able to stop taking their prophylactic drugs after six months of successful therapy. Of course, only your health care practitioner can help you make that decision.

When are prophylactic drugs indicated? Who should take them? Most headache experts agree that headache sufferers who fail abortive therapy and who experience flare-ups more than two or three times a month should receive preventive drugs.[4] Additionally, individuals unable to take abortive drugs due to medical conditions (for example, those allergic to codeine and unable to use NSAIDs due to an ulcer) are candidates for preventive therapy.

Myriad drugs from a number of different classes of medication are used to prevent recurrent tension-type, migraine, and cluster headaches.

The most common classes of drugs used to prevent persistent headache include the beta-blockers, calcium channel blockers, antidepressants, and corticosteroids. We'll list only some of the most common ones here.

BETA-BLOCKERS

Beta-blockers are the most commonly used agents to prevent migraine headache.[5] These drugs, commonly used to treat high blood pressure, angina, and other medical conditions, act on tiny receptors in the blood vessels, heart, and lungs that are under the influence of adrenaline. The chemical reactions that occur during a vascular headache lead to narrowing of blood vessels; beta-blockers work by blocking the effects of these chemicals and maintaining blood vessels at a relatively dilated size.

Some beta-blockers include:

- Propranolol (Inderal)
- Atenolol (Tenormin)
- Metoprolol (Lopressor)
- Nadolol (Corgard)

The prototypical beta-blocker, propranolol, has been in use in the United States since the 1960s. Since then, about twelve other agents of this class have been formulated and are currently available by prescription only. Because of their ability to open up blood vessels, beta-blockers are ideal agents to lower blood pressure and to treat a number of other cardiovascular conditions. If you happen to have high blood pressure in addition to chronic headaches and are in need of a headache prophylactic drug, a beta-blocker may be a good choice for you. Ask your health care provider.

The most commonly reported side effects of beta-blockers include fatigue, reduced exercise tolerance, loss of memory, and impotence. Beta-blockers slow the metabolism of some users, reducing the rate of caloric burning and preventing weight loss. If you are trying to lose weight, ask your health care provider if it is at all possible to avoid these agents. People who suffer from depression may also want to avoid these drugs, as they can worsen depression. Pregnant and breast-feeding women should not take beta-blockers.

Because beta-receptors are located in the lungs, beta-blockers may narrow bronchial tubes. Normally, the narrowing of the bronchial tubes is a problem only for persons with asthma; however, selective beta-blockers are now available that "select out" the receptors in the heart and blood vessels for beta blockade. Don't stop taking these drugs suddenly, especially the short-acting agents, because that can lead to a rebound rise in blood pressure and the return of severe headaches.

Among diabetics, beta-blockers can impair the ability to sense a fall in blood sugar levels. Therefore, Type 1 (insulin-dependent) diabetics should avoid taking these drugs. People maintained on theophylline for chronic bronchitis, asthma, and emphysema should be monitored closely by their doctors for potential theophylline toxicity.

CALCIUM CHANNEL BLOCKERS

Calcium channel blockers (CCBs), also referred to as calcium blockers, date back to 1962 when Ulrich Von Heidland and his colleagues discovered that the drug verapamil hydrochloride lowered blood pressure in persons with high blood pressure. Additional research showed that CCBs relax the muscles in blood vessel walls by reducing calcium flow into muscle cells, resulting in the dilation of blood vessels. By relaxing blood vessels, CCBs prevent them from undergoing the dilation that characterizes the vascular-type headaches, making these agents ideal for vascular headaches such as migraines and cluster headaches. Doctors also prescribe these drugs to lower blood pressure and to control the heartbeat in people with irregular heart rates.

Calcium channel blockers include:

- Verapamil (Calan, Verelan, or Isoptan tablet)
- Nimodipine (Nimotop tablet)
- Diltiazem (Cardizem or Tiazac tablet)
- Nifedipine (Procardia or Adalat tablet)
- Nicardipine (Cardene tablet)

Headache specialists Drs. Alan Rapoport and Fred Sheftell of the New England Center for Headache in Stamford, Connecticut, found that migraineurs with auras had better results with CCBs than did their counterparts without auras. Verapamil appears to be the most effective CCB for migraine prophylaxis, while Nimotop works better for cluster headaches.

Most people tolerate these medications very well. The most common side effects of CCBs are temporary headaches, low blood pressure, retained fluid, and constipation. In the majority of users, these side effects clear up after a few weeks of taking the drug. The vast majority of CCB prescriptions are written for the long-acting (taken once daily) forms of the drugs. In 1993, researchers found a possible link between an increased risk of heart attacks and the short-acting (taken multiple times daily) CCBs, and the FDA issued a caution to doctors and patients. Studies are currently underway to evaluate the safety of these agents. If you are taking the short-acting CCBs, check with your doctor for further guidance.

CCBs may block the electrical activity in the heart when combined with beta-blockers in people with a condition called atrioventricular block. CCBs may also increase the blood levels of theophylline and quinidine. Grapefruit or grapefruit juice can impair the enzyme responsible for breaking down CCBs; therefore, you should not take these medications within twenty-four hours of consuming grapefruit products.

ANTIDEPRESSANTS

Many headache experts recommend antidepressants as part of the management of chronic headaches, especially for people with chronic daily headaches and migraines. These agents are also helpful for headache sufferers with concurrent depression. Currently, there are four main classes of antidepressants available in the United States, the tricyclic and tetracyclic agents, the selective serotonin reuptake inhibitors, and the monoamine oxidase inhibitors.

Tricyclic Antidepressants

The tricyclic antidepressants (TCAs) have been used in the United States since the 1960s, but have given way to the newer selective serotonin reuptake inhibitors (see page 200) in recent years. TCAs work by increasing the level of the neurotransmitter serotonin in the brain by preventing its reabsorption into the nerve terminals (see chapter 1). These drugs are ideal for headache sufferers with coincidental depression and sleep disorders, because all three conditions are related to brain serotonin levels.

Tricyclic antidepressants include:

- Amitriptyline (Elavil, Endep)
- Nortriptyline (Pamelor, Aventyl)
- Doxepin (Sinequan)
- Trazodone (Desyrel)
- Imipramine (Tofranil)

The most common adverse effects of the TCAs are sedation, dry mouth, constipation, loss of libido, and weight gain. These drugs should not be taken if you have heart rhythm disturbances, a recent heart attack, or a history of epilepsy. Other contraindications to taking TCAs include enlarged prostate gland and glaucoma. Because of the sedation these drugs cause, they should not be used when driving, operating heavy machinery, or taking other sedating drugs.

TCAs are generally prescribed to be taken at bedtime, and these drugs can take about two to four weeks to achieve their maximum therapeutic benefits. Monitoring the blood levels of nortriptyline may be indicated in some individuals.

Tetracyclic Antidepressants
This class of antidepressants, which includes mirtazapine (Remeron) and maprotiline (Ludiomil), has not enjoyed the widespread popularity for use as headache prophylactic agents as have the other antidepressants. No study has shown their efficacy in preventing recurrent headaches. However, they work in similar fashion to the TCAs.

The most common side effects of the tetracyclic agents are drowsiness, increased appetite, weight gain, dry mouth, and constipation. As with the TCAs, you should not drive, operate heavy machinery, or take other sedative drugs while taking tetracyclic antidepressants. These drugs can take about two to four weeks to achieve their maximum therapeutic benefits.

Selective Serotonin Reuptake Inhibitors
The selective serotonin reuptake inhibitors (SSRIs) represent a revolutionary way to treat depression. Like vascular headaches (and possibly, tension-type headaches), the major biochemical dysfunction in depression is a reduction in brain serotonin levels. SSRIs work on the 5-HT receptors to increase the concentration of brain serotonin levels. Besides depression and chronic headache prevention, some SSRIs are used to treat obsessive-compulsive disorder and bulimia nervosa.

Some selective serotonin reuptake inhibitors include:

- Fluoxetine (Prozac)
- Paroxetene (Paxil)
- Sertraline (Zoloft)

- Nefazodone (Serzone)
- Venlafaxine (Effexor)

The most common side effects of the SSRIs are insomnia, weight loss, reduced libido, male sexual dysfunction, and increased depression. These drugs are contraindicated for concurrent use with the monoamine oxidase inhibitor class of antidepressants (see below). The SSRIs may increase or decrease the blood levels of other drugs such as lithium, digoxin, theophylline, and phenobarbital.

Monoamine Oxidase Inhibitors
The monoamine oxidase inhibitors (MAOIs) are the oldest class of antidepressants. These drugs have significant side effects and they interact with many other drugs. For these reasons, MAOIs are rarely used today, having been replaced by newer antidepressants, especially the SSRIs. MAOIs are effective in managing migraines and cluster headaches not responsive to other prophylactic drugs. The side effects of these drugs and their potential to interact with many foods and drugs, however, limit their use. The most common side effects of MAOIs include low blood pressure, headaches, impotence, and drowsiness.

Monoamine oxidase inhibitors include:

- Tranylcypromine (Parnate)
- Phenelzine (Nardil)
- Isocarboxazid (Marplan)

MAOI users should not consume tyramine-containing foods, such as aged cheese, red wine, and yeast extract, as this combination can result in severe elevation of blood pressure. MAOIs should not be used with tricyclic antidepressants or with antidiabetic and anti-Parkinson's drugs. Finally, don't start MAOIs within five weeks of taking an SSRI.

SEROTONIN-RECEPTOR ANTAGONISTS

Methysergide
As discussed earlier, methysergide maleate (Sansert) is used to treat cluster headaches and to prevent migraines. It's reserved for use by individuals who fail other preventive drug treatments.

The most common side effects of methysergide are nausea, drowsiness, dizziness, insomnia, muscle cramps, and pain or swelling in the extremities. The most troubling adverse effect, the accumulation of excess connective tissue, is less likely to occur if you take the drug for less than six months, stop for one month, and resume taking it for another six-month stretch.

ANTICONVULSANTS

Anticonvulsants or antiepileptic drugs can also be used to prevent vascular headache. Anticonvulsants may work by quieting the electrically irritable migraine brain.[6] Carbamazepine has been shown to be effective in preventing cluster headaches, while phenytoin is suited for childhood migraines.

Anticonvulsants include:

- Phenetoin (Dilantin)
- Carbamazepine (Tegretol)
- Divalproex sodium (Depakote)

The most frequent anticonvulsant-induced side effects include nausea, drowsiness, weight gain, and hair loss. Phenytoin can cause thickening of the gums, especially in individuals with poor dental hygiene. If you take anticonvulsants, your provider may order periodic blood tests to monitor the function of your liver. You shouldn't take these drugs if you have liver disease.

NONSTEROIDAL ANTI-INFLAMMATORY DRUGS

As discussed earlier in this chapter, nonsteroidal anti-inflammatory drugs (NSAIDs) are successful abortive agents that have also been shown to be effective in preventing recurrent headache, especially menstrual migraines.[7] (See pages 188–190 for the side effects and contraindications of NSAIDs.)

Some nonsteroidal anti-inflammatory drugs include:

- Ibuprofen (Advil, Nuprin, Motrin)
- Naproxen sodium (Anaprox, Naprosyn)
- Meclofenamate (Meclomen)
- Ketoprofen (Orudis)
- Aspirin

Corticosteroids

Corticosteroids or glucocorticoids are also used to prevent cluster headache. Again, the most common adverse effects of corticosteroids are ulcers and elevation of blood pressure. Long-term use of steroids can suppress the immune system, making the user susceptible to infections. Over time, these drugs can also cause glaucoma and cataracts.

Corticosteroids include:

- Prednisone (Deltasone)
- Dexamethasone
- Prednisolone (Pediapred)

MISCELLANEOUS HEADACHE PREVENTION AGENTS

Cyproheptadine (Periactin) is an antihistamine (treats hay fever and hives) with chemical properties resembling the tricyclic antidepressant drugs. Periactin has also been effective at preventing recurrent migraines. The most common side effects of this drug are sedation, increased appetite, weight gain, dry mouth, and dizziness. Children seem to tolerate Periactin better than do adults.[8]

Lithium salt (Lithotabs and Lithonate) is normally used to treat bipolar disease but is also effective in preventing cluster headaches. The most common side effects of this drug are drowsiness, tremor, nausea, blurred vision, and dry mouth. Lithium can affect the blood levels of many drugs including the NSAIDs, calcium channel blockers, and diuretics.

DRUGS USED TO TREAT SPECIFIC MEDICAL CONDITIONS

As we discussed in chapter 10, a number of medical conditions can cause head and neck pain. These conditions include allergies, sinus problems, high blood pressure, and TMJ syndrome. In this section, we'll very briefly list some general information regarding drugs used to treat these conditions.

TMJ syndrome is usually treated with local heat, modified activities, dental mouth guards, NSAIDs, and in rare instances, narcotics. We discussed the use of NSAIDs and narcotics earlier in this chapter when we talked about drugs to treat and prevent primary headache syndromes.

ANTIHISTAMINES/DECONGESTANTS

As was discussed in chapter 3, hay fever and other allergies are common headache triggers. These conditions are treated with environmental control measures (avoidance) and antihistamines and decongestants directed to combat the effects of allergies (runny nose, sneezing, and headache). Additionally, these drugs are used as adjunctive treatment along with an antibiotic for sinus infections. (See the discussion of antibiotics on pages 205 and 206.)

Some antihistamine/decongestants include:

- Fexofenadine (Allegra)
- Fexofenadine and pseudoephedrine (Allegra-D)
- Loratadine (Claritin)
- Loratadine and pseudoephedrine (Claritin-D)
- Cetirizine (Zyrtec)
- Chlopheniramine and pseudoephedrine (Deconamine)
- Brompheniramine and phenylpropanolamine (Dimetapp)

The most frequent side effects of antihistamines and decongestants are drowsiness, dry mouth, dizziness, anxiety, depression, thickening of bronchial secretions, and palpitations. Fexofenadine and loratidine are nonsedating agents; Zyrtec is a relatively nonsedating antihistamine.

Antihistamines/decongestants are contraindicated in persons with narrow-angle glaucoma, urinary retention, and severe high blood pressure; they should not be taken within two weeks of taking an MAOI.

ANTIBIOTICS

You may recall from chapter 3 that sinus infections can cause headache; when bacteria cause these infections, antibiotics are used to treat the condition. The most commonly used antibiotics to treat sinusitis are amoxicillin/clavulanic acid (Augmentin), sulfamethoxazole/trimethoprim (Bactrim or Septra), and clarithromycin (Biaxin). Viral sinusitis is a self-limited condition and requires only supportive care.

Each antibiotic has its own side effect. For example, the most common side effects of Augmentin are upset stomach, and in the case of women, yeast infections. Bactrim and Septra can also cause upset stomachs, along with hypersensitivity to sunlight and pseudomembranous colitis (inflammation of the colon). Biaxin is associated with upset stomachs, taste disturbance, and headaches.

As with other medications, individuals allergic to antibiotics should not take these drugs. In addition, individuals with megaloblastic anemia should not take Bactrim or Septra. Biaxin should not be taken together with cisapride, pimozide, and other drugs metabolized by the liver.

HIGH BLOOD PRESSURE DRUGS

High blood pressure is treated with many classes of drugs that work differently to lower abnormally high pressure of circulating blood.[9] (See table 16.2.) The most commonly used classes of antihypertensive drugs are calcium channel blockers, beta-blockers (also used to manage vascular headaches), diuretics (water pills), angiotensin-converting enzyme inhibitors, and angiotensin-blocking agents. Alpha-blockers, peripheral antiadrenergics, and direct vasodilators are less frequently used.

We'll briefly list general information and side effects of these agents and summarize their interaction profiles. There are over one hundred blood pressure drugs in use in the United States, making it impossible to discuss everything there is about these drugs in this book. However, the suggested reading section lists well-written hypertension references.

Each class of antihypertensive has its own side effect profile. For example, the beta-blockers can cause fatigue, reduced exercise tolerance, loss of memory, and impotence. Calcium channel blockers can cause temporary headaches, low blood pressure, fluid retention, and constipation. Angiotensin-converting enzyme inhibitors can cause a chronic cough in a small percentage of users. The alpha-blockers can cause lightheadedness.

TABLE 16.2 HIGH BLOOD PRESSURE DRUGS

Calcium Channel Blockers
Verapamil (Calan, Verelan)
Nimodipine (Nimotop)
Nifedipine (Procardia, Adalat)

Beta-Blockers
Propranolol (Inderal)
Atenolol (Tenormin)
Metoprolol (Lopressor)

Diuretics
Hydrochlorothiazide (Oretic)
Furosemide (Lasix)

Angiotensin-Converting Enzyme Inhibitors
Linsiopril (Prinivil, Zestril)
Quinapril (Accupril)

Angiotensin II Blocking Agents
Losartan (Cozaar)

Central-Acting Alpha-2 Inhibitors
Clonidine (Catapress)

Peripheral Antiadrenergics
Reserpine (Serpalan)

Alpha-1 Adrenergic Antagonists
Terazosin (Hytrin)

Direct Vasodilators
Minoxidil

COMPLEMENTARY AND ALTERNATIVE THERAPY

As we discussed in chapters 14 and 15, complementary or alternative medical practices are rapidly becoming an adjunct to, and sometimes a substitute for, conventional medicine. Similar to the way in which garlic has been used to lower high blood pressure, several healing herbs and other nonconventional agents have been effectively used for the treatment of chronic headache.[10] Naturopathic physicians usually prescribe herbal agents.

Among these agents are feverfew, valerian root, skullcap, chamomile, ginger root, and omega-3 fatty acids. Because contraindications for these substances have not been clearly established, it is wise to check with your health care provider to see if you are a candidate for these substances.

FEVERFEW (TANACETUM PARTHENIUM)

Feverfew, an herbal product used extensively in Europe, has been shown in several studies to reduce the severity and frequency of migraines.[11] Derived from a plant in the chrysanthemum family, this agent was used in medieval Europe to treat fever and headache.[12] This naturopathic medicine works by inhibiting the release of substances that dilate blood vessels.

Feverfew is available in a capsule or as a tincture for the treatment of migraines; however, the tincture has a distinctly unpleasant taste. The most common side effects are nausea, mouth ulcers, lip swelling, loss of taste, and rash. Maximum efficacy may take several weeks. Consult your doctor before using this as a headache-preventive agent.

VALERIAN ROOT (VALERIANA OFFICINALIS)

This herb has been shown to be effective in relieving migraine and tension headaches. Other conditions treated with this herb include insomnia, mental fatigue, and generalized pain. Valerian can be taken as a tea or tincture and can be mixed with other herbs to treat coincidental conditions. This herb may be toxic at high doses and often causes headaches.

SKULLCAP (SCUTELLARIA LATERIFOLIA)

This herb is indicated for the treatment of anxiety, stress, and tension. Skullcap is a good substitute for patients not responsive to valerian root. It comes in a tea or tincture, and there is no toxicity related to its use.[13]

CHAMOMILE (MATICARIA CHAMOMILLA)

This highly aromatic herb is effective in the treatment of headaches related to anxiety.[14] It is also used to treat respiratory mucus, joint pain, intestinal spasm, and mouth ulcers. Chamomile comes as a tea as well as a tincture.

GINGER ROOT (ZINGIBER OFFICINALE)

Regular household ginger has many uses, including lowering cholesterol, and its antinausea and antivomiting properties make it effective for the treatment of migraine headaches. Ginger root tea can be steeped or boiled; because no toxicity has been reported, it appears safe during pregnancy.[15]

OMEGA-3 FATTY ACIDS

Omega-3 fatty acids are unsaturated fats found in cold-water fish such as sardines and cod. They probably work by preventing platelet clumping in the blood, just as aspirin does.[16] Taken in capsule form, this fat has been shown to be effective in reducing the severity, frequency, and duration of migraines.

The main side effect of omega-3 fatty acids is increased stomach acid. These fats may lower blood sugar in some people, potentially causing headache flare-ups. Consult your health care provider before taking this product.

IN SUMMARY

- Your physician or nonphysician provider is the only person positioned to determine whether you are a candidate for any headache drug.
- Headaches are managed with painkillers to abort an episode in progress or with prophylactic drugs to reduce the frequency and intensity of headache flare-ups.
- Abortive medications include NSAIDs, ergotamines, triptans, sympathetic agents, barbiturates, and narcotics. Prophylactic drugs include beta-blockers, calcium channel blockers, antidepressants, serotonin-receptor antagonists, anticonvulsants, and NSAIDs.
- Alternative agents used to treat headaches include feverfew, valerian root, skullcap, chamomile, ginger root, and omega-3 fatty acids.
- Antihistamines/decongestants, antibiotics, and antihypertensive drugs are examples of drugs used to treat specific medical conditions that can cause headaches.

CHAPTER SEVENTEEN

How to Be a Savvy Consumer

Chances are good that you'll buy products or services to monitor or treat your chronic headaches. Whether you buy headache medications or exercise equipment or consult an acupuncturist, you can potentially spend more than necessary unless you carefully research your purchases. If you fall prey to people promising dubious headache remedies, you can potentially spend huge sums of money or worse, be irrevocably harmed by dangerous products or procedures.

> THE PROBLEM IS TO INDUCE PEOPLE TO PAY TWENTY-FIVE CENTS FOR THE LIVER-ENCOURAGING, SILENT-PERAMBULATING, FAMILY PILLS, WHICH COST THREE CENTS.
> **THOMAS HUXLEY**

In this chapter, we'll help you to become an informed consumer of medical products and services. We'll list a variety of consumer-safe strategies and tell you how these can save you money and prevent you from being taken in by quacks. Alternative medicine is gaining popularity and new products will eventually gain approval from the scientific community. This will undoubtedly herald a flood of ingenious scam artists jumping on the new-product bandwagon. The informed consumer will know which therapies are legitimate and which are bogus and will be able to make informed choices. We're not going to compare prices of exercise equipment or painkillers, but we'll provide you with a list of sources from which to obtain this information.

THE FINANCIAL EFFECTS
OF YOUR HEADACHES

Health care in the United States today is big business. Unlike thirty years ago, there are now very few sources of charitable health services. Most Americans pay for their care through health insurance carriers or fee-for-service (out-of-pocket) arrangements. The costs can quickly add up if you have a chronic medical problem that requires recurrent purchases of health care services and devices.

Society also shoulders a tremendous financial burden caused by high health care charges. As we said in the preface, recurrent headaches—the number-one reason for lost productivity in the United States and the biggest reason for disability payments to American workers—cost businesses a staggering fifty billion dollars annually due to absenteeism and payment of medical benefits to headache sufferers.[1] Migraine headaches alone cost a whopping eleven billion dollars annually to treat.[2] By any standards, chronic headaches are an expensive proposition.

As a consumer of health care services and products, it behooves you to get the best deal for your hard-earned dollar. In today's complex health care market, consumers are faced with a litany of issues, including dealing with insurance companies and managed care organizations, the high cost of prescription and nonprescription drugs, dealing with quackery and health care fraud, and recognizing legitimate complementary and alternative practices. Those who do their homework and research the intricacies of the marketplace come out ahead.

ARE YOU COVERED?

How about health insurance coverage? How do you purchase it and what's the going rate? People with chronic headaches are at a tremendous disadvantage when it comes to getting health insurance coverage.[3] Not only is their condition expensive to evaluate and treat, but insurance companies make it difficult to collect on claims. Because no blood tests or X-rays specifically diagnose headaches and testing is done to simply rule out other conditions that can present with recurrent headaches, health insurers invariably question physicians' medical evaluations of headache patients. What can you do to survive this tremendously frustrating situation? How can you ensure that you get reimbursed for headache-related diagnosis and treatment?

The first order of business is to understand the various types of health insurance available and the benefits they offer. The most common type of health insurer is the indemnity insurer. This insurance company typically reimburses you for a portion of your medical bill above and beyond the copayment. When you start a new job, there are some medical problems, referred to as *preexisting conditions,* which the insurer will not cover for up to twelve months. This can include chronic headaches.

Even when a medical condition is covered, the insurer may reject claims for procedures and tests ordered to rule out other conditions. Claims adjusters usually interpret the rules in the strictest sense when a claim is filed, but they are willing to listen to a valid appeal. The best solution for combating claims rejection is persistence. Repeated appeals may be the difference between getting the insurance company to pay or being stuck with a prohibitively large medical bill. Recent state and federal governmental interventions have led to substantial reforms in the health insurance industry, and a number of successful lawsuits have also forced the industry to rethink its business practices. Insurance company bureaucrats are now willing to sit down with patients to work out reasonable compromises.

Don't let your policy lapse. Be sure to pay your premiums on time. Insurance companies are precluded from dropping a policyholder because of a newly developed problem, but you can be dropped if your policy lapses. It can be very difficult to get new health insurance after you've been diagnosed with a chronic condition.

If you plan to change jobs, do your research. You may not be able to transfer your insurance from one job to the next. If you can't take your insurance to your new job, check to make sure your new job will cover your preexisting condition. In some cases, if you have to leave your job, you may be entitled to continued coverage if you pay the premium and an administrative fee.

If you are unemployed and don't have health insurance, you may be able to purchase individual health plans through some insurance carriers such as Blue Cross/Blue Shield. These insurance plans can be quite expensive and typically list a number of limiting clauses. Whatever your status, check with your state's insurance commission about what's available, the rules of the game, and available recourse when things go awry.

TIPS ON DEALING WITH MANAGED CARE NETWORKS

Most Americans with health insurance now get their health care from health maintenance organizations (HMOs), preferred-provider organizations (PPOs), and independent practice associations (IPAs). The basic aim of these for-profit health plans, dubbed managed care providers, is to provide quality, comprehensive health care at the lowest possible cost. Care from these plans revolves around a primary care physician who serves as the "gatekeeper," referring patients to medical and surgical specialists only when necessary. For example, if you are an HMO enrollee with migraine headaches, a family physician will care for you and consult a headache specialist only after your headaches prove to be very resistant to the standard management.

By and large, managed care providers provide excellent quality of health care for the vast majority of uncomplicated health problems such as ear infections and sprained ankles. Criticisms leveled at these organizations have to do with the quality and volume of care available to patients with complicated health problems. Many patients with complex illnesses, such as unmanageable, recalcitrant migraine headaches, charge that HMOs and other managed care providers make it difficult for them to obtain timely care from specialists.

If your primary care physician has current expertise in taking care of headaches and your headaches are responsive to usual treatments, you will likely have a positive experience with your managed care provider. Even if your assigned physician seems disinterested in taking care of chronic headaches, you may be able to switch doctors. Most health plans now allow patients to choose a different clinician in cases of poor doctor/patient relationships. As we said earlier, persistence and repeated appeals may be the difference between settling for a less-than-appealing doctor/patient relationship and getting a better deal within your managed care organization.

Recent state and federal governmental interventions have led to substantial reforms among managed care organizations. A number of successful lawsuits have also inspired an industrywide review of business practices. HMO and other managed care bureaucrats are now willing to listen to members who press their cases for reviews and hearings.

DEALING WITH MEDICARE AND MEDICAID

Like managed care providers and health insurance companies, government-sponsored Medicare and Medicaid insurance coverage can be very annoying, as Medicare and Medicaid are huge bureaucracies invariably frustrating for the average user.[4]

Medicare is a federally funded program that pays part of the health care cost for individuals sixty-five years old and older and people with a disability that qualifies them for Social Security Disability Insurance (SSDI).

Medicaid is a combination of local, state, and federally funded insurance programs that cover people with income levels below the poverty line. People who qualify for SSDI and Aid to Families with Dependent Children are also eligible for Medicaid.

REDUCING MEDICATION COSTS

Taking one drug every day for the rest of your life can prove costly, and it really adds up if you need to take multiple medications daily. Statistics compiled by the National Center for Health Statistics show that one in ten patients with a chronic condition takes three or more different drugs daily. Buying multiple medicines need not leave you broke. Like everything else, both over-the-counter and prescription drug prices vary greatly, depending on what you buy and where you make your purchase.

Selling drugs is big business. A *Time* magazine investigative report exposed a war of painkiller drug advertisements fought between the two largest producers of over-the-counter painkillers.[5] These pharmaceutical companies embellish their products and vilify rival products (which are often equally potent and effective), trying to sway consumers and garner a larger share of the $2,700,000,000 over-the-counter painkiller market. Naive consumers invariably fork over inflated sums to the company with the most convincing advertisement but aren't necessarily getting the superior product.

Your doctor and pharmacist can help you save money on drugs. If you're being prescribed medications for the first time, ask your doctor for samples. This allows you time to get your dosage adjusted and to see if you'd respond to this particular agent or develop adverse reactions to the drug, before investing your money. Sometimes, the medication you are originally prescribed is not the one on which you stay. This is especially true for painkillers, which sometimes cause intolerable side effects, forcing the user to switch to other drugs.

When you are given a prescription, ask your provider to allow refills on the prescription. Refills will avoid the expense of additional doctor visits just to get a new prescription written. However, under certain circumstances, such as when you are first diagnosed with a chronic condition, your health care provider may prefer to examine you when your prescription runs out before deciding whether the drug can be safely continued or if a new drug or a change in dosage is indicated.

Using coupons can also help you save with each purchase. Ask your doctor, nurse, or pharmacist for the coupons they frequently get from drug salespersons. Also ask your pharmacist for the address of the drug company and write to its sales/public relations department for discount coupons.

BUYING IN BULK

There are now many reputable mail-order pharmacies and distribution outlets that sell medications at reduced prices. Advocacy groups such as the American Association of Retired Persons and the American Geriatrics Society endorse many of these organizations. Your pharmacist may be able to help you compare the cost of buying your medication from a traditional pharmacy to the cost of buying from a clearinghouse. Mail-order drug prices are usually 10 to 35 percent cheaper than prices at local pharmacies. The biggest advantages of buying in bulk are the convenience of mail-order shopping and the availability of a list of prices for comparison.

One drawback to buying in bulk is the risk of your drug expiring before you are able to take it. To prevent this, buy only what you know you'll use within three to six months, and always check the expiration date when your drugs arrive in the mail. Most mail-order drug companies will exchange pills if you anticipate that they will expire before you can use them.

GENERIC DRUGS

After a drug company's patent on a drug runs out (usually after seventeen years), other companies are free to make the drug from its basic chemical components. Generic drug manufacturers are required to ensure that each product adequately absorbs and distributes in the body, but they are not required to conduct rigorous testing to see if the drug is comparable to the original agent. The question remains whether the generic form of the drug is equally as potent as the brand-name form of the drug. This is an issue that has been hotly debated for some time now and one you should bring up with your doctor.

Generic drugs are usually cheaper than the brand-name forms of the same drug. If your physician feels that the generic form of the drug you are prescribed is comparable to the brand-name form, you may want to buy the generic and save some money. The proof will be in the pudding; if your headaches return after you've switched to a generic, you'll want to stick to the brand-name drug.

If you switch to generics, remember that the pill will likely be a different color and shape than your brand-name drug. It is also possible that the generic may cause new drug-associated symptoms like heartburn or diarrhea. If this occurs, voice your concern to a member of your health care team. Conversely, the generic may have fewer side effects yet be as effective as the brand-name form of the drug.

LET'S TALK ABOUT QUACKERY

The Federal Trade Commission, the National Fraud Information Center, the Better Business Bureau, and many other consumer advocacy groups are united in the fight to uncover health care fraud and to bring the perpetrators to justice. Quacks come in all colors, shapes, and sizes. In most cases, they sing a familiar theme: "My product is endorsed by a government

agency (such as the FDA), initially rejected by a Wall
Street drug company, cured millions around the
world, and now, it is available to you for only $89.95
(a $55 savings!)." Show this advertisement to a room-
ful of desperate chronic pain sufferers and more than
half the time you'll get their attention, especially if
they have the financial means to assuage their curiosity. This crime is per-
petrated more often and with more success that you can imagine, as reported in a recent issue of *Consumer Reports*:

> QUACKS ARE THE GREATEST
> LIARS IN THE WORLD EXCEPT
> THEIR PATIENTS.
> **BENJAMIN FRANKLIN**

> Today, quackery is a multibillion-dollar business, but the money wasted
> each year on quack products and treatments is only part of the problem.
> No one knows how many people have died because they relied on quack
> treatments until it was too late for conventional therapy to be of help. Or
> how many arthritis victims have dissipated their life savings chasing false
> hopes—while their disease and disability grew worse.[6]

Hope springs eternal. The promise of "quick cures" and "miraculous
relief" sounds great to someone with a chronic medical condition. After all,
a cure would mean no more daily medications, no more lifestyle restric-
tions, and an end to pain and suffering. Many unscrupulous individuals
are aware of this collective vulnerability and actively and aggressively court
unsuspecting, desperate people for financial gain, touting miracle cures for
everything from arthritis to AIDS.

Chronic headache has its own quacks who make grandiose claims
about products that have "permanently cured" migraines in an impressive
number of people. Most "revolutionary products" (drugs, dietary supplements, equipment, and mechanical devices) are usually expensive, often
worthless, and sometimes harmful.

We always tell our patients that if "a hot, new treatment" were a true god-
send, every newspaper and magazine editor and television news producer
in the country would be clamoring to extol its virtues. You'd have to live in a

cave not to hear about this great miracle cure. Viagra, the revolutionary impotence drug released for marketing in 1998, received widespread press coverage. Everyone heard of it, even people with the most primitive media access. Every newspaper, magazine, and television station worth their keep reported on Viagra. This drug's phenomenal success is unrivaled so far, partly due to the publicity it garnered from diverse publications.

Similarly, when and if a revolutionary headache cure becomes available, you'll be constantly bombarded with information about how it works, why it works, and how many headache sufferers have regained control over their lives. Until such time, our advice is "buyer beware." Do your homework when contemplating the purchase of unconventional headache drugs, dietary supplements, equipment, or mechanical devices.

RECOGNIZING QUACKERY

Quackery involves deception on the part of charlatans peddling an unproven product or service with the same skills employed by Madison Avenue advertising firms. Advertising is the single most effective way these people perpetrate dubious schemes on unsuspecting individuals. Be leery of outlandish advertisements that tout a cure for a condition you know is chronic and incurable. Usually, the more grandiose the claim, the more attention the product will get, and unfortunately, the more likely that desperate people will give it a try. If you keep up with current events even minimally, you know that there is no cure for arthritis, AIDS, or most chronic headaches; these conditions can only be effectively managed.

When in doubt about a product's claim, check with your health care practitioner or consumer advocate organization. Inventors, or companies who discover medical cures approved for marketing by the FDA, mail product information to a large percentage of physicians and other practitioners. These products are also widely advertised in many of the commonly read medical journals, and most audiovisual media do feature stories on these products. Chances are, if your doctor or consumer advocate has never heard of a purported miracle cure, it's a fake.

TESTIMONY FROM NEIGHBORS, FRIENDS, AND RELATIVES

Many people with acute and chronic illnesses hear anecdotes from friends, neighbors, and relatives who were "cured" by unconventional products. To understand why phony products work for some people, you have to understand what placebos are and why they work.

Placebos are inert substances (substances having no active pharmacological properties) that are sometimes used in clinical practice and in almost all scientific studies involving drugs. A certain percentage of people will derive pharmacological benefits from placebos. The placebo effect is extremely powerful and has to do with the recipient's belief system. If a person believes that he is getting a powerful drug, he will be psychologically and physically prepared for its helpful effects. As a result, some benefits may accrue.

Most clinical and scientific studies of a medicinal product compare that product to a placebo. Predictably, there will be subjects given placebo who will show improvement or a cure. In fact, pharmacological agents that fail to perform better than placebos are disapproved for use due to lack of efficacy.

CURIOSITY

In a frank discussion about the lure of fraudulent health care claims, noted author and clinician Dr. Isadore Rosenfeld observed, "It's only human to wonder whether maybe, just maybe, there is something to such a claim, however preposterous."[7] Curiosity is a healthy instinct. An important aspect of healthy curiosity is doing your own research. Inquire how the product works, what its side effects are, how long it has been on the market, what scientific scrutiny it has undergone, and if applicable, if it has FDA approval.

Besides your health care practitioner, a number of nonprofit health information clearinghouses and professional medical organizations are more than willing to provide information on health devices and products. If these organizations, like the Consumer Information Center, are unfamiliar with or unaware of a product or device, chances are that the product in question is phony and should be avoided.

When your curiosity is sparked, a good dose of caution is advisable. The old Latin adage *caveat emptor* ("buyer beware") is a healthy attitude to adopt when dealing with advertisements that smack of snake-oil salesmanship. Suppress your curiosity, stick to tried-and-true treatments, and save your money for important things.

COMPLEMENTARY AND ALTERNATIVE THERAPIES

Mainstream medical practitioners are becoming increasingly receptive to alternative ways of treating certain acute and chronic illnesses. For example, some mainstream physicians, such as Harry G. Preuss, M.D., of Georgetown University Medical School, believe that garlic can lower blood pressure in some individuals. These beliefs were previously based on anecdotal evidence, but recent scientific research suggests that some alternative therapies may be beneficial in treating conditions such as chronic headaches.

Many nonmedical practitioners perform therapy that improves overall health and may also relieve headaches. These practitioners include reflexologists, acupuncturists, acupressurists, massage therapists, naturopaths, homeopaths, hypnotists, and herbalists. As we discussed in chapters 14 and 15, these unconventional therapists perform maneuvers and treatments that aim to restore normal body functions.

The establishment of the Office of Alternative Medicine by the National Institutes of Health in 1992 has been instrumental in the recent surge of interest in subjecting alternative medical practices to scientific study. A number of mainstream researchers have been given grants to study the merits of incorporating acupuncture, chelation therapy, hypnosis, prayer, biofeedback, and other alternative approaches to treating problems such as pain, wound healing, heart disease, and stress reduction. In the coming years, the safety, efficacy, and indications of alternative practices will be determined and will undoubtedly find their way into mainstream medical practices.

IN SUMMARY

- Chronic headache medications and other products can prove expensive unless careful research is undertaken to find the best buys.
- Buying drugs in bulk and purchasing generic drugs may help reduce costs.
- People with chronic headaches are susceptible to sales pitches by unscrupulous individuals touting a "cure" for the condition.
- Quackery can be recognized by grandiose claims about products that have not received widespread and mainstream media coverage.
- Some unconventional therapies, such as biofeedback and progressive muscle relaxation, may have merit in headache treatment. Reflexologists, acupuncturists, and herbalists may provide effective headache relief.

CHAPTER EIGHTEEN

Living Well with Chronic Headache

By now you have realized that managing chronic headache is a full-time commitment. We suggest that you pursue nondrug strategies and take your medication each and every day as prescribed by your health care practitioner. We also suggest that your pursuit of a headache-free life can be made easier if your family and friends support your efforts.

> LONG AILMENTS WEAR OUT PAIN, AND LONG HOPES JOY.
>
> STANISLAS I (LESZCYNSKI) OF POLAND

In this chapter, we'll review tips on being an effective self-manager and ways to astutely purchase health care services. We'll also outline the roles of your loved ones and coworkers in helping you conquer your chronic headache. Spouses, children, parents, cousins, and others in your extended family are important players in helping you competently manage your condition. According to surveys of people with chronic medical conditions, the involvement of family and friends provides great comfort as one works to achieve optimal control of a long-term problem.

AN EMOTIONAL ROLLER COASTER

By all accounts, chronic illnesses can take a tremendous toll on the quality of life of patients and their loved ones, and chronic headache is no exception. Relationships, self-esteem, confidence, and economic solvency suffer. Many chronic pain victims bristle at the inability to be good fathers, mothers, husbands, and wives. The vast majority of sufferers become chronically irritable, anxious, and depressed.

The physical disability is only one issue that can send one into an emotional tailspin. Other emotionally harrowing factors faced by chronic headache sufferers include the inability to find a doctor with whom to work toward effective management, medication side effects, isolation, and financial troubles. In addition, they face misunderstandings and a lack of sympathy from family members, friends, coworkers, and supervisors due to society's overall skepticism regarding the legitimacy of headaches as a biological disease.

Combating these adverse situations requires a complete plan that brings to bear all available social resources: your employer, family, and friends.

BECOMING A COMPETENT SELF-MANAGER

When confronted with a problem, your level of success in solving it is largely determined by how motivated you are to research, plan, and pursue the solutions.[1] How you think about the problem is also vitally important. For example, if you think that the only way to cope with chronic headaches is by crawling under a rock and playing dead, chances are you'll give up trying and suffer needlessly. If you decide, however, that chronic headaches can be conquered, you'll be armed with the most important ingredient in the recipe for success: hope.

The first order of business on the road to success is to determine exactly what you want to accomplish. Be both realistic and very specific. Do you want to become headache free or would you be happy with one headache each month as opposed to one a week? Is it likely that you'll completely get rid of migraines that are triggered by almost everything you eat, or is it more realistic to lower your ideal frequency and intensity by 50 percent?

A very important element in getting rid of recurrent headaches is a workable plan with both short-term and long-term timetables. Again, you'd have to be realistic. Chances are that a twenty-year history of migraine headaches has also wreaked havoc on your physical and psychological health, as well as economic wherewithal. This will not be cured in two weeks.

SHORT-TERM GOALS

Setting short-term goals involves delineating things you want to do or accomplish in the next few weeks or months. The timetable will be determined by the extent of your disease and the resources available to you. Be specific: what, how much, when, and how often. What stumbling blocks do you foresee? What about an old knee injury that has led to your leading a sedentary life the past eight years? How about the financial output for good exercise equipment?

Remember to start slowly and work your way toward a realistic goal. An example of a short-term goal for a chronic headache sufferer is to start a walking exercise program that begins with walking one city block three times weekly the first two weeks and gradually increasing the distance to twenty city blocks five times weekly by three months. Have an alternative plan (for example, riding a stationary bike) for days when the weather is bad.

LONG-TERM GOALS

One of the best motivators for continuing to work toward your goal is to monitor and record your progress. There is nothing more encouraging than looking back at your diary entries and seeing that in two months you've progressed from walking one city block three times per week to walking ten city blocks five days per week.

DETERMINING RESULTS

It is important to periodically gauge the results of your efforts. You'll have to decide what yardstick you want to use to measure the results of your program. Based on your efforts, are your headaches now less frequent and intense, say, 50 percent less frequent and 30 percent less severe?

EDUCATING
YOUR EMPLOYER

If you are like most people, maintaining a job is an important part of your daily living. You work to pay your bills, to maintain your professional or technical skills, to get intellectual and emotional support, and to maintain your overall self-esteem. Anything that threatens to negatively affect your work endangers the very essence of your existence. Small wonder that chronic illness, including recurrent headache pain, is a source of worry for those unfortunate enough to be afflicted.

Recurrent headache sufferers often have a tough time juggling the demands of a job and a chronic medical condition. Workers who have to interact with others in crucial situations are often less effective during headache flare-ups. Suboptimal performance means poor job evaluations, slower promotions, and possible discrimination. Many bosses, especially those without personal experience with headaches, subscribe to the headache myths we delineated in chapter 2. A supervisor who regards a migraineur as a hypersensitive person with poor coping skills trying to use a fake disorder to get sympathy is bound to be less than understanding during a headache flare-up.

As a headache sufferer, how do you deal with this situation? How do you excel in your job while dealing with the restriction imposed by your chronic condition? Should you even tell your boss?

THE ROLE OF LOVED ONES

Chronic headaches can be disabling and demoralizing, and no one knows that more than the headache sufferer. Only the migraine sufferer knows the frustration of lying absolutely still in a dark room during a migraine attack. Only the sufferer feels the piercing pain of a cluster attack. Don't underestimate, however, the effects your headache can have on your family and friends.

Research has shown that family members and friends experience the same emotional upheaval as does the chronic pain sufferer.[2] In their efforts to help monitor the patient's condition and activity level, loved ones may suffer burnout. They experience a number of psychological and behavioral responses, including fear, anger, and guilt. Initially, loved ones may be fearful about the cause of your symptoms. When your condition fails to disappear, they may feel angry that you and the family are victims of a chronic medical problem. Finally, family members and loved ones may have guilt at being angry about the situation.

How can you help your family cope with their emotions and help them help you on your road to recovery? First, silence will not help; it will cause more resentment and frustration.[3] Your best option is to fully educate friends and relatives about your condition and delineate your treatment plan. The next best thing is for you to effectively institute your treatment plan so your chronic headaches are no longer the focus of everyone's attention.

SUPPORT GROUPS

As social beings, we have an innate need to feel connected to others. Research has shown that people who are socially isolated develop illnesses at a higher rate than those who have a strong network of family and friends. Modern living constantly threatens this very important social network; chronic illnesses further rob us of the ability to stay socially connected.

LOVE AND INTIMACY ARE AT A ROOT OF WHAT MAKES US SICK AND WHAT MAKES US WELL, WHAT CAUSES SADNESS AND WHAT BRINGS HAPPINESS, WHAT MAKES US SUFFER AND WHAT LEADS TO HEALING.

DEAN ORNISH, M.D.[4]

Support groups have effectively filled the need to connect with others for people with chronic conditions. These gatherings provide the perfect forum to discuss the physical, psychological, and spiritual issues of the illness in question. These groups, such as "First Connection," sponsored by the Leukemia Society of America, have effectively provided emotional ballast for chronically ill patients as well as for their families and friends. Chronic headache support groups can foster a healthy exchange of ideas regarding diet, exercise, stress management, and medication usage, among others.

Group members are united in the knowledge that "I'm not in this by myself; I'm face to face with others who share my health problems, feelings, and frustrations." The group can be energized by the knowledge that everyone has to cope with similar challenges, and members experience a similar range of emotions such as depression, anxiety, and anger. There is nothing more therapeutic than seeing and listening to someone with a similar problem relate her trials and tribulations and offer practical solutions. People learn more coping strategies from support group members than from the best-written book on the subject.

Persons who attend support groups often feel more obligated to comply with their prescribed treatment. They also realize, after listening to others in the group, that the only way to conquer a chronic condition is to treat it every day of the year. Support groups also expose bogus cures as disappointed group members tell of treatments that fail to deliver on lofty promises.

An added benefit of support groups is the availability of experts as guest lecturers. Physicians, nurses, pharmacists, dietitians, and others are always eager to offer their expertise to such groups. These health professionals can discuss the latest information in their respective fields and can answer questions in a setting free from the time constraints typical of a medical office visit.

Support groups aren't for everyone, however.[5] To be successful, support group members have to be willing to openly share their thoughts and feelings. Members must be willing to learn about and to help each other. Some people aren't comfortable talking about their private thoughts and feelings and may have a hard time fitting into these programs. People who are severely depressed may feel worse after attending group sessions, especially groups that are not moderated by health professionals.

IN SUMMARY

- Family and friends can lend invaluable support to your pursuit of a headache-free life.
- Take the time to educate your extended family and friends about your headaches: what they are, how they develop, why you get them, and how you treat them.
- Support groups can bolster the physical, psychological, and spiritual needs of chronic headache sufferers as well as their families and friends.
- The most current information can be obtained through support group members and experts invited as guest speakers.

Epilogue

This is a book of hope. We hope that *The Headache Sourcebook* came close to fulfilling its goal: to serve as a single-source self-help manual to assist individuals with chronic headaches to better understand and manage their disease. We also hope that this manual gave you enough information to help foster a collaborative relationship between you and your health care team. If you've hoped for complete relief from your head pain for years, we trust that this handbook will be the pivotal resource to fulfill your dream.

We've shared our knowledge about the clinical features, diagnosis, and management of various headaches, such as tension-type, migraine, cluster, and mixed head pain. We've listed the purported causes, cutting-edge treatments, and preventive strategies of the various primary and secondary headache syndromes, based on the most current research. We hope that you now have a complete understanding of:

- The type of headaches you get
- What factors trigger your headaches
- How to keep a headache diary
- What steps you can take to prevent your headaches
- What nondrug strategies you can adopt to manage your headaches
- How your headache medicines work
- What questions to ask your physician or other health care practitioners and how to get the most out of your health care visit

DEVELOPING A COMPREHENSIVE PLAN

I DO NOT THINK YOUR DISEASE SHOULD ALARM YOU. BY FOLLOWING ALL THE ABOVE DIRECTIONS, I THINK YOUR RECOVERY IS AS CERTAIN AS PHYSICIANS DARE TO PRONOUNCE ANY EVENTS TO BE THAT RELATE TO THE ISSUE OF DISEASE.

BENJAMIN RUSH

We hope that you now are armed with the information needed to confidently enter into a coequal relationship with your physician, physician assistant, nurse practitioner, physical therapist, chiropractor, acupuncturist, or other health care professional. If you haven't already done so, write down a plan of action that takes you from having recurrent headaches to becoming headache free. Starting with the type of headaches you get, your plan should include when they occur, why they occur, which foods trigger an attack, which drug and nondrug therapies work best for you, and when to consult your health care providers. We hope you realize your goal to conquer your recurrent headaches.

A LOOK TO THE FUTURE

What's next for you as you embark on your crusade to rid yourself of recurrent head pain? We suggest a step-by-step implementation of as many strategies as you can adopt. Please understand that it takes time to conquer chronic medical problems. If you've suffered with migraines for fifteen years, it'll take more than a few days to develop and implement a successful treatment plan. Be patient, ask all the right questions of your health care team, seek its members' advice, reread this book as necessary, and do what it takes to end your suffering.

Headache researchers and clinicians are working feverishly to uncover all the biochemical mechanisms and other factors that cause head pain and to develop new ways of treating recurrent headache. Over just the past two decades, the fundamental philosophy about the management of chronic headache has dramatically changed. Because scientific research and clinical observation continually provide new insight and improved ways of managing old problems, we expect that some information in this book will soon become obsolete. We'll stay abreast of these changes and will include them in future editions of *The Headache Sourcebook.* Meanwhile, you should also keep abreast of current headache information and watch for developments put out by print and television media, as well as information to be found in cyberspace. More important, remember to keep your health care provider informed if you're considering any of the recommendations described in this or any other book or information source.

In the meantime, please feel free to write down your comments, thoughts, or suggestions on how we can improve future editions of this book. Send your letters directly to us at the following address:

JOEL PAULINO, M.D.
CEABERT J. GRIFFITH, P.A.

Headache Symptom Diary

Your headache symptom diary (page 238) helps you detail your headache pain and associated symptoms. It need not be elaborate, but accuracy is important. Write down all your observations for about four to six weeks. The importance of your symptoms may not make sense at the time they occur, but after you've recorded everything, the pattern and timing of your symptoms may tell a compelling story. In addition to helping your doctor diagnose the type of headache you might have, it will also help her plan a treatment strategy that's right for you.

HEADACHE SYMPTOM DIARY

PATIENT'S NAME: _____ DATE: _____

TIME HEADACHE BEGAN: _____ ENDED: _____

WEATHER CONDITIONS:_____

WARNING SIGNS OR SYMPTOMS (AURA): _____

_____

ASSOCIATED SIGNS OR SYMPTOMS: _____

_____

1ST DAY OF MENSTRUAL PERIOD: _____

INTENSITY OF PAIN:

   (MILD) 1   2   3   4   5   7   8   9   10 (SEVERE)

LOCATION OF HEADACHE: _____

FOODS AND DRINKS CONSUMED TODAY: _____

ACTIVITIES AND TIME OF DAY: _____

_____

_____

MISCELLANEOUS OBSERVATIONS: _____

_____

_____

SELF-TREATMENTS AND THEIR EFFECTS: _____

_____

_____

Chronic Headache Resources

An important aspect of being a proactive partner in the management of any chronic disease is knowing where to find additional information. Fortunately, many consumer, governmental, and health organizations offer invaluable information about chronic headache. These organizations provide information at little or no cost to consumers. Feel free to contact these organizations by writing or calling them.

HEADACHE INFORMATION

American Council for Headache Education (ACHE)
875 Kings Highway, Suite 200
Woodbury, NJ 08096
Tel: 1-800-255-ACHE
www.achenet.org

ACHE is a nonprofit support organization for headache sufferers and their families. It dedicates its resources to educate the public, health care professionals, insurance companies, and legislators about headaches, and supports research about all forms of headaches.

National Headache Foundation
5252 North Western Avenue
Chicago, IL 60625
Tel: 1-800-843-2256; in Illinois, 1-800-523-8858

A consumer advocacy group dedicated to headache education and research.

American Medical Association
515 North State Street
Chicago, IL 60610
Tel: (312) 464-4804
Fax: (312) 464-4184

The largest physician advocate organization in the United States, the AMA maintains a comprehensive clearinghouse on a wide range of health topics, including recurrent headaches.

American Academy of Pediatrics
141 Northwest Point Boulevard
P.O. Box 927
Elk Grove, IL 60009-0927
Tel: 1-800-433-9016
Fax: (708) 228-5097

The largest organization representing the interests of American pediatricians, the AAP maintains a large catalog of topics on diseases affecting children, including headaches.

The American Chiropractic Association
1701 Clarendon Boulevard
Arlington, VA 22201
Tel: (703) 528-5000

The largest organization representing the interests of American chiropractors, the ACA provides information on diseases that are amenable to chiropractic care, and facilitates referrals to chiropractors.

The Migraine Association of Canada
365 Bloor Street
Suite 1912
Toronto, Ontario M4W 3L4
Tel: (416) 920-4916 or 1-800-663-3557

The Migraine Foundation of Australia, Ltd.
464 Glenferrie Road
Hawthorn 3122, Victoria, Australia
Tel: (03) 9818-7844
Fax: (03) 9818-1566

SPECIALIZED HEADACHE CENTERS

New England Center for Headache
778 Long Ridge Road
Stamford, CT 06902

Jefferson Headache Center
The Gibson Building
111 South 11th Street, Suite 8130
Philadelphia, PA 19107

Houston Headache Clinic
1213 Herman Drive, Suite 360
Houston, TX 77004

DRUG INFORMATION

The Food and Drug Administration (FDA)
HFD-8
Rockville, MD 20857
Tel: (301) 295-8012

The FDA regulates the research, manufacture, sale, and consumption of all drugs in the United States.

The Nonprescription Drug Manufacturers Association (NDMA)
1150 Connecticut Avenue, N.W.
Washington, DC 20036

A national organization representing companies dedicated to providing consumers with over-the-counter medications. NDMA also is an excellent resource for information about the indication, contraindication, efficacy, safety, and adverse effects of over-the-counter drugs.

NUTRITION INFORMATION

American Dietetic Association
216 West Jackson Boulevard
Chicago, IL 60606
Tel: 1-800-877-1600
www.eatright.org

This organization provides information about nutrition and can help you find a registered dietitian in your area.

GENERAL CONSUMER INFORMATION/ CONSUMER FRAUD

Consumer Product Information Center
Consumer Information Center—6D
P.O. Box 100
Pueblo, CO 81002
Fax: (719) 948-9724
www.pueblo.gsa.gov

Governmental clearinghouse publishes a consumer information catalog of more than two hundred free and low-cost pamphlets on many subjects, including headaches.

Federal Trade Commission (FTC)
Bureau of Consumer Protection
Division of Food and Drug Advertising
Washington, DC 20580
Tel: 1-877-FTC-HELP (382-4357)
www.consumer.gov/idtheft

The FTC is one of three federal agencies charged with stamping out health care fraud and other quackery. If you suspect that you may have been a victim of a health rip-off, contact the FTC.

COMPLEMENTARY AND ALTERNATIVE HEALTH INFORMATION

National Center for Homeopathy
801 North Fairfax, Suite 306
Alexandria, VA 22314
Tel: (703) 548-7790

This nonprofit organization, dedicated to the advancement of the practice of homeopathy, provides a directory of pharmacies and practitioners specializing in homeopathic medicine.

National Commission for the Certification of Acupuncturists
1424 16th Street, N.W., Suite 601
Washington, DC 20036
Tel: (202) 232-1404

This organization certifies acupuncturists via a standard examination. The organization provides information on the practice of acupuncture.

American Massage Therapy Association
1130 West North Shore Avenue
Chicago, IL 60626
Tel: (312) 761-AMTA

This association advocates on behalf of practitioners of massage therapy, provides information to the public, and facilitates referrals to massage therapists.

International Association of Yoga Therapists
109 Hillside Avenue
Mill Valley, CA 94941
Tel: (415) 383-4587

This nonprofit organization, dedicated to the advancement of the practice of yoga, funds research and educates the public about yoga.

International Institute of Reflexology
P.O. Box 12642
St. Petersburg, FL 33733-2642
Tel: (813) 343-4811

This institute disseminates general information, books, and pamphlets about reflexology. It also conducts seminars and training on reflexology and makes referrals to reflexology practitioners.

The Institute of Transpersonal Psychology
744 San Antonio Road
Palo Alto, CA 94303
Tel: (415) 493-4430

Provides information and conducts imagery training and certifies persons interested in mind/body consciousness.

Notes

PREFACE

1. The American Council for Headache Education with L. M. Constantine and S. Scott, *Migraine: The Complete Guide.* New York: Dell Publishing Group, 1994.
2. The National Headache Foundation, *Managing Headaches: What You Need to Know.* National Headache Foundation, 1999.
3. See note 1.
4. P. E. Stang and J. T. Osterhaus, "Impact of Migraine in the United States: Data from the National Health Interview Survey," *Headache* 33 (1993): 29–35.
5. S. L. Burks, *Managing Your Migraine: A Migraine Sufferer's Practical Guide.* New Jersey: Humana Press, 1994.

INTRODUCTION

1. A. M. Rapoport and F. D. Sheftell, *Headache Relief.* New York: Fireside, 1991.

CHAPTER ONE

1. A. M. Rapoport and F. D. Sheftell, *Headache Relief.* New York: Fireside, 1991.
2. C. Gorman, "Oh, My Aching Head!" *Time* 30 (June 1997): 62.
3. M. B. Stevens, "Tension-Type Headaches," *American Family Physician* 47 (1993): 799–805.
4. See note 2.

5. See note 2.
6. Headache Classification Committee of the International Headache Society, "Classification and Diagnostic Criteria for Headache Disorders, Cranial Neuralgias, and Facial Pain," *Cephalgia* 8 (1988): 1–96.
7. P. Maas and D. Mitchell, *Guide to Headache Relief.* New York: Pocket Books, 1997.
8. See note 6.
9. W. J. Stoffey, "Headaches," *PA Today* 6 (1998): 8–13.
10. The National Headache Foundation, *Managing Headaches: What You Need to Know.* National Headache Foundation, 1999.
11. J. W. Lance, *Headache: Understanding Alleviation.* New York: Charles Scribner's Sons, 1975.
12. E. H. Ackernecht, *A Short History of Medicine.* Baltimore: The Johns Hopkins University Press, 1982.
13. See note 11.

CHAPTER TWO

1. A. M. Rapoport and F. D. Sheftell, *Headache Relief for Women.* Boston: Little, Brown and Co., 1995.
2. A. M. Rapoport and F. D. Sheftell, *Headache Relief.* New York: Fireside, 1991.
3. The National Headache Foundation, *Managing Headaches: What You Need to Know.* National Headache Foundation, 1999.
4. The American Council for Headache Education with L. M. Constantine and S. Scott, *Migraine: The Complete Guide.* New York: Dell Publishing Group, 1994.
5. See note 1.

CHAPTER THREE

1. The American Council for Headache Education with L. M. Constantine and S. Scott, *Migraine: The Complete Guide.* New York: Dell Publishing Group, 1994.
2. P. Maas and D. Mitchell, *Guide to Headache Relief.* New York: Pocket Books, 1997.

3. G. Selby and J. W. Lance, "Observation of 500 Cases of Migraine and Allied Vascular Headache," *Journal of Neurological and Neurosurgical Psychiatry* 23 (1960).
4. A. M. Rapoport and D. Sheftell, *Headache Relief for Women.* Boston: Little, Brown and Co., 1995.
5. See note 4.
6. See note 2.
7. See note 1.
8. See note 2.
9. See note 2.
10. See note 2.
11. See note 2.
12. S. L. Burks, *Managing Your Migraine: A Migraine Sufferer's Practical Guide.* New Jersey: Humana Press, 1994.
13. S. D. Silberstein and J. Saper, "Migraine: Diagnosis and Treatment," in *Wolff's Headache and Other Head Pain.* New York: Oxford University Press, 1993.
14. See note 2.
15. F. Fracchinetti et al., "Magnesium Prophylaxis of Menstrual Migraine Effects of Intracellular Magnesium," *Headache* (1991): 298–301.
16. See note 2.
17. A. M. Rapoport and F. D. Sheftell, *Headache Relief.* New York: Fireside, 1991.
18. See note 2.
19. See note 2.
20. See note 2.
21. See note 18.
22. See note 2.
23. See note 12.
24. See note 12.
25. See note 1.
26. See note 2.

CHAPTER FOUR

1. W. J. Stoffey, "Headaches," *PA Today* 6 (1998): 8–13.
2. M. B. Stevens, "Tension-Type Headaches," *American Family Physician* 47 (1993): 799–805.

3. A. M. Rapoport and F. D. Sheftell, *Headache Relief.* New York: Fireside, 1991.
4. M. A. Aminoff, *Current Medical Diagnosis and Treatment.* Stamford, Conn.: 1996.
5. See note 2.
6. See note 3.
7. Headache Classification Committee of the International Headache Society, "Classification and Diagnostic Criteria for Headache Disorders, Cranial Neuralgias, and Facial Pain," *Cephalgia* 8 (1988): 1–96.

CHAPTER FIVE

1. J. Adler and A. Rogers, "The New War Against Migraines," *Newsweek* (11 January 1999).
2. F. Sicuteri, A. Testi, and B. Anselmi, "Biochemical Investigations in Headache," *International Archives of Allergy* 19 (1961): 55–58.
3. The American Council for Headache Education with L. M. Constantine and S. Scott, *Migraine: The Complete Guide.* New York: Dell Publishing Group, 1994.
4. R. S. Kunkel, "Managing Primary Headache Syndromes." Patient Care 2000: 100–122.
5. Headache Classification Committee of the International Headache Society, "Classification and Diagnostic Criteria for Headache Disorders, Cranial Neuralgias, and Facial Pain," *Cephalgia* 8 (1988): 1–96.
6. See note 3.
7. A. M. Rapoport and F. D. Sheftell, *Headache Relief.* New York: Fireside, 1991.
8. S. L. Burks, *Managing Your Migraine: A Migraine Sufferer's Practical Guide.* New Jersey: Humana Press, 1994.

CHAPTER SIX

1. A. M. Rapoport and F. D. Sheftell, *Headache Relief.* New York: Fireside, 1991.
2. Headache Classification Committee of the International Headache Society, "Classification and Diagnostic Criteria for Headache Disorders, Cranial Neuralgias, and Facial Pain," *Cephalgia* 8 (1988): 1–96.
3. C. J. Griffith, "Cluster Headache: Breaking the Cycle of the Most Painful Headache," *Physician Assistant* 22 (1998): 24–45.

CHAPTER SEVEN

1. N. T. Mathew, "Transformed Migraine, Analgesic Rebound, and Other Chronic Daily Headaches," *Neurologic Clinics* 15 (1997): 167–186.
2. See note 1.
3. N. T. Mathew, K. Ravishanker, and L. C. Sanin, "Coexistence of Migraine and Idiopathic Intracranial Hypertension without Papilledame," *Neurology* 46 (1996): 1226–1230.
4. See note 1.
5. S. D. Silberstein, "Drug-Induced Headache," *Neurologic Clinics* 16 (1998): 107–123.
6. See note 1.
7. A. M. Rapoport and F. D. Sheftell, *Headache Relief for Women.* Boston: Little, Brown and Co., 1995.
8. See note 7.
9. See note 7.
10. See note 7.
11. See note 7.

CHAPTER EIGHT

1. C. Peterson, *The Women's Migraine Survival Guide.* New York: Harper-Collins,1999.
2. Ibid.
3. The American Council for Headache Education with L. M. Constantine and S. Scott, *Migraine: The Complete Guide.* New York: Dell Publishing Group, 1994.
4. See note 1.
5. P. Maas and D. Mitchell, *Guide to Headache Relief.* New York: Pocket Books, 1997.
6. See note 1.
7. A. M. Rapoport and F. D. Sheftell, *Headache Relief.* New York: Fireside, 1991.
8. Ibid.
9. Ibid.
10. Ibid.
11. Ibid.
12. Ibid.

CHAPTER NINE

1. A. M. Rapoport and F. D. Sheftell, *Headache Relief.* New York: Fireside, 1991.
2. I. Abu-Arefeh and G. Russell, "Prevalence of Headache and Migraine in Schoolchildren," *British Medical Journal* 309 (1994): 765–769.
3. B. V. Singh and E. S. Roach, "Diagnosis and Management of Headache in Children," *Pediatrics in Review* 19 (1998): 132–136.
4. P. Mass and D. Mitchell, *Guide to Headache Relief.* New York: Pocket Books, 1997.
5. The American Council for Headache Education with L. M. Constantine and S. Scott, *Migraine: The Complete Guide.* New York: Dell Publishing Group, 1994.
6. See note 5.
7. See note 1.
8. S. Dyson, *Migraines: A Natural Approach.* Berkeley, Calif.: Ulysses Press, 1998.
9. See note 5.
10. See note 1.
11. C. J. Griffith, "Cluster Headache: Breaking the Cycle of the Most Painful Headache," *Physician Assistant* 22 (1998): 24–45.
12. See note 5.
13. See note 5.

CHAPTER TEN

1. P. Mass and D. Mitchell, *Guide to Headache Relief.* New York: Pocket Books, 1997.
2. The American Council for Headache Education with L. M. Constantine and S. Scott, *Migraine: The Complete Guide.* New York: Dell Publishing Group, 1994.
3. C. Peterson, *The Women's Migraine Survival Guide.* New York: Harper-Collins, 1999.
4. See note 1.
5. See note 1.
6. A. M. Rapoport and F. D. Sheftell, *Headache Relief.* New York: Fireside, 1991.
7. See note 1.
8. See note 6.
9. See note 3.
10. See note 3.
11. See note 1.

CHAPTER ELEVEN

1. P. Maas and D. Mitchell, *Guide to Headache Relief.* New York: Pocket Books, 1997.
2. C. Peterson, *The Women's Migraine Survival Guide.* New York: Harper-Collins. 1999.

CHAPTER TWELVE

1. A. M. Rapoport and F. D. Sheftell, *Headache Relief for Women.* Boston: Little, Brown and Co., 1995.
2. The American Council for Headache Education with L. M. Constantine and S. Scott, *Migraine: The Complete Guide.* New York: Dell Publishing Group, 1994.

CHAPTER THIRTEEN

1. The National Headache Foundation, *Managing Headaches: What You Need to Know.* National Headache Foundation, 1999.
2. A. M. Rapoport and F. D. Sheftell, *Headache Relief for Women.* Little, Brown and Co., 1995.

CHAPTER FOURTEEN

1. P. Maas and D. Mitchell, *Guide to Headache Relief.* New York: Pocket Books, 1997.
2. U. Stone, *Homeopathy for Headaches.* New York: Kensington Publishing, 1999.
3. I. Rosenfeld, *Guide to Alternative Medicine.* New York: Random House, 1996.
4. D. W. Swanson, ed., *Mayo Clinic on Chronic Pain.* Rochester, Minn.: Mayo Foundation, 1999.

CHAPTER FIFTEEN

1. P. Maas and D. Mitchell, *Guide to Headache Relief.* New York: Pocket Books, 1997.

2. See note 1.

3. S. Wood and B. Griffith, *Conquering High Blood Pressure.* New York: Insight Books, 1997.

4. See note 3.

5. See note 3.

6. See note 3.

7. See note 1.

8. See note 1.

9. See note 1

10. See note 1.

11. I. Rosenfeld, *Guide to Alternative Medicine.* New York: Random House, 1996.

12. A. M. Rapoport and F. D. Sheftell, *Headache Relief for Women.* Boston: Little, Brown and Co., 1995.

13. C. N. Alexander et al., "People with High Blood Pressure May Want to Medicate and Meditate," *Hypertension* 20 (1996).

14. See note 3.

15. See note 11.

CHAPTER SIXTEEN

1. C. C. Tollison and J. W. Tollison, *Headache: A Multimodal Program for Relief.* New York: Sterling Publishing, 1982.

2. A. M. Rapoport and F. D. Sheftell, *Headache Relief for Women.* Boston: Little, Brown and Co., 1995.

3. See note 3.

4. See note 3.

5. See note 3.

6. See note 3.

7. See note 3.

8. C. Peterson, *The Women's Migraine Survival Guide.* New York: Harper-Collins, 1999.

9. S. Wood and B. Griffith, *Conquering High Blood Pressure.* New York: Insight Books, 1997.

10. E. Urbaniak, *Natural Healing for Headaches.* Gig Harbor, Wash.: Harbor Press, 2000.

11. J. J. Murphy et al., "Randomized Double-Blind Placebo-Controlled Trial of Feverfew in Migraine Prevention," *Lancet* (1988): 189–192.
12. See note 9.
13. See note 11.
14. See note 11.
15. See note 9.
16. S. L. Burks, *Managing Your Migraine: A Migraine Sufferer's Practical Guide.* New Jersey: Humana Press, 1994.

CHAPTER SEVENTEEN

1. The National Headache Foundation, *Managing Headaches: What You Need to Know.* National Headache Foundation, 1999.
2. The American Council for Headache Education with L. M. Constantine and S. Scott, *Migraine: The Complete Guide.* New York: Dell Publishing Group, 1994.
3. See note 2.
4. See note 2.
5. S. Perman, "Bitter Ads to Swallow," *Time* 150 (1996): 48–49.
6. Editors of Consumer Reports, *Health Quackery.* New York: Holt, Rinehart, and Winston, 1980.
7. I. Rosenfeld, *Guide to Alternative Medicine.* New York: Random House, 1996.

CHAPTER EIGHTEEN

1. K. Lorig et al., *Living a Healthy Life with Chronic Conditions.* Palo Alto, Calif.: Bull Publishing Company, 1994.
2. D. W. Swanson, ed., *Mayo Clinic on Chronic Pain.* Rochester, Minn.: Mayo Foundation, 1999.
3. See note 2.
4. D. Ornish, *Love & Healing: The Scientific Basis for the Healing Power of Intimacy.* New York: HarperCollins, 1998.
5. See note 2.

Glossary

abortive headache drug A type of medication used to stop (abort) headache pain after the pain has begun. (*See* prophylactic headache drug.)

adrenaline Also called epinephrine, adrenaline is the "fight or flight" hormone secreted by the adrenal glands, which sit atop the kidneys. It can quickly increase heart rate and blood pressure in response to emotional or physical threats.

aerobic exercise Physical activity that enhances the body's intake and utilization of oxygen. An important aspect of cardiovascular fitness, aerobic exercises include jogging, running, swimming, walking, and bicycling. (*See* anaerobic exercise.)

anaerobic exercise An exercise whose energy comes from burning fat without the use of oxygen. Examples are isometrics and weight lifting.

analgesics A class of medications, commonly known as painkillers, that are used to relieve pain. Examples of these medicines are aspirin, acetaminophen (for example, Tylenol), and ibuprofen.

aneurysm A bulge in the wall of an artery due to weakening of the wall by disease or birth defect that is at risk of rupturing.

angiogram A specialized study of the carotid and other arteries in which dye is injected into the bloodstream and X-rays are taken as the fluid travels through the blood vessels to the head and neck. The dye enhances the structures within the arteries. (*See* arteriogram.)

aorta The largest artery in the body; receives blood from the left ventricle and distributes it to the body.

arteries A type of blood vessel that carries blood away from the heart to different parts of the body.

arteriogram A diagnostic X-ray of the arteries taken after injecting contrast dye into the bloodstream to make the blood vessels more visible. (*See* angiography.)

arterioles Small arteries that carry blood from the arteries to the capillaries. Narrowing of the arterioles increases resistance to blood flow, driving up blood pressure in the larger arteries.

arteriosclerosis Hardening of the arteries caused by, in most cases, mineral and fatty deposits (called *plaques*) that eventually lead to blockages that impair blood flow in the arteries. (*See* atherosclerosis.)

atherosclerosis The most prevalent form of arteriosclerosis, atherosclerosis involves a buildup of hard plaques (consisting of cholesterol, fat, calcium deposits, and other debris) on the inside lining of the arteries. (*See* arteriosclerosis.)

aura A symptom or set of symptoms, such as flashing lights, zigzag lines, or temporary loss of vision, that can signal the onset of some migraines.

baroreceptors Tiny structures (nodes) in the walls of the blood vessels that monitor the volume and flow of blood and regulate the width of the blood vessels. When blood volume drops, baroreceptors send a message to the brain to narrow the blood vessels; when blood volume increases, they send a message to dilate the blood vessels. This causes the blood pressure to either rise or fall depending on the body's needs.

basilar artery migraine A rare form of migraine, occurring mostly in young women, adolescents, and children, that is caused by disturbance in a major brain artery. Symptoms include loss of balance, difficulty speaking, double vision, poor muscle coordination, and occasionally loss of consciousness.

beta-blocker A drug that blocks the effects of selective body hormones (e.g., epinephrine) on the heart and blood vessels. These agents slow the heart rate, lower blood pressure, and reduce the heart's oxygen requirements. This last effect makes them ideal for treating patients with angina pectoris. Some beta-blockers narrow the bronchial (airway) tubes and may exacerbate asthma.

biofeedback Immediate information about a bodily function (such as heartbeat and muscle tension) through audiovisual feedback that allows a person to change the level of that body function through relaxation and other methods of operant conditioning.

biological Having to do with the body and its functional and chemical processes.

blood pressure The pressure created by the circulating blood on the walls of the arteries. Blood pressure results from the contraction, or squeezing, of the heart vis-à-vis the resistance put up by the circumference of the blood vessels. Many hormones, enzymes, and blood vessel structures influence blood pressure. Blood pressure is also influenced by the volume of circulating blood.

blood vessels The network of tubes (arteries, veins, and capillaries) that carries blood throughout the body.

blood volume The total amount of blood circulating in the body.

brain scan A specialized study in which a radioactive chemical (called a *radionuclide*) is injected into the arm and travels to the brain, enhancing its outline when X-rays are taken.

calcium channel blocker A blood pressure–lowering drug that works by blocking calcium from entering through microscopic channels in the walls of arteries. This blockade results in relaxation of the arterial walls, thus lowering blood pressure.

capillaries The smallest blood vessels that conduct blood between the arterioles and the veins. Capillaries have thin walls that allow the exchange of oxygen and other vital substances and carbon dioxide and other waste products.

cardiac arrest Cessation of the heartbeat, which causes loss of consciousness because blood can no longer reach the brain.

cardiovascular Relating to the heart (cardio) and the body's network of blood vessels (vascular). Cardiovascular disease refers to diseases of the heart and blood vessels, including arteriosclerosis.

carotid arteries The two main arteries that supply blood to the head and neck.

catecholamines Powerful chemicals, including dopamine, epinephrine, and norepinephrine, produced by the body to help regulate numerous bodily processes, including heart rate and blood pressure.

cephalgia The medical term for headache or pain in the head.

cervicogenic headache A type of secondary headache caused by arthritis and other conditions of the bones and joints in the neck.

cholesterol A waxy substance produced by the body, and found in animal fat and dairy products, that is necessary for cell function and the production of hormones.

circadian rhythm The rhythmic pattern of bodily functions, based on a twenty-four-hour cycle, that regulates the sleep/wake cycle and the body's responses to daylight and night. Factors that interrupt this rhythm, including certain medications, changes in the amount of daylight, and stress, can cause a change in the body's immune system, blood pressure, and seizure and pain thresholds.

cluster headache A type of vascular headache so named because of its repeated occurrences in groups or clusters. These severely painful headaches, most common among men, are typically located around one eye and are associated with tearing and a runny nose.

computerized axial tomography Commonly referred to as a CAT scan, this X-ray procedure produces a computer-enhanced picture of a cross section of the body, creating three-dimensional images of internal organs and body structures.

constriction Narrowing of blood vessels caused by contraction of their muscles.

coronary artery disease Diseases affecting the arteries that supply blood to the heart muscle. The most common type of coronary artery disease is atherosclerosis, the deposit of fat, cholesterol, and calcium on the inner walls of the coronary arteries.

corticosteroids Steroid hormones secreted by the adrenal glands that help to prevent or reduce inflammation. These drugs are used to prevent and treat vascular headaches.

diabetes mellitus Commonly referred to as diabetes, this disease has to do with the body's inability to properly produce or utilize insulin, causing too much glucose (sugar) in the blood. There are two types of diabetes mellitus: in Type 1, the body doesn't produce enough insulin; in Type 2, the body produces enough insulin but is unable to use it efficiently.

diastole The relaxation phase of the heart cycle, when the heart chamber fills in preparation for systole (contraction).

diastolic blood pressure The bottom number of a blood pressure reading. It reflects the pressure inside the arteries when the heart is relaxed between beats. If the blood pressure is 110/68 mm Hg, the diastolic pressure is 68 mm Hg.

dihydroergotamine A drug used to treat migraine and cluster headaches.

diuretics A group of drugs, also called "water pills" that enhance salt and water loss via the kidneys. This in turn lowers the blood volume and blood pressure.

echocardiogram Also called *ultrasound*, this test outlines the size, structure, and function of the heart and major blood vessels by using high-frequency sound waves bounced off these structures.

eclampsia High blood pressure and seizures occurring during pregnancy.

electrocardiogram Also referred to as an EKG or ECG, it is a graphic record of the electrical activity of the heart and can provide information regarding the heart's muscle thickness and the presence of a heart attack and other problems.

electroencephalography Also referred to as an EEG, this test, akin to an

EKG, delineates the electrical activity of nerve cells in the brain via electrodes applied to the scalp. EEG can provide information regarding disorders of the brain such as seizures, tumors, and blood clots.

electrolytes Dissolved minerals carried by the blood that are important for muscle and other vital body functions. Electrolytes include sodium, chloride, potassium, and carbon dioxide.

electromyogram Also referred to as an EMG, this test, akin to an EEG, delineates the electrical impulses in a muscle via electrodes applied to various muscle groups. EMG can provide information regarding disorders that can cause muscle weakness or paralysis.

electronystagmography Also referred to as an ENG, this test records eye movements by measuring the electrical impulses of the eye muscle. Generally, ENGs are used to detect tumors on the nerves that serve the eye muscles.

endocrine system A system of glands that manufacture hormones. Endocrine glands include the thyroid gland, the adrenal glands, the ovaries, and the testes.

endorphins Morphinelike chemicals naturally secreted by the nervous system. These amino acid–based chemicals are produced abundantly during aerobic exercise and have an important role in pain reduction.

epinephrine Also called adrenaline, this hormone has important functions in regulation of your blood pressure. (*See* adrenaline.)

ergotamine tartrate A drug used to treat migraine headaches.

estrogen One of the female sex hormones that is produced primarily by the ovaries during a woman's childbearing years. Estrogen prepares the wall of the uterus for implantation of the fertilized egg. Estrogen is used in birth control pills to prevent pregnancy and in hormone replacement pills to treat the effects of menopause.

exercise stress test An electrocardiogram used to measure heart rate and its electrical activity while the participant exercises on a treadmill or stationary bike. The test is used to detect advanced coronary artery disease prior to starting an exercise program.

heart rate Reflected by the pulse, the heart rate refers to the number of times the heart pumps blood per minute.

hereditary The genetic transmission of a trait (for example, blue eyes) or disease (for example, diabetes) from parent to offspring.

high blood pressure (*See* hypertension.)

high-density lipoprotein (HDL) cholesterol The so-called good cholesterol that has been shown to protect against coronary heart disease by removing extra fatty material from the blood vessels.

hormone replacement therapy (HRT) Hormones taken by women after hysterectomy or menopause to prevent osteoporosis (bone thinning) and heart disease.

hormones Substances secreted by an endocrine gland that influence the activities of various organs (for example, estrogen secreted by the ovaries helps give a woman her feminizing features).

hypercholesterolemia A blood cholesterol level exceeding the desirable level of 200 mg/dL (dL = deciliter = one-tenth of a liter) in both men and women.

hypertension Abnormally high blood pressure within the blood vessels caused by increased volume of circulating blood or decreased diameter of the blood vessels, among other factors. Hypertension and high blood pressure are interchangeable terms.

hyperthyroidism Abnormally high production of thyroid hormone by the thyroid gland that sits at the base of the front of the neck.

hypotension Low blood pressure, defined as blood pressure below 100/60.

internists Physicians who have at least three years of training beyond medical school. These doctors restrict their practice to matters of internal medicine, which include conditions such as high blood pressure, diabetes, and headaches. Do not confuse these practitioners with interns, who are newly graduated physicians-in-training.

interns Newly graduated physicians-in-training doing their first year of post–medical school training.

intravenous pyelogram (IVP) Special X-ray in which an injected dye goes to the kidneys, enhancing its outline and that of its associated structures.

ischemia A condition in which an organ (for example, the heart muscle) gets a reduced amount of oxygen due to compromised blood flow.

isometric exercise The type of exercise that involves applying bodily force against stable resistance (for example, weight lifting).

kidneys Bean-shaped organs that detoxify the body by removing poisonous waste products. The kidneys also regulate electrolyte, acid-base, water, and salt balance in the body.

left ventricle The lower-left chamber of the heart that is essentially its main pump.

lipid profile A blood test that measures the levels of the various fats in the blood.

lipids A name for various fats found in the body that include cholesterol and triglycerides.

lipoproteins The complex of cholesterol and fat joined with protein carriers. The types of lipoproteins are high-density lipoproteins (HDL), low-density lipoproteins (LDL), and very low density lipoproteins (VLDL).

low blood pressure (*See* hypotension.)

low-density lipoprotein (LDL) cholesterol The so-called bad cholesterol that has been shown to cause coronary heart disease by accumulating within the blood vessel walls.

lumbar puncture Commonly referred to as a spinal tap, this diagnostic test involves removing a small amount of spinal fluid using a needle inserted into the spinal canal in the lower back. Spinal taps are used to help diagnose problems such as meningitis, brain hemorrhage, and other life-threatening conditions.

magnesium A metallic element crucial to the function of bones, muscles, nerves, and other bodily tissues.

magnetic resonance imaging (MRI) A highly specialized imaging technique that uses magnets and computers to form a three-dimensional image of internal organs, such as the brain.

migraine headache A type of vascular headache caused by widening and narrowing of blood vessels that feed the head and neck.

monoamine oxidase inhibitor (MAOI) A group of antidepressants that increases the body's levels of mood-elevating chemicals (e.g., norepinephrine) by preventing their breakdown.

musculoskeletal Having to do with the body's bones, muscles, ligaments, tendons, and other components of the skeletal system.

myocardial infarction Also called a heart attack, it refers to infarction (death) of heart muscle cells.

nephropathy Reduction in the kidneys' ability to clear the body of waste products due to damage from a number of factors including certain drugs, diabetes mellitus, or other diseases.

neurotransmitters The chemical messengers (serotonin, dopamine, and norepinephrine) that facilitate communication among brain cells.

nonsteroidal anti-inflammatory drugs (NSAIDs) Drugs used to treat pain and inflammation associated with headaches. Ibuprofen and naproxen are examples of NSAIDs.

nurse practitioner A nurse with advanced training who performs many health care tasks traditionally provided by a physician.

obesity Defined as 20 to 30 percent over ideal body weight.

ophthalmoplegic migraine A rare form of migraine that causes double vision and the eyelids to droop.

oral contraceptive pill Birth control pills.

osteoporosis Thinning of the bones related to a drop in estrogen levels that occurs in women as they approach menopause and that continues after menopause. Osteoporosis leads to bones breaking with minimal physical stress.

PA (*See* physician assistant.)

pain threshold The weakest stimulus at which a sensation is felt and interpreted by an individual as pain.

pain tolerance The degree of severity each person assigns a pain stimulus.

palpate The act of feeling with the hands, as when a physician feels for the consistency and size of a mass in the abdomen.

parasympathetic nervous system (*See* autonomic nervous system.)

percuss The act of tapping, as when a physician taps over the liver to determine its size. Percussion uses the physical characteristics of various body structures (for example, tapping over the liver produces a dull sound) to decide if abnormalities exist.

physician assistant (PA) A health care professional who, by formal training and experience, performs many medical functions traditionally performed by physicians. Studies have shown that primary care PAs can effectively carry out 80 to 90 percent of the tasks performed by general practice physicians.

phytoestrogens Substances found in soy and soy products that are similar in chemical structure to the female hormone estrogen. Some women may be able to substitute phytoestrogens if they are unable to take regular estrogen after menopause.

pituitary gland A pea-sized gland situated at the base of the skull. It secretes numerous hormones, including vasopressin and others that regulate blood pressure.

plaque Fatty deposits in the blood vessels that reduce the free flow of blood.

polycystic kidney disease An inherited disorder in which both kidneys contain numerous cysts that interfere with their normal function, resulting in many problems, including high blood pressure.

polymyalgia rheumatica A syndrome characterized by pain, stiffness, and weakness of the muscles in the neck, shoulders, back, hips, and thighs. The symptoms are worse on rising in the morning. The condition is classified as a rheumatoid disease and its cause is unknown. It is associated with a condition called temporal arteritis.

positron emission tomogram (PET) scan A computer-enhanced study that uses radioactive particles (called *positrons*) to study the function of the brain. A sugar solution containing a radioactive "tag" is swallowed and carried to the brain. X-rays are then taken of the areas tagged with positrons looking for brain tumors, blood clots, and other conditions.

postural hypotension A sudden drop in blood pressure (hypotension) on changing body positions (postural), usually upon standing. This occurs because gravity tends to pull most of the circulating blood to the feet, reducing the flow of blood to the brain.

potassium A vital electrolyte found in the blood and cells that plays a key role in the function of nerves and muscles, including the heart muscle. Potassium can be found in foods such as orange juice and bananas.

prednisone An artificial cortisone drug used to prevent and treat vascular headaches. (*See* corticosteroids.)

pre-eclampsia An abnormal condition of pregnancy marked by acute hypertension, swelling of the extremities, and urinary excretion of protein.

prognosis A prediction regarding the expected course of a disease process.

prophylactic headache drug A type of medication used to prevent headache pain. The objective of headache prophylactic therapy is to reduce the frequency and severity of recurrent headache attacks and to enhance the efficacy of headache painkillers. (*See* abortive headache drug.)

pseudotumor cerebri A condition in which there is abnormally high pressure in the spinal fluid that bathes the brain and spinal cord. The exact cause of pseudotumor cerebri is unknown but the condition is associated with certain conditions (for example, pregnancy and head injury), vitamin A deficiency, and the use of certain medications (e.g., tetracycline, sulfonamides, and indomethacin).

reflexology A form of massage therapy that applies pressure to the feet, palms, and ears to cause relaxation. Practitioners of this therapy claim to help treat chronic constipation, asthma, and chronic headaches, among other conditions.

REM The abbreviation for rapid eye movement, REM refers to the period of sleep when dreaming occurs. REM sleep alternates with the four stages of non-REM sleep.

renal Relating to the kidneys.

renal artery stenosis A narrowing of the main artery that feeds the kidneys.

renin An enzyme found in the kidneys that, in excess amounts, can narrow blood vessels and elevate blood pressure.

retina The light-sensitive layer lining the back of the eye that receives images through the lens and sends them to the brain via the optic nerve.

risk factor A condition or habit that increases the likelihood of developing a disease. Obesity, smoking, high alcohol intake, and excessive sodium consumption are among the most prevalent risk factors for high blood pressure.

salt A crystallized form of sodium chloride. Sodium causes fluid retention and elevated blood pressure.

saturated fat A fatty acid that is "saturated" with hydrogen atoms and thus cannot combine with any more hydrogen. Solid at room temperature, this fat is found in cheese, butter, red meat, and eggs, among other foods. Saturated fats have been shown to raise blood cholesterol levels.

secondary hypertension High blood pressure caused by a specific disease such as hyperthyroidism (overactive thyroid gland) and pheochromocytoma (a tumor that secrets adrenaline). Approximately 10 percent of all people diagnosed with hypertension have secondary hypertension.

selective serotonin reuptake inhibitors (SSRIs) A class of antidepressants that selectively concentrates in the part of the brain influenced by serotonin. SSRIs have fewer side effects than the older antidepressants such as the MAOIs.

sequelae A secondary disorder or condition resulting from disease or injury.

serotonin A neurotransmitter that transmits information such as blood flow in the brain and pain chemicals found in brain fluids.

sinusitis Inflammation of the series of sinus cavities located around the eyes and nostrils.

sleep apnea Transient cessation of breathing while asleep. Its causes include obesity, and it can lead to high blood pressure.

sodium A mineral element that, in the body, controls water balance, nerve impulse, muscle contraction, and acid-base balance. Approximately 40 percent of table salt is sodium. People who are salt sensitive run the risk of developing high blood pressure if they take in large quantities of sodium.

spinal tap (*See* lumbar puncture.)

steroids (*See* corticosteroids.)

stress The response to a perceived threat to our psychological or physical well-being and the realization that we lack the resources necessary to cope with that threat.

stroke Also referred to as cerebrovascular accident (CVA). Stroke is a sudden loss of function of a part of the brain due to cessation of blood flow caused by a blood vessel rupture (hemorrhage) or blockage (by a clot). Strokes can lead to paralysis and death. Hypertension is the most important risk factor for stroke.

sympathetic nervous system (*See* autonomic nervous system.)

symptom A pain, weakness, or something felt or noticed by the patient that indicates a disease or disorder is affecting the body.

syncope Fainting as a result of reduced blood flow to the brain.

systole The contraction phase of the heart cycle when the heart squeezes out blood into its large blood vessels.

systolic blood pressure The top number of a person's blood pressure reading that reflects the pressure within the arteries when the heart contracts. If a person's blood pressure is 118/66, his systolic blood pressure is 118.

temporal arteritis A condition caused by the thickened walls of the arteries that feed the temples and eyes. Its cause is unknown and it produces headaches, scalp sensitivity, and altered vision. It is associated with a condition called *polymyalgia rheumatica*.

temporomandibular joint dysfunction Also referred to as TMJ syndrome, it is inflammation of the joint between the temporal bone and lower jaw (located just in front of the ear) that can cause headaches. Symptoms include pain and clicking and locking of the jaw.

thrombosis A condition in which the blood produces solid particles or clots (thrombus). Thrombus in a blood vessel blocks blood flow through that vessel.

tic doulourex (*See* trigeminal neuralgia.)

tricyclic antidepressants A group of antidepressants that elevate mood by manipulating the body's levels of the mood-elevating chemical norepinephrine. (*See* MAOIs and SSRIs.)

trigeminal neuralgia A painful condition of the trigeminal nerve. Symptoms include intense facial pain. Also referred to as tic douloureux.

triggers Factors that set off a condition. In the case of cluster headaches, alcohol and nicotine are common triggers. Some migraine headaches are triggered by noise and flickering lights.

triglycerides One of the various types of fat that circulates in the blood and is used for energy or stored in the body as fat. Triglycerides are manufactured in the liver or obtained from dietary sources.

unsaturated fats Liquid at room temperature, these fats are found in corn, sunflower, and other vegetable oils. Unsaturated fats help lower blood cholesterol levels.

vascular Refers to blood vessels (arteries, veins, arterioles, and capillaries) that carry blood throughout the body.

vascular headaches Headaches caused by abnormal function of the body's blood vessels. Migraine and cluster headaches are considered vascular headaches.

vasoactive Refers to the ability to cause the widening or narrowing of a blood vessel. Caffeine, nicotine, and adrenaline are vasoactive substances, as are the medications nitroglycerine, hydralazine, and nitroprosside.

vasodilators Drugs that dilate the circumference of the arteries and veins in the body, resulting in a lowering of blood vessel resistance and a reduction in blood pressure.

veins Blood vessels that carry blood from the body back to the heart for oxygen replenishment.

vertebrogenic headache (*See* cervicogenic headache.)

vertigo A sensation of spinning of one's self or surroundings. This can be caused by any number of conditions, including inner ear inflammation and elevated blood pressure.

X-ray The use of high-energy beams of electrons to image bones and other body parts. X-rays are also used to kill cancer cells.

yoga A technique that teaches deep relaxation through proper posture, ture, breathing, and medication. Based on teachings of Hinduism, yoga induces relaxation and improves circulation, memory, and concentration.

Suggested Readings

The following books and pamphlets discuss chronic headaches and offer practical strategies for pharmacological and nonpharmacological management of chronic head pain.

AMERICAN COUNCIL ON HEADACHE EDUCATION. *Migraine: The Complete Guide.* Dell, 1994.

BURKS, SUSAN L. *Managing Your Migraine: A Migraine Sufferer's Practical Guide.* New Jersey: Humana Press, 1994.

ELIOT, R. S. *From Stress to Strength: How to Lighten Your Load and Save Your Life.* New York: Bantam Books, 1994.

MAAS, PAULA and DEBORAH MITCHELL. *Guide to Headache Relief.* New York: Pocket Books, 1997.

Physicians' Desk Reference, 52d ed. Oradell, N.J.: Medical Economics Company, 1998.

RAPOPORT, ALAN M. and FRED D. SHEFTELL. *Headache Relief.* New York: Fireside, 1990.

———. *Headache Relief for Women.* Boston: Little Brown, 1996.

ROTER, D. L. and J. A. HALL. *Doctors Talking with Patients, Patients Talking with Doctors: Improving Communication in Medical Visits.* Westport, Conn.: Greenwood Publishing Group, 1992.

VICKERY, D. M. and J. F. FRIES. *Take Care of Yourself.* New York: Addison-Wesley, 1995.

WOOD, S., and B. GRIFFITH. *Conquering High Blood Pressure.* Phenum Books, 1997.

Index

ML